The Persian Presence in Victorian Poetry

Reza Taher-Kermani

D1615608

EDINBURGH
University Press

Edinburgh University Press is one of the leading university presses in the UK. We publish academic books and journals in our selected subject areas across the humanities and social sciences, combining cutting-edge scholarship with high editorial and production values to produce academic works of lasting importance. For more information visit our website: edinburghuniversitypress.com

© Reza Taher-Kermani, 2020, 2022

Edinburgh University Press Ltd
The Tun – Holyrood Road, 12(2f) Jackson's Entry, Edinburgh EH8 8PJ

First published in hardback by Edinburgh University Press 2020

Typeset in 11/13 Adobe Sabon by
IDSUK (DataConnection) Ltd, and
printed and bound by CPI Group (UK) Ltd,
Croydon, CR0 4YY

A CIP record for this book is available from the British Library

ISBN 978 1 4744 4816 1 (hardback)
ISBN 978 1 4744 4817 8 (paperback)
ISBN 978 1 4744 4818 5 (webready PDF)
ISBN 978 1 4744 4819 2 (epub)

The right of Reza Taher-Kermani to be identified as the author of this work has been asserted in accordance with the Copyright, Designs and Patents Act 1988, and the Copyright and Related Rights Regulations 2003 (SI No. 2498).

Contents

Series Editor's Preface

'Victorian' is a term, at once indicative of a strongly determined concept and an often notoriously vague notion, emptied of all meaningful content by the many journalistic misconceptions that persist about the inhabitants and cultures of the British Isles and Victoria's Empire in the nineteenth century. As such, it has become a by-word for the assumption of various, often contradictory habits of thought, belief, behaviour and perceptions. Victorian studies and studies in nineteenth-century literature and culture have, from their institutional inception, questioned narrowness of presumption, pushed at the limits of the nominal definition, and have sought to question the very grounds on which the unreflective perception of the so-called Victorian has been built; and so they continue to do. Victorian and nineteenth-century studies of literature and culture maintain a breadth and diversity of interest, of focus and inquiry, in an interrogative and intellectually open-minded and challenging manner, which are equal to the exploration and inquisitiveness of its subjects. Many of the questions asked by scholars and researchers of the innumerable productions of nineteenth-century society actively put into suspension the clichés and stereotypes of 'Victorianism', whether the approach has been sustained by historical, scientific, philosophical, empirical, ideological or theoretical concerns; indeed, it would be incorrect to assume that each of these approaches to the idea of the Victorian has been, or has remained, in the main exclusive, sealed off from the interests and engagements of other approaches. A vital interdisciplinarity has been pursued and embraced, for the most part, even as there has been contest and debate amongst Victorianists, pursued with as much fervour as the affirmative exploration between different disciplines and differing epistemologies put to work in the service of reading the nineteenth century.

Edinburgh Critical Studies in Victorian Culture aims to take up both the debates and the inventive approaches and departures from convention that studies in the nineteenth century have witnessed for the last half century at least. Aiming to maintain a 'Victorian' (in the most positive sense of that motif) spirit of inquiry, the series' purpose is to continue and augment the cross-fertilisation of interdisciplinary approaches, and to offer, in addition, a number of timely and untimely revisions of Victorian literature, culture, history and identity. At the same time, the series will ask questions concerning what has been missed or improperly received, misread, or not read at all, in order to present a multi-faceted and heterogeneous kaleidoscope of representations. Drawing on the most provocative, thoughtful and original research, the series will seek to prod at the notion of the 'Victorian', and in so doing, principally through theoretically and epistemologically sophisticated close readings of the historicity of literature and culture in the nineteenth century, to offer the reader provocative insights into a world that is at once overly familiar, and irreducibly different, other and strange. Working from original sources, primary documents and recent interdisciplinary theoretical models, Edinburgh Critical Studies in Victorian Culture seeks not simply to push at the boundaries of research in the nineteenth century, but also to inaugurate the persistent erasure and provisional, strategic redrawing of those borders.

Julian Wolfreys

Acknowledgements

I finished the first draft of this monograph in 2014 at the University of Bristol. But I completed it five years later at Nazarbayev University. The seeds of the study were, however, sown during my MA year which coincided with the bicentenary of the birth of Edward FitzGerald and the commemorative publication of the Oxford University Press edition of Edward FitzGerald's *Rubáiyát of Omar Khayyám* (2010), edited by Daniel Karlin, who was at the time a Professor in the School of English at the University of Sheffield, and who later became my MA and PhD supervisor and a lifelong mentor and advisor. As someone who had always wanted to incorporate the literary-cultural significance of his Iranian heritage within the scope of his literary studies, this was a good opportunity to make a long-held dream a reality. As such, I wrote my thesis on the hybrid (Anglo-Persian) nature of FitzGerald's translation and later decided to prepare a longer study on the British cultural and imaginative engagements with Persia in the nineteenth century.

The cheeriest, and the most challenging, moments of preparing this study have been shared with many people, to whom I am indebted indefinitely. My first and foremost debt of gratitude goes to my teacher and professor, Daniel Karlin. Without his erudition, support and guidance, I would have never been able to complete this monograph. I would also like to thank members, past and present, of the Department of English in Bristol, especially Professor David Hopkins, Dr Jane Wright, Dr John Lyon and Dr Stephen Cheeke. I would like to particularly thank Dr Samantha Matthews for her mentorship and guidance, both in Bristol and Sheffield. Her instruction and supervision helped me begin my graduate studies and academic career on the right foot. I am also indebted to Professor Joe Phelan (De Montfort University) for his support and critical commentary on various sections of this study. Thanks are also due to Dr Andrew Reynolds (Wisconsin-Madison) for his mentorship and critical engagement with my work. I would like to express my gratitude to my friends in Sheffield, Bristol, London, and Tehran for providing the encouragement and friendship I needed. Especial thanks go to Craig Savage, Danny Adams, Mohammad Nassaji, and Dr Gavin Schwartz-Leeper (University of Warwick).

I would also like to thank my parents, Mohammad-Ali (Shahpoor) Taher-Kermani and Shahnaz Saeedvarnia. It was under their watchful eyes that I gained the ability to tackle challenges head on, that I learned about commitment, perseverance, consistency and dedication. My brother Ali with his infinite support and friendship has also been a great source of joy and inspiration. To these people, I owe a lifelong debt, and I can only hope that I can one day show how much I love and appreciate them.

Reza Taher-Kermani

Edinburgh Critical Studies in Victorian Culture

Series Editor: Julian Wolfreys

Recent books in the series:

For a complete list of titles published visit the Edinburgh Critical Studies in Victorian Culture web page at www.edinburghuniversitypress.com/series/ECVC

Also Available:
Victoriographies – A Journal of Nineteenth-Century Writing, 1790–1914, edited by Diane Piccitto and Patricia Pulham
ISSN: 2044-2416
www.eupjournals.com/vic

To Mum and Dad

Introduction

This book sprang from my desire to study Victorian poetry alongside classical Persian poetry. My initial plan was to examine nineteenth-century English translations of medieval Persian poetry, to explore the ways in which some of the more 'exotic' ideological and aesthetic elements of classical Persian poetry (that is, the poetry written in Persia from the tenth to the sixteenth century) were introduced and assimilated into the poetry of nineteenth-century Britain. But during the course of my preliminary research, I came to realise that the presence of Persia in nineteenth-century English poetry transcends the mere category of translation, that Persia to the Victorians stood not just as the poetry of Hafiz or Omar Khayyám (though this formed a substantial part of their conception of the country), but as a complex and paradoxical embodiment of different notions, created and crafted by a range of oral and written stories, themes, and tropes. Knowledge of Persia had reached the discursive realms of the British imagination through many centuries and from a variety of sources, including classical and biblical texts, histories, and travel-writings. This effectively transformed the word 'Persia' into something more than the name of a territorial entity. Persia became a cultural imaginary, a mental landscape formed over time and subject to change. The Victorians responded to this landscape from different perspectives, marked by every shade of social class, religious affiliation, and political allegiance.

The manifold nature of the Victorians' conception of, and response to, Persia is most clearly shown in their depiction of it in their imaginative writings. Persia appears in a variety of roles in nineteenth-century English poetry. It may appear as a land of charming rose gardens, filled with poets, nightingales, and young lovers, as in Henry Alford's 'Henry Martyn at Shiraz' (1851); or as a despotic monarchy in Augustine Hickey's 'On to Freedom' (1865); or as the enemy of the Greeks in Elizabeth Barrett Browning's 'The Battle of Marathon' (1820); or, further still, as a fallen empire whose former greatness is the subject of elegy in Edward Henry Bickersteth's 'A Lament for Persia' (1848). Persia also appears in different measures in English poetry of the nineteenth century. It may dominate a poem, determining subject matter, form, or tone, or it may make only a fleeting, casual appearance; although the scale itself can be deceptive, because a poem that seems to be devoted in its entirety to Persia, as with Henry Kendall's 'Persia' (1888), may contain very little that directly involves Persia or is related to it; whereas, a single, succinct image in another poem may convey a moment of far greater knowledge, such as the 'rose of Iran on an English stock' in Grant Allen's 'A Special Occasion' (1894), written to commemorate the planting of a rose from Omar Khayyám's tomb on the grave of Edward FitzGerald.

To chart the diversity of perceptions associated with Persia in Victorian literary culture is my primary purpose in this book. Poetry is clearly the medium through which I have surveyed the Victorian conception of Persia; but in examining the ways in which Persia figures in Victorian poetry, I have not confined myself to a corpus of works that were written specifically on or about Persia; instead, I have taken account of a broader selection of poems incorporating literary, historical, and cultural material. Such material may shape the structure of a poem, or its verbal texture, and may do so at different levels of intensity and significance. I also do not aim at complete bibliographical coverage; instead, I intend to explore the complex network of cultural exchange that is behind the construction of the Victorian notion of Persia. To do so, I move from context to text, and from general to specific: I begin with the provision of necessary contextual information on the presence of Persia in English literary-historical culture before the nineteenth century, move on to consider some of the ways in which Persia was mediated in nineteenth-century poetry, and then offer case-studies of three major Victorian works: Matthew Arnold's 'Sohrab and Rustum' (1853), Edward FitzGerald's *Rubáiyát of Omar Khayyám* (1859), and Robert Browning's *Ferishtah's Fancies* (1884).

Although my primary focus is on the manifestations of Persia in writings from the Victorian period, I engage, where necessary, with significant texts from outside this period, such as Sir William Jones's 'A Persian Song of Hafiz' (1772). Such critical engagements are necessary and inevitable given the significance of certain non-Victorian texts in carving the Victorian image of Persia. A large part of the study is, nevertheless, dedicated to the examination of the contours of the Victorian literary image of Persia. But within that framework, I am primarily interested in poems in which Persia emerges indirectly or obliquely, as opposed to translation or more explicit forms of 'influence'. My goal in the *Persian Presence* is not to study what is visibly Persian but to disclose the unnoticed, the unobserved, and, so to speak, the hazy Persian particles of Victorian poetry. This is, of course, not to deny the importance of translation as such; Edward FitzGerald, after all, presented his *Rubáiyát* as a translation, and the poem had a major role in shaping British perceptions of Persia (it took several decades before the accuracy of FitzGerald's rendition was challenged). Arnold's 'Sohrab and Rustum' was also an indirect translation, though Arnold himself might not have wanted his poem to be identified as such. Nevertheless, my examination of these poems, and the lesser-known poems that are discussed in the earlier part of the book, is to uncover the unheeded Persian dimension of Victorian poetry, is to unveil the ways by which Persia became not a travesty or a misreading in the nineteenth century, but a discourse, a language that was shared, whether knowingly or unknowingly, amongst Victorian authors. My dual (Anglo-Persian) readings in this book are to illuminate this process of influence and exchange. This is a process full of misperception, but misperception can itself be a source of creative possibility, and can develop in unexpected ways as in Browning's *Ferishtah's Fancies*.

My readings in the *Persian Presence* also provide historical, cultural, and linguistic depth to a growing body of scholarship on the processes of cultural exchange between Persia and the West. A number of significant works have been published in recent years on this topic: Laetitia Nanquette's *Orientalism Versus Occidentalism: Literary and Cultural Imaging Between France and Iran Since the Islamic Revolution* (2013), Jane Grogan's *The Persian Empire in English Renaissance Writing, 1549–1622* (2014), and Hamid Dabashi's *Persophilia: Persian Culture on the Global Scene* (2015) have focused exclusively on the perennial theme of Persia's cultural relevance and longevity within the discursive realms of the Western imagination. The aim of the *Persian Presence* is of the same nature: its exploration of the Victorian conception of Persia is to explain how and why Persia has remained a constant, yet mobile, facet of Western cultural memory.

A word also needs to be said about my choice of the word 'presence' over the more common designation, 'influence'. As noted at the start, the manifestation of Persia in Victorian poetry is prolific, and not uniform. Some poems are, for example, direct translations, such as Edward Robert Lytton's 'The Roses of Saadi' (1865). Others, such as James Clarence Mangan's 'An Ode by Hafiz' (1848), claim to be translations but have no direct counterpart in Persian. There are also adaptations that are rendered indirectly or through a third intermediary language, such as 'Sohrab and Rustum', whose source in Firdausi's *Shahnameh* reached Arnold via a French translation. There are poems that make direct and specific reference to Persia such as Tennyson's 'Persia' (1827), and poems in which Persia appears in the background or the margins, though this less obvious presence may still be richly significant, as in the opening lines of the pope's mono-logue in Robert Browning's *The Ring and the Book* (1868–9), and in sonnet 8 of Christina Rossetti's 'Monna Innominata' (1881), both of which allude to the biblical story of Esther and Ahasuerus. The term 'presence' is, therefore, more suited to my purpose, as it encompasses a wider spectrum of literary engagements including translation, imita-tion, interpretation, representation, conscious allusion, and indirect borrowing. No study of the representation of Persia in nineteenth-century English poetry can, nevertheless, pretend to be comprehen-sive. The word Persia with its multi-layered construction is too diverse for that to be feasible. The range of its connotations may, however, be suggested so that the reader gains some perspective on this vast, com-plex landscape. This has been my aim in the more general chapters that discuss broad thematic tendencies in the representation of Persia; my case-studies offer more intensive, detailed discussion of aspects of the Victorian engagement with Persia that are of particular interest.

Although I am mostly concerned with poetry, in my study of the meanings of Persia in the Victorian imagination I have found it help-ful to refer, at various points in this study, to a number of prose works including Sir John Malcolm's *History of Persia* (1815), James Morier's *The Adventures of Hajjî Baba of Ispahan* (1824), and Arnold's 'Persian Passion Play' (1871). My choice of such works refers both to their general significance and to the ways in which they influence the perception of Persia in the period. However fictional and satirical, Morier's *Hajjî Baba* is, for instance, one of the first attempts in the nineteenth century to offer an account of the life and the habits of the Persians, opening up a channel of communication between romance and modernity which FitzGerald, though with very different aims, was later to exploit in the *Rubáiyát*. Similarly, Malcolm's *History* not only enhances the British knowledge of Persian history but also initi-ates the narrative of Persia's decline and decay, which, however true, remains popular amongst British writers throughout the nineteenth century.

One other defining choice here concerns my exclusion of transla-tion proper. The closing decades of the nineteenth century saw the advent of a more learned type of engagement with Persia and Persian literature than had been the case in previous decades. Scholarly writings and translations by specialists and enthusiasts such as Edward Cowell, Edward H. Palmer, Edwin Arnold, H. Wilberforce-Clarke, Jesse Cadell, and Gertrude Bell expanded the British understanding of authentic Persian literature. These writers were conversant with the Persian language, and their first-hand knowledge enabled them to give a more accurate representation not just of the texts they translated, but of the historical and cultural contexts in which those texts had been produced. Jesse Cadell's stringent critique of FitzGerald's *Rubáiyát* in 1879, which was the first by a Persian-speaking critic, is emblematic of this new approach.[1] A more erudite understanding of Persian literature, history, and culture led to a more discerning identification of certain tenets such as Islamic mysticism (Sufism) and its idiosyncratic place in Persian poetry. Towards the end of the nineteenth century, a continuing interest in Persian poetry and particularly in the work of certain figures such as Hafiz and Rumi appeared in Britain that has continued to this day. The study of this great field of cultural production, however, lies beyond the boundaries of this book. Most writings on Persia or translations of Persian from the latter half of the nineteenth century claimed to be, and in most cases were, authentic; they were faithful to their Persian originals in their conception, structure, and diction. Works such as Herman Bicknell's *Ḥáfiẓ of Shíráz* (1875), Gertrude Bell's *Poems from the Divan of Háfiz* (1897), Walter Leaf's *Versions from Hafiz: an essay in Persian meter* (1898) or Edwin Arnold's *The Gulistán: being the Rose-garden of Shaikh Sà'di; the first four Babs, or "Gateways"* (1899) were grounded in authentic Persian texts, or at least in texts which were thought to be authentic; their analysis would, therefore, require a different mode of critical engagement in which translation studies would have a more central role.

This book is not the first work of scholarship to recognise the influence of Persia and Persian poetry in English literature. As well as two essays, Laurence Lockhart's 'Persia as Seen by the West' in A. J. Arberry's *The Legacy of Persia* (1953) and Farhang Jahanpour's 'Western Encounters with Persian Sufi Literature' in Leonard Lewisohn and David Morgan's *The Heritage of Sufism* (1999), there have been three books in recent decades that have focused exclusively on this topic: Marzieh Gail's *Persia and the Victorians* (1951), John D. Yohannan's *Persian Poetry in England and America: A Two Hundred Year History* (1977), and Hasan Javadi's valuable work, *Persian Literary Influence on English Literature, with special reference to the*

Nineteenth Century (2005). There also exists Cyrus Ghani's *Shakespeare, Persia, and the East* (2007) which looks exclusively at the manifestations of Persia in the work of Shakespeare and other Elizabethan writers. I have benefited from critical engagement with all of the above works, especially those of Gail, Yohannan, and Javadi, whose methods in situating the influence of Persia and Persian cultural materials in English literature are more literary than the others and, therefore, closer to mine. Nevertheless, there are differences of emphasis: both Yohannan and Javadi, for example, allocate a chapter to the study of the influence of Persian themes in Romantic literature, whereas my focus is more on mid-Victorian poetics. Romantic notions of Persia, transmitted by works that purported to be Persian, such as Thomas Moore's *Lalla Rookh* (1817), do, of course, form part of the conceptual background of this monograph, although arguably they had less importance for the major writers I study than, for instance, the deeper-rooted conceptions of Persia transmitted by classical and biblical texts.

There are methodological distinctions between the current work and its critical precursors too. As I have indicated, the concept of 'presence' has led me to consider less obvious, more oblique ways in which Persia manifests itself in Victorian poetry. A further distinctive feature of this book is the bilateral, Anglo-Persian nature of its critical enquiry. The close readings in this book seek to make Persia visible to anglophone readers, but they are mindful of British literary traditions, too. It is, for example, because the vocabulary and idiom of FitzGerald's *Rubáiyát*, and its literary affiliations, are so recognisably English that its engagement with Persia is so powerful and prominent. *Ferishtah's Fancies*, similarly, has the recognisable characteristics of Browning's poetry: it is formally complex, verbally dense and intricate, polemical, and provocative; and it is this quintessentially 'Browningesque' design of the poem that makes its oblique historical and cultural Persian presence more intriguing. The 'Englishness' of the poetry I explore is thus crucial to an understanding of its 'Persian' construction and connotations, and, accordingly, a hybrid, Anglo-Persian criticism that is attentive to Persia (Iran) and Britain's history, literature, and language is required for what this study aims to accomplish.

My methodology is neither that of conventional literary history, in which questions of direct influence are of primary concern, nor of cultural history, in which literature is seen as part of a broader analysis of the history of ideas. The poems themselves, whether considered in categories or as individual works, are the object of attention. Particular emphasis is placed on elements that might be less visible to readers who lack knowledge of Persian literature and culture in its original forms. The aim is to examine the ways in which Persia was received, circulated, and represented in Victorian poetry. The term 'Persia' itself has multiple and shifting associations, but one strong connecting thread may be discerned in the poems that are discussed in this study: the persistence, through a period in which British encounters with modern Persia were increasing in the areas of diplomacy and trade, and in which knowledge of the country's language, history, and culture was becoming more exact and more detailed, of a fantasised Persia, or Persian imaginary, compounded of ancient and in some cases mythic elements. This is my underlying argument in this study: the Persia of Victorian poetry, however diverse in concept and construction it might have been, is imaginary; it is fantastical with little connection with historical reality.

In my analysis of the poetic adaptation of Persian themes and tropes, I do not engage with any single theoretical model, though I recognise the significance of recent works on cross-cultural appropriations, including Patrick Brantlinger's *Rule of Darkness* (1988), Chris Bongie's *Exotic Memories* (1991), Robert J. C. Young's *Colonial Desire* (1995), and the primary work in this field, Edward Said's *Orientalism* (1978). A few more words, however, may need to be said about my approach to Said, particularly in light of the ideological alignment that one may draw between my exploration of the Victorian reception and representation of Persia and the theoretical frameworks that were first described in *Orientalism*. Part of Said's overall argument is that positive, sympathetic articulations, as manifest expressions of Orientalism, are still discursively placed within its broader, latent structures. With that in mind, one may argue that the underlying idea in the *Persian Presence* is in accordance with, and indebted to, Said's way of thinking. But it would be surprising if this were not the case, considering the pervasiveness, and the earliness, of Said's critical framework. *Orientalism* laid the foundations of an intellectual debate which is still current in our day. Since its appearance, there has been almost no work of scholarly merit on Orientalism that has not engaged, either favourably or adversely, with Said's frame of reference. The *Persian Presence* is no exception; it adheres to Said's employment of the key terms 'Orient' and 'Orientalism', but does not wholly support his polemic, nor does it intend to provide an Orientalist analysis of its chosen texts. There are two main reasons for this divergence. The first concerns the scope of Said's argument, which, as Robert Irwin's states, is limited to 'the Arab heart-land' and offers 'no substantial discussion of Persian or Turkish studies'.[2] The second concerns the somewhat reductive nature of Said's framework in its own terms. The summing up of a complex network of cultural, social, and literary interactions under one heading is inimical to the method I have adopted in this monograph, even allowing for the fact that Said's actual critical practice was often less intransigent than what his master-narrative would dictate or his detractors claim. In the work of many authors who incorporated the Orient into their writing (Morier, Tennyson, Arnold, FitzGerald, Browning, among many other examples) there is a manifold set of responses to the Orient, some of them arrogant and stupid, *colonial* in the most hidebound sense of that term, but others sympathetic, generous, hospitable, self-questioning; the fixities of identity and class are destabilised in these works as often as they are reinforced, and in ways that ask *Orientalism* to be set aside, and for the texts themselves to be reconsidered.

This book begins by surveying a range of sources from which the British derived their knowledge of Persia, and emphasises the persistent, and, at times, concurrent, influence of two main currents of thoughts, that is, 'mythic' and 'modern', in shaping the British perception of Persia in the nineteenth century. The opening chapter follows a chronological pattern and its historical contextualisation is key to the close readings it makes. Moving forward from the Greek and biblical representations of Persia, it then explores the reasons behind the persistence of this ancient understanding in the early modern period, particularly as against the gradual emergence of direct contacts with the country. The main corrective to these ingrained structures of thought and feeling about Persia in this period comes from trade and diplomacy, empirical narratives of travel, and the literary by-products of these encounters with the Orient such as those that were written on and about the Sherley brothers in England. An analysis of the growing British interest in Persian studies in the final quarter of the eighteenth century also forms part of the design of this chapter. The chief figure here is Sir William Jones, the founder of the academic study of Oriental literatures; the chapter examines Jones's 'A Persian Song of Hafiz' as one of the earliest examples of the scholarly treatment of Persian poetry in English, before moving on to look at the dynamic between the nineteenth-century politicised vision of Persia and the narrative of its decline and decay through studying James Morier's popular fiction, *The Adventures of Hajjî Baba of Ispahan* (1824).

The second chapter provides the first systematic analysis of the presence of Persia in nineteenth-century English poetry. In doing so, the chapter relies on the categories of texts and typologies that are outlined in Chapter 1 as a conceptual basis to describe the environments of knowledge within which the image of Persia was defined and disseminated in the nineteenth century. In discerning the image of Persia, the chapter employs keyword searches of literary databases, principally Literature Online (LION), with additional data from the British Library Catalogue. Although LION is admittedly not comprehensive (it does not, for example, include newspaper and magazine verse), it is still large enough to serve as a representative corpus. Methodologically, using LION also allows for the significant contours of the book's subject to be mapped out. A preoccupation with certain classical or biblical texts, for example, will show up even in the broad, undifferentiated findings of a keyword search, and will suggest the compelling force of such texts in shaping people's perception of Persia in nineteenth-century Britain. The range of designs and discourses that Persia embodies can then be distinguished using the data that LION provides. The poems explored in this chapter are also both the result *of*, and in direct communication *with*, the discussions in Chapter 1. It is, in fact, through the historical contextualisation of the opening chapter that we are able to propose a taxonomy, however partial and provisional, of nineteenth-century English poetic portrayal of Persia. But the poems I cite here also look forward to the case-studies of the following chapters. The imaginary Persia of myth and fable, which dominates the mass of nineteenth-century poems I have found in my study, is present in the 'modern' poems of Arnold, FitzGerald, and Browning. 'Sohrab and Rustum' draws Persia in the light of the past as an ancient place of legends and heroes. FitzGerald envisions Persia in his *Rubáiyát* as an imaginary 'garden'.[3] Browning in *Ferishtah's Fancies* relies, as the title intimates, on his own 'fancy', and on his polemical reading of the *Rubáiyát*, to create a mythical medieval Persia. Of course, a poem such as the *Rubáiyát* does more than recycle familiar tropes and conventions, but it is still working within their domain; FitzGerald's historical scholarship, not negligible in itself and certainly well in advance of that of many of his contemporaries, is, in the end, subject to an idea of Persia shaped by the past.

The second part of the book, consisting of three case-studies, shows in greater depth and detail how conceptions of Persia entered into major works of British literature. The case-studies follow a chronological order of publication, beginning with 'Sohrab and Rustum'. Arnold's long narrative poem comprises of a variety of components, many of which he had borrowed from secondary sources. Accordingly, the chapter approaches Arnold's epic narrative from various angles: it first considers the poem's Persian origin, looking at Firdausi's background, his *Shahnameh*, the history of its composition, and the political context in which it was created. The chapter then focuses on the episode of 'Sohrab'. Knowledge of Firdausi's original is crucial here not because Arnold knew it but because he did not. Arnold never read Firdausi. He wrote his version of 'Sohrab' after he read, in French, Charles Augustin Sainte-Beuve's 'Le Livre des Rois' (1850), a review of Julius von Mohl's translation of Firdausi's *Shahnameh*. In the chain of interpretation from Mohl to Sainte-Beuve to Arnold, only Mohl had read the Persian text. This complex process of transmission, in which Mohl's poetics, and Sainte-Beuve's cultural politics, play a significant role, has shaped Arnold's appropriation of Firdausi's characters, setting, and mythical substance. My aim in this chapter is to unravel the complexity of this process of literary appropriation, exposing the paradoxical nature of Sainte-Beuve's role, since he both enabled Arnold to write the poem and implicitly challenged the authority of any modern poet to rival a 'primary' epic poet such as Firdausi.

The claim of the penultimate chapter in the book is that FitzGerald, without being literal in his rendition of the quatrains attributed to Khayyám, succeeded in transmitting a Persian spirit in his *Rubáiyát*. One might suppose that this has always been received wisdom: FitzGerald himself speaks of it in his letters and in his preface of 1859. Charles Eliot Norton also confidently repeated the claim in his 'Review of *Rubáiyát*' in 1869 (and Norton did not know Persian). The same claim was put forward, on a more informed basis, by Edward Heron-Allen in 1898, and then again by the prominent Persian scholar Arberry in 1959. And it has been the working assumption of most critics of the poem. But there exists no single study of FitzGerald's *Rubáiyát* that reinforces this long-standing notion by providing evidence of FitzGerald's attunement to idiomatic nuance in the original quatrains. English-speaking critics have provided extensive and commendable literary and historical scholarship on the poem, and credited FitzGerald for matching a work of Oriental literature to Western tastes; but their unfamiliarity with the Persian language has inevitably hindered them from fully appreciating the Persian dimension of the poem. Those who know Persian, on the other hand, have given FitzGerald the credit he deserves for the profundity and peculiarity of his translation but have not provided direct evidence of his remarkable importation of Persian linguistic, literary, and cultural elements in his poem. In its detailed comparison of FitzGerald's *Rubáiyát* to his Persian original(s), this chapter offers new insights into FitzGerald's translation practice and the poetics. The emphasis is almost wholly on these specific comparisons, which supplement the work done on the poem by previous critiques such as Arberry's *The Romance of the Rubaiyat*. Yet my argument here goes beyond a comparative literary analysis. FitzGerald succeeded in transfusing a Persian soul into his re-writing of the *Rubáiyát* by importing matter of peculiar Persian significance, elements that may look foreign to English readers of the poem, but familiar to those who are acquainted with the particulars of Persian literary and cultural traditions. In order to unearth these hidden peculiarities, the *Rubáiyát* ought to be read with, so to speak, a Persian eye; it has to be read as a native critic would, for instance, study the poetry of Hafiz.

The final chapter in the book is, at first sight, a peculiar one. One might wonder why *Ferishtah's Fancies* has been chosen over the other, and more notable, Persian poems of the second half of the nineteenth-century which have a greater claim to authenticity. True, *Ferishtah's Fancies* has no counterpart or original Persian source, nor is it a translation or adaptation of any kind. It is a work of English literature with, in Browning's language, a 'thin' layer of Persian disguise. But this seemingly thin layer of Persian-ness is the main reason behind my choice of the poem: the implicit nature of the presence of Persia in *Ferishtah's Fancies* makes it an apt choice for the kind of Persian presence that I seek to unveil in this monograph. The poem's Persian surface, apparently decorative and making no claim to historical or literary authenticity, conceals another, less demonstrative layer of allusion, some of which may be the result of an unconscious, or unintended infusion of knowledge about Persian culture picked up from many sources, among them FitzGerald's *Rubáiyát*, to whose hero Browning's Ferishtah is polemically opposed. Close reading of the poems – of a kind rarely accorded to this work, which has mainly been seen as a repository of Browning's religious and philosophical ideas – uncovers its deeper, less visible Persian presence.

A few points need to be clarified with regard to the Persian side of this study. The first one relates to the age-old question of Persian versus Farsi. In this book, I use 'Persia' and 'Persian' when I refer to texts from the period under study, since these were the terms in common use in the nineteenth century. I use 'Iran' and 'Iranian' when I refer to modern scholarship. An exception with regard to 'Iran' and 'Iranian' concerns Firdausi's use of these terms to designate the ancient Persia of the *Shahnameh*. I make a similar distinction with regard to 'Persian' as against 'Farsi' for the name of the language. While acknowledging that no system of reference is perfect, this seems the best way of respecting both historical context and modern developments. The second point relates to my transliterations of Persian. I hope I may be forgiven for adopting a simple method of transliteration. Almost all Persian words in this work are transliterated without diacritics. The only exception is when I use Victorian transliterations of certain Persian words such as Khayyám, *rubáiy*, or *Rubáiyát*. With the translation of Persian poetry, instead of attempting a literal but unembellished translation myself, I have decided to rely, where possible, on professional translators. For the *Shahnameh*, I have relied on Dick Davis's *nameh: the Persian Book of Kings* (2007). For the translation of the *Rubáiyát*, I have used Peter Avery and John Heath-Stubbs's *The Ruba'iyat of Omar Khayyam* (2004). There are also a few lines from Hafiz in the first two chapters. In the opening chapter, I have used Dick Davis's translation in *Faces of Love: Hafez and the Poets of Shiraz* (2012); in one instance in the second chapter, for a lack of a better rendition, I have relied on H. Wilberforce-Clarke's translation from *Dīvān-i-Hāfiz* (1891). For the meaning of words in Persian, I have used *Dehkhoda Dictionary* (1998). All the biblical excerpts in this study are taken from the King James Bible, and all the translations of the Qur'an are from Arberry's *The Koran Interpreted* (1955).

Notes

1. Cadell, 'The True Omar Khayyam'.
2. Irwin, *For Lust of Knowing*, p. 282.
3. In his letter of 2 November 1858 to Edward B. Cowell, FitzGerald described his translation as 'a sort of Epicurean Eclogue in a Persian Garden'; see Terhune and Terhune, *Letters*, vol. 2, p. 322.

Chapter 1

Persia in the West

The aim of this chapter is to trace the development of the image of Persia which shaped, and was shaped by, nineteenth-century English poetry. In order to do this, it is necessary to give some account of how knowledge about Persia was acquired and disseminated in the West from (roughly) the fourteenth century onwards; and, just as important, we need to understand the different *kinds* of knowledge that were available. Generalisations about such broad cultural-historical matters are difficult, and must be put forward with caution. Categories such as 'the West' are themselves not uniform or stable; 'Persia' itself meant different things in the sixteenth century to a subject of Queen Elizabeth and a citizen of the Venetian Republic. Nevertheless, and with due regard for such differences, this chapter attempts to give some idea of the Persian imaginary as it took hold in Western culture over the course of several centuries. This narrative and descriptive account, however, is not neutral. My argument is that there were two main currents of knowledge about Persia, which sometimes flowed alongside each other, and sometimes met and interpenetrated. One derived from ancient sources, from the Bible, from classical Greek history and literature, and, a little later, from romance. The other derived from what might be called 'modern' real-world contacts with Persia, conducted through trade, diplomacy, and travel. Of course, these two currents are not entirely separate, since merchants, diplomats, and missionaries went to Persia with ideas already formed by the older tradition. But the latter modes of engaging with Persia was never able to supersede the former ways of thinking about it. Historical and linguistic scholarship, accelerating from the mid-eighteenth century onwards, and driven in part by a new-found interest in Persia's geopolitical position, did bring the biblical and classical accounts and associations under critical scrutiny. But what is surprising (or perhaps, on reflection, it is not so surprising) is the persistence of an ancient or mythic Persia through the very period in which actual knowledge of the country was increasing. Numerous books and essays were published in the nineteenth century in which Persian history, geography, religion, and social customs were treated in the 'modern' spirit of systematic inquiry; translations of major literary works trace an arc from adaptation and appropriation to a more scholarly effort at linguistic and contextual fidelity. But the reference points for 'Persia' in English poetry of the nineteenth century show another kind of fidelity, to an enduring image of Persia as an antitype to Western concepts, whether in the domain of politics, or religion, or aesthetics, or the relations between the sexes.[1] The clash, or intermingling, of ancient and modern ideas of Persia lies at the heart of the readings of major works of English literature undertaken in subsequent chapters of this book.

The account that follows of the history of Anglo-Persian cultural and material contacts cannot claim to be comprehensive. Excellent studies of this field exist. Those on which I have mainly relied are named in the Introduction; they also appear in the Bibliography and several are specifically acknowledged in the notes to this chapter. My aim is to give a selective but, I trust, fair-minded survey of the general framework of knowledge about Persia leading up to the nineteenth century, with an emphasis on those features that mattered most – that made the deepest impression – on literary works. I begin with the ancient world, and move through the voyages, travel literature, and other forms of imaginative thinking about Persia in the early modern period, to the turning point of 'modern' Persian scholarship in the West at the end of the eighteenth century, whose representative figure in Britain was the great Orientalist Sir William Jones. The chapter concludes with a brief discussion of early nineteenth-century Anglo-Persian political contacts and their cultural and imaginative ramifications, including one of the most remarkable and indicative works of the time, James Morier's *Hajjî Baba of Ispahan* (1824). Morier's picaresque novel, a fascinating blend of observation and fantasy, embodies the contradictions that continued to animate the image of Persia in British writing in the decades that followed.

Persia and the Greeks

Victorian thinking about Persia was steeped in the discourse of two ancient cultures, that of the Greeks and that of the Hebrew Bible (the 'Old Testament'). In studying their influence, certain factors, however, need to be considered. First, what we know today of both the Greek world and the Bible is evidently different from what the Victorians

knew: a mass of sociocultural knowledge generated by modern historical and archeological discoveries, and by the advances of textual
scholarship, has shaped our understanding of ancient Greek and biblical narratives. Our image of ancient Athens, for example, takes more
account of the position of women, and of the question of slavery, than
that of the Victorians – though, it would be wrong to imply that such
issues were wholly absent from the discussion of Athens as the 'cradle'
of democracy. Another example relates to the question of historicity,
particularly that of the Bible. The 'Higher Criticism' of biblical writings, led by German scholars, had been making its way into popular
consciousness since the end of the eighteenth century. But this was a
slow process; the arguments of the biblical criticism were by no means
universally accepted and, more to the point, not widely disseminated.
The chronology and historical veracity of books such as Ruth and
Esther were taken for granted, except by specialists whose scholarly
research had not yet changed the dominant public perception.[2] In
what follows this difference between modern and Victorian perspective needs to be constantly borne in mind.

Ancient Greek writings on Persia can be divided into two main
categories. The first group, dominated by Herodotus' *Histories*
(c. 440 BCE), takes its impetus from the wars between the Persian
empire and the Greek city-states in the sixth and fifth centuries BCE,
beginning with the defeat of Croesus, king of Lydia, by Cyrus in
547, and the conquest of Ionia by his general Harpagus in the following year. The invasions of Darius I and his son Xerxes in 492 and
481 were marked by a series of battles (Marathon, Thermopylae,
Salamis, Plataea) that acquired quasi-mythological status, not just
for their descendants but for the Christian inheritors of the Greek
political and philosophical tradition. Herodotus himself, and those
historians who followed him, though, had a sense of the grandeur
of their theme, and aimed to offer a detailed narrative of the past
and contemporary events in an impartial way, or at least in a way
that presented itself as impartial. It is not my aim here to discern
how unbiased these texts were but it is worth remembering that a
notion such as historical veracity, if existed at all, must have carried a
different connotation in antiquity.[3] As Michael Flower explains, the
modern distinctions that we carefully draw today between subjectiv-
ity and objectivity, or fictional and non-fictional, cannot be applied
without qualification to a work such as the *Histories*; 'Herodotus'
conception of "historical truth" is unlikely to be exactly the same
as ours', although the narrative of *Histories* is still considered 'to be
based on a core of hard facts'.[4]

Herodotus, the most renowned classical author on the Persian affairs, was originally from Greece but was raised as a Persian subject. His writing on Persia, later divided into nine books (named after the muses), traces the development of the Persian empire, starting with Croesus of Lydia, through Cyrus and Xerxes. In the last three books, the narrative focuses largely on the Persian campaign against Greece (the earlier books mostly contain geographical and anthropological information on ancient Persia). In writing his book, Herodotus relied on existing written narratives and oral stories of those who had served as mercenaries in the Persian army.[5] For his account of the Persian invasions, which he was documenting several decades later, he collected various data on the number of armies and individuals involved in these battles. Curiously, this systematic approach in writing history has brought Herodotus both praise and criticism. The use of quantifiable data in reconstructing history is certainly a distinctive, and an original, trait of his genius: Herodotus is arguably the first quantitative historian. But on the other hand, he has been rebuked for his acceptance of all sorts of unusually colourful and dramatic narratives. There is also an argument that his account features fictitious sources.[6] But then there is another peculiarity to Herodotus' approach, though this makes him a reliable, and rather unusual, source for his time. The account of the Persian affairs that the *History* provides is far from what we would call 'triumphalist'.[7] Herodotus does not conform to the ethnically prejudiced intellectual milieu of its time; his narrative is less concerned with, or manipulated by, racial or ethnic prejudice. As such, the stereotype of the Persians as enslaved effeminate barbarians, as against the strong and spirited Greeks, is less evident in his narrative (although, by the nineteenth century, even this relatively unbiased narrative was pressed into service to reinforce the opposing, and the more pervasive, image of the Persians).[8]

The same might be said of Xenophon's *Cyropaedia* (c. 370 BCE), a flamboyant biography of Cyrus the Great (580–529 BCE). *Cyropaedia* describes, in eight volumes, Cyrus' upbringing, education, kingship, military campaigns, and death. But within the boundaries of its biographical framework, it also explores many other aspects of ancient Persia, including the formation of the Persian empire, its military structure, political administration, and education system. There is, however, something distinctive about Xenophon's narrative; *Cyropaedia*, while it offers a detailed narrative of the life of Cyrus and, more generally of Persian affairs, is not simply a historical account. It is fictive; it is feigned. Xenophon did have a first-hand experience of Persian life; he served as a mercenary, fighting for Cyrus the Younger (c. 423–401), the son of the Achaemenian king, Darius II, in his attempted coup in 401 BCE against his brother, the newly acceded king, Artaxerxes II.[9] He also had access to the writings of his predecessors such as those of Herodotus or Antisthenes.[10] But his 'historical' treatment of Cyrus, despite his exposure to Persia and access to earlier sources, is not entirely accurate and is predisposed in its own peculiar way. The Cyrus of *Cyropaedia* is too good to be true. He is an outstanding hero, a living legend who appears in almost every episode in the book. There are, however, reasons for this colourful and overwhelmingly strong presence of Cyrus in the book. Although he was long dead, Cyrus' eminence and achievements were known to the Greeks of Xenophon's time. Herodotus' full account of his life, including details of his birth, youth, wars, and triumphs, was already available, not to mention that the Greeks of the fourth century BCE had a fascination for all things Persian.[11] Cyrus was then a safe object for commendation at the time. This assumption becomes more credible if we take note of what appears to have been Xenophon's main purpose for writing *Cyropaedia*. Xenophon's special interest in, and lavish praise for, Cyrus springs from something other than conventional, and excessive, admiration. To him, Cyrus is an architype that can exemplify a set of moral, philosophical, and political principles; he is, in Deborah Gera's language, 'a convenient framework, a peg upon which Xenophon hangs reflections and ideas of his own'.[12] But there is one thing about Xenophon's Cyrus: the ideas that he incarnates had a Greek (Western) reach; they were embodied in the figure of Cyrus, not for the sake of Persia or its people, but for the enhancement of contemporary and future Greeks. In other words, the Cyrus of *Cyropaedia* is a carefully crafted figure, an imaginary construct whose administration of his vast empire offered an ideal model for future princes – something that came to be highly valued in Renaissance England.[13]

Neither Herodotus nor Xenophon set out to write 'revisionist' works as we would understand the term today, nor were they writing fully from 'within' the Persian culture they described. But Herodotus' ambition to reconstruct the past from the accounts of those who had witnessed it, and Xenophon's choice of a Persian monarch as his idealised subject, meant that, in different ways, they were not predisposed to further a narrative in which 'Persia' simply stood as the antithesis to 'Greece', whether in terms of personal qualities (courage, loyalty, friendship) or public and political virtues. The effect is markedly different from that of the second major group of Greek writings on Persia, consisting of plays and tragedies that were inspired by historical events, but in which the depiction of these events was swayed by personal feelings and communal perceptions. The career of Phrynichus is instructive in this respect. His *Sack of Miletus* (498 BCE) was a tragedy on the conquest of Miletus by Darius, which had taken place the year before; it was so harrowing that, according to Herodotus, the Athenians fined Phrynichus for reminding them of the loss of their colony.[14] In 476, by contrast, Phrynichus produced the *Phoenissae*, which told the story of the defeat of Xerxes I at the battle of Salamis (480). This was a reminder not of defeat but of glorious victory; the play won first prize at the Dionysia. The *Phoenissae* was followed by Aeschylus' *Persae* (472), also based on the defeat of Xerxes and including, besides an account of Salamis, a 'prophecy' of the victory in the battle of Plataea (479).[15] To add insult to injury, the prophecy is delivered by the ghost of Darius, Xerxes' father.

The *Persae* is the only extant play whose author had a first-hand experience of the Persian wars. Aeschylus' hostility to Persia is not unusual, given the concurrency of his life (c. 525–455/6 BCE) with the brutal conduct of these wars, epitomised by the conquest of Miletus, with the slaughter of the men, and enslavement of the women. Many of Aeschylus' fellow Athenians were killed in the battles against the Persians. Darius' invasion of mainland Greece took place when Aeschylus was almost thirty-five years of age. He and his brother are both said to have been involved in the battle of Marathon in 490 (Aeschylus' brother is said to have been killed in that conflict). But the struggle with Persia continued even after Marathon. For over a decade, Athens had to deal with its own political turmoil, while at the same time being dominated by the unending threat from the Persians. Aeschylus eventually witnessed the march of Xerxes into Athens after the Persians captured the city and evacuated its people in 480, before the naval victory at Salamis unexpectedly redressed the balance of the war. But this victory did not in itself resolve matters; the aftermath of the war was both politically and economically difficult.[16] In such circumstances, it is hardly surprising that the Persians and their king, Xerxes, are treated with such animosity in Aeschylus' play. Considered simply as a communal, and, in view of Aeschylus' personal history, subjective, response to years of Persian military oppression, the play has its own validity. However, the historicity of the play is another matter. Scholars have often doubted the legitimacy of Aeschylus' narrative, especially when set against that of Herodotus. They have instead taken the *Persae* as an example of the Greeks' projection of themselves, based on their grand perception of their own ethnic and cultural status. Today, we know that the Greeks' representation of the 'other' was shaped largely by ethnic stereotyping. Anyone who was not Greek was considered uncivilised, savage, barbaric.[17] War, as it always does, facilitated the formation and circulation of this opposition between civilisation and barbarism, especially when no understanding of the ideological factors that are involved in the social and imaginary 'construction' of one culture by another could have existed.[18]

Taken as a whole, the Greek writings on the Greco-Persian wars were significant, though not just because they documented the history of one of the greatest military conflicts of antiquity, but because they formed an undying ideological impression. Whether through the relative impartiality of historians such as Herodotus, or the subjective passion of dramatists such as Aeschylus, the story that emerged was that of the triumph of freedom and self-government; although the 'example' of Greece in this sense differed from that of Rome, which tended towards the validation of conquest and empire. Towards the end of the eighteenth century, and particularly after the French Revolution, while Europe was pondering its future, circumstances urged the need for an appropriate history and genealogy. With advances in the understanding of Greek art and philology, in which German and British scholars of the Romantic period played a leading role, Europe was able to connect its history to ancient Greece through uncovering linguistic and philological ties. This breakthrough led to the advent of a series of complex ideological, cultural, and historical understandings; though it also became both a tool for propaganda and a forceful element in the academic and political discourse in the nineteenth century. In the case of ancient Persia, the military warfare of the Persians with Greece came to be interpreted not just as an armed clash, but as an emblematic conflict between monolithic and theocratic tyranny, and political and intellectual liberty. The clash of a democratic government and a tyrannical regime in the context of the Greco-Persian war came to be taken as a validation of the supremacy of principles such as democracy, liberty, and republicanism, with which Europe, through its affiliation with ancient Greece, would associate itself, over notions such as tyranny, despotism, and barbarism, for which the Persians, through the Greeks' identification of them, had come to be known.

Persia and the Bible

Persia enters largely into the historical portion of the Bible, and its connections with the fortunes of the Jews are particularly close and direct. There is an array of information on Persia in the Old Testament, predominantly in relation to the end of the biblical period when the Persians became a dominant force in the Near East, including in the land of Israel, after the defeat of the Babylonian empire in the sixth century BCE. The early Persian kings are all named in the Bible, notably in books which were probably composed in the period, such as Ezra, Nehemiah, and Esther. There are also important references in some of the prophetic books: for example, Isaiah, Haggai, Zachariah, and Malachi.[19] The Old Testament image of Persia is, however, mixed. The Persians are at times praised for their benevolence, for their benefactions, yet this very quality has its dangerous side, as in the story of Esther where the vulnerability of the Jews as a minority is exposed. But overall, the account of the Persians given by the Jewish prophets is more approving than condemnatory. An example of this appears in Isaiah, where Cyrus is referred to as the Lord's 'shepherd' (44: 28) and his 'anointed [. . .] whose right hand I have holden, to subdue nations before him' (45: 1). The term 'anointed' associates Cyrus with the great deliverer for whom the Jews longed. In his conquest of Babylonia in 539 BCE, Cyrus showed mercy to the captive Jews. Perhaps, though evidence is lacking, he looked at the Jewish God and that of his people's monotheistic religion (Zoroastrianism) as a manifestation of one God.[20] He may have also been thinking politically ahead of his time. Cyrus' empire was still young at the time; protecting the Jews would bring not only the good will of his subjects but also the support of the Jews. But more important than any other consideration, from the point of view of the Jews themselves, was the decree that Cyrus issued ordering the rebuilding of the Temple at Jerusalem, and thus the reversal, in part at least, of the Babylonian captivity. Cyrus' decree – eventually confirmed by his successor, Darius – establishes the Persian monarch as God's agent, placing his royal power at the service of God's providential design.[21] The concept of royal absolutism is crucial to this story: the image of Persia as a land ruled by decrees that could not be questioned plays into the narrative of a different, higher form of absolute power, that of the God of Israel. But one consequence of shaping history in this way was to create a stereotype of Oriental absolutism which endured for centuries, and which indeed has not disappeared. As we will see, the idea of Oriental despotism became a link between the very different kinds of Persia envisioned in the Bible and in Greek history and literature.

The persona of the absolute monarch also dominates the book of Esther, but it does so with a curious twist.[22] Ahasuerus, the Persian king, is all-powerful, yet at crucial moments is incapable of acting on his own initiative, and is swayed by the advice, or the wiles, of his courtiers. The story begins with the Queen Vashti disobeying the king's royal command and refusing to show her beauty.[23] Vashti's royal place, after this, is given to someone else. Ahasuerus then consults with seven princes of Media and Persia. Seven virgins are sought out and brought into the house of women, among whom is Mordecai's cousin, Esther (or Hadassah in Hebrew).[24] Mordecai discovers an assassination plot against the king; he is not immediately rewarded, but his service is documented in an official record which becomes the hinge on which the reversal of the narrative turns. Meanwhile, a feud develops between him and Haman, the king's prime minister, because Mordecai refuses to render Haman the quasi-divine homage to which he is entitled. Knowing that Mordecai is a Jew, Haman decides to get rid of him and the entire Jewish people. Ahasuerus is persuaded to issue a decree ordering the annihilation of the Jews, but Haman's plot is foiled by a series of ironic mishaps, which end with him being hanged on the gallows he had prepared for Mordecai. Esther plays her part, under Mordecai's direction, by daring to appear before Ahasuerus without being summoned (supposedly a capital crime) and pleading for the salvation of her people. In the Jewish tradition, the story is the origin of the festival of Purim; for both Jews and Christians, it is one of the great emblems of divine providence, and it stands as one of the few stories in which a woman's heroism is central to the plot.[25] But these features depended on the way the ambivalence with which the figure of the Oriental despot is treated in the story. Ahasuerus is as arbitrary, capricious, and cruel as one could wish from such a stereotype, yet also pliable and willing to do justice. Mordecai's cleverness and Esther's courage work within the boundaries of a regime whose authority is not questioned. Unlike Pharaoh in Exodus, Ahasuerus never confronts the God of Israel; the salvation of the Jews is achieved not by defying an absolute monarch but by manipulating him. Ahasuerus' 'reach', his ability to decide what happens throughout his vast empire, is as formidable as that of Cyrus or Darius; yet though his decrees cannot be disobeyed, they can be circumvented or even, as Haman discovers, turned inside out. The image of the Persian king is thus a double one, embodying absolutism and weakness, sexual potency and subjugation to a 'favourite'. It is an image which casts a long shadow.

Persia and the Early Modern Contact

Ancient Greece and the Bible represent the 'mythic' strand of knowledge about Persia in the West before the nineteenth century. What of 'real-world' contacts? Persia in the early middle ages was an entity lost to the Christian West; its landscapes, notwithstanding its national characteristics, were unknown to medieval Europe. But from the middle of the thirteenth century, things changed; writings and reports from envoys, missionaries, and merchants slowly started to enhance Europe's knowledge of the Orient, expanding its geographical boundaries to territories beyond Jerusalem and biblical lands. Persia's distinct geographical and cultural identity came to be recognised for the first time in the writings of the Europeans who were travelling through the region, often on their way to, and from, territories further east.[26] Among the many medieval conduits of this process were Marco Polo's *Devisement du Monde* (c. 1298), Odoric of Pordenone's *Relatio* (1330), and John Mandeville, the supposed author (or compiler) of *The Book of John Mandeville* (c. 1356/7).[27]

The practice of collecting voyages continued into the early modern period.[28] By this time, these writings were treated as repositories of information about land beyond Europe where only a few had visited. Amongst the most notable compilations in England were those of Richard Eden, the translator of *A Treatyse of the Newe India* (1498–1552) and *The Decades of the Newe Worlde or West India* (1555);[29] Richard Willes's *History of Travayle* (1577), a sequel to Eden's *Decades* which included substantial materials on Japan and China;[30] Richard Hakluyt's *Divers Voyages Touching the Discoveries of America* (1582) and *Principal Navigations* (1589 and 1598–1600) and Samuel Purchas's *Purchas his Pilgrimage* (1625).[31] However infused with traditional attitudes to the Orient, the travel writings that appeared in this period bear witness to the growth of a new desire for 'modern' information about actual people and places, a sort of empiric specificity that previously had no precedent in the European treatment of the Orient. As far as England is concerned, it is no coincidence that this development overlapped with the emergence in the sixteenth century of commercial companies such as the Muscovy Company, the Levant Company, and the East India Company. Literary allusions reflect this shift of emphasis: classical and biblical motifs are by no means abandoned, but a more contemporary Persia also comes into view. As an example, take two passages that speak of Persia's wealth. The first, from Spenser's *The Faerie Queene* (1590), is rooted in the traditional image of Persia as a land of fabulous wealth and luxury:

By them they passe, all gazing on them round,
And to the Presence mount; whose glorious vew
Their frayle amazed Senses did confound:
In liuing Princes court none euer knew
Such endless richesse, and so sumptuous shew;
Ne *Persia* selfe, the nourse of pompous pride,
Like euer saw. (I, iv, 7)[32]

The second is from Shakespeare's *Twelfth Night* (c. 1601/2): 'I will not give my part of this sport for a pension of thousands to be paid from the Sophy' (II, v, 156–7).[33] Note the difference in emphasis: Spenser's mythic and generic label ('the nourse of pompous pride') has been replaced by a modern, concrete vocabulary: 'a pension of thousands to be paid from the Sophy', an extravagant but not impossible wish. The word 'sophy', which was a European designation, or a misnomer, for the Safavid monarchs, is indicative of the existence of a more current type of knowledge about Persia in early modern England, though the word also says something of the extent of this knowledge.[34] The Safavids were neither Sufis, nor in favour of Sufism. They saw Sufism as a threat, even though it was arguably Sufism that had given rise to their dynasty.[35]

Before looking further at the kind and the complexity of the English Renaissance perception of Persia, a word needs to be said about the study of Oriental languages in Europe in this period. Europe came to learn about the significance of Oriental languages through the success of its missionaries in the fourteenth century. The council of Vienne (1311–12) decreed that chairs of Arabic, Chaldee (the language of ancient Chaldeans), and Hebrew needed to be established in five European universities: Avignon, Paris, Bologna, Salamanca, and Oxford.[36] The Oxford chair was instituted in 1320, though evidence is lacking as to how systematically, or seriously, these languages were being studied there at the time. It was, in fact, not until two hundred years later that the study of Oriental languages gained relative importance in England. Oxford launched the Regius Professorship of Hebrew in 1535. The Thomas Adams Professorship of Arabic was founded at Cambridge in 1632, and another chair of

Arabic, the Laudian Professorship, was inaugurated in Oxford in 1636.[37] But even then, there were many, including the Orientalists (mostly Arabists) themselves, such as Abraham Wheelocke, the first man who held the Thomas Adams Chair in Cambridge, who did not think highly of the subject that they taught. Arabic was deemed not only difficult but also unserviceable; its only use, as Robert Irwin explains, was to study 'the manner of life of Abraham and Moses' in Arabic texts, 'to identify the flora and fauna of the Bible and map out the topography of ancient Palestine'.[38] In the meantime, Persian was being treated even more superficially. Because of its Perso-Arabic script, it was often mistaken for a Semitic language; though the study of it did not even receive the puny significance of Arabic. There was a lack of incentive for learning Persian. Compared to Turkish or Arabic, Persian carried much less significance in furthering the English commercial or political objectives. In 1699, William III, for instance, ordered the acceleration of the study of Turkish because the English needed the language in their commerce with the Ottomans.[39] But there was no such mandate with Persian, and this remained to be the case until the dawn of the nineteenth century.

Notwithstanding this comparative linguistic deficit, the reign of Queen Elizabeth, especially its later years, saw the beginning of a more direct type of engagement with Persia. A number of English emissaries and merchants started to arrive in Persia in the sixteenth century, though the attempts of many to reach the country were also thwarted by the hardship of the journey. One of the earliest, and more iconic, examples of these Anglo-Persian contacts happened in 1561, when Anthony Jenkinson, a representative of the Muscovy Company, arrived at the Safavid capital, Qazvin, with the new Queen Elizabeth's letter of recommendation to Shah Tahmasp. The queen's letter had a modern intent: the support of the Safavids was needed to facilitate trade, not necessarily with Persia but with China. Yet the content of the queen's letter had an ancient tone; Tahmasp was addressed as 'the Emperour of the Persians, Medes, Parthians Hircans, Carmanians, Margians, of the people on this side, and beyond the river of Tygri, and of all men, and nations, betweene the Caspian sea, and the gulfe of Persia'.[40] These appellations were outdated, as if the letter was written to an Achaemenid king rather than a Safavid shah. Tahmasp refused Jenkinson's request, not because of the naivety of the language of the letter but because he did not want to trade with non-Muslims.[41] The parallels between their monarch and those of ancient Persia were not unknown to the Safavids, not to mention that their empire was almost as sizable as that of their pre-Islamic predecessors.[42] But however ineffective at the time, the queen's letter is of value here: it is exemplary because it embodies the English Renaissance thinking about Persia. There was, indeed, a notable empire ruling over Persia in the sixteenth and seventeenth centuries. The Safavids had the largest (and the longest) administration in Persia since the fall of the Sasanian empire in the seventh century. Yet the Persia that permeated the literary consciousness of Renaissance England was not that of the contemporary Safavids (1501–1722) but that of the ancient Achaemenids (559–330 BCE) particularly Cyrus'. Of course, the English were not unmindful of Safavid Persia. They had first-hand contacts with it, albeit small and sporadic.[43] They also had access to a number of recent travel narratives on it, including William Thomas's translation (c. 1550) of the Venetian Giosafat Barabaro's *Travels to Tana and Persia* (c. 1543–5), Richard Willes's *History of Trauayle* (1577) which featured an account of Jenkinson's visit, or Hakluyt's *Principal Navigations* (1598) which included accounts of embassies such as those of Jenkinson and Ralph Fitch (who accompanied the English merchant, John Newberie, in his second journey to Persia in 1581).[44] But despite the availability of these recent sources, in their approach to Persia, the English preferred the ancient imaginary to the actual contemporary. Put differently, the English perception of Persia in the sixteenth century was still largely shaped by the more primitive and the more recognised sources such as *Cyropaedia* whose first English translation was made available in 1522 by William Barker. Nevertheless, compared to the Safavids', the Persia of someone like Cyrus was better known, more accessible, more flexible, and more relevant.[45]

A central ideological aspect of the English engagement with Persia during the Elizabethan age was its inward-looking nature. To men like Thomas More, Philip Sidney, or Edmund Spenser, Persia in its ancient monarchical form was a vehicle 'to explore imaginatively the moral and political nature of empire'; it was a model for 'English Renaissance self-fashioning as a nation, culture, and society'.[46] To someone like Sidney, who would have studied *Cyropaedia* in his schooldays, Xenophon's Cyrus was thus not only a familiar topic but an obvious example to make.[47] Xenophon has given 'us *effigiem justi imperii*, the portraiture of a just empire under the name of Cyrus', writes Sidney in his *The Defence of Poesy* (c. 1579).[48] Of course, the fictive nature of Xenophon's Cyrus was not lost to Renaissance readers. It was this very quality of his conception that, in fact, made him relevant to Sidney's purpose. Even more pertinent was the effect and instrumentality of this creative design, that Xenophon had bestowed 'a Cyrus upon the world to make many Cyruses, if they will learn aright why and how that maker made him'.[49] This is the essence of Xenophon's intention in reinventing Cyrus: to make him stand as an exemplary model for the leaders of future Greece; though, at this point, Xenophon's forward-looking rhetoric was adopted for the progress of a set of political and philosophical debates that had a uniquely English aim.

With the advent of nationalist debates in the 1530s and 1540s on governmental sovereignty, the English began to search for ideal imperial models in the hope of defining the nature of their own nascent imperial identity. But to them, 'ideal' did not necessarily mean perfect; it meant non-Roman. Given the scarcity of scholarly findings on Anglo-Roman genealogical ties, not to mention their bruised historical recollection as a former 'barbaric' Roman colony, the English wanted to look beyond Rome to find appropriate monarchical architypes. The ancient Persian empire of Cyrus was the right fit for their purpose, not just because of its non-Roman pedigree, but because of its adaptability and the availability of a range of 'sacred' classical sources, texts such as Xenophon's *Cyropaedia*, Herodotus' *History*, and, to a lesser extent, the narratives of the Old Testament. The versatile nature of the ideas associated with ancient Persia in these texts would allow the English to incorporate the concept of Persia into an array of moral, political, and educational discourses. Herodotus' *Histories*, for instance, was taken as a cautionary tale against imperial insatiety (*koros*); whereas Xenophon's pseudo-imaginary biography of Cyrus was read as a handbook for *speculum principis* (the mirror-for-princes tradition). At the same time, ancient Persia's isolated (non-Western) heritage would also allow the English to maintain a sense of autonomy in their imperial rhetoric; the language of empire needed to reflect historical and cultural independence. But ancient Persia was also a viable choice because of the ethnological speculations surround it, not to mention the affinity that Europe had for the Safavids. Shah Abbas's engaging foreign policy had even made some Europeans to think of him of as a Christian convert (hence the notable interest in him in nineteenth-century English poetry); a Portuguese priest, Francisco da Costa, who had travelled through Persia on his way back from India, for instance, told the Pope that Shah Abbas 'was willing to undergo instruction in the Christian religion'.[50] Renaissance ethnography, nevertheless, thought of ancient Persia as England's barbaric ancestor – prefiguring a stronger, and a more intellectual, nineteenth-century racialist paradigm that took the Persians as Europe's Aryan kinsmen.[51] Although disputed in coteries with strong classical affinities, such Anglo-Persian identifications were well received in Renaissance England, particularly in light of the English perception of Cyrus, through *Cyropaedia*, which took the legendary king as someone who had single-handedly led his people out of barbarism to imperial prosperity. To an England embroiled in uncertainties over the nature of its imperial identity and ashamed of its own barbaric past, Persia was thus, in Jane Grogan's language, 'an appealing alternative to Rome, and a reason to imagine a new imperial history for itself to exorcize its colonial past'.[52]

Persia and the Sherleys

The most iconic English presence in Persia in the early modern period was that of the Sherleys.[53] The arrival of Anthony and Robert Sherley in the Safavid court at the end of the sixteenth century marked the beginning of a new era in the history of Anglo-Persian contacts, underpinned by the military, diplomatic, and commercial aims of modern nation states. The Sherleys were unquestionably two of the earliest Englishmen who visited Persia with such aims.[54] But since they were operating independently of the English state, their legacy had little actual bearing on 'modern' Anglo-Persian relations, which were developing as Robert's second mission to Europe was coming to an unsuccessful end. The Sherleys' Anglo-Persian enterprise was, nevertheless, momentous because of its unprecedented nature both in Persia and abroad: they were the first to exploit the resources of Persia's diplomatic and military power, even if that exploitation was unsuccessful, and they were the first, and the only, *English* ambassadors of Persia to Europe. The Sherleys' venture was also historic because of its duration (Robert stayed in Persia for almost ten years, from 1598 to 1607) and its geographical reach (the Sherleys, especially Robert, visited more than half a dozen states while in the Persian service). But more importantly, and most relevant to our purpose, the Sherleys' contact was significant because of the originary nature of its cultural repercussions. It is ironic that the Sherleys themselves had little interest in the arts and literature of Persia; their presence there was largely political.[55] But in spite of that, they generated in England a pioneering literary-imaginative interest in Persia as a contemporary country, one that bore at least some resemblance to the actual Persia of the Safavids; although, as both the history and the literary representations of the Sherleys' adventures have made clear, it was still not immune to fantasy and romance.

In order to study this 'modern' rendition of Persia, it is necessary to review the history of the Sherleys' travels. The latter is featured in almost every major work of critical scholarship on the history of Anglo-Persian cultural and material exchange. My interest in the Sherleys, however, is topical; it concerns the larger thematic framework of this study, highlighting the unprecedented role that their Persian expeditions came to play in England. Alongside the diplomatic nature of their mission, the Sherleys created an interest in Persia at home which was inventive and intellectual. This process of thought and creativity, where political aims in Persia lead to imaginative manifestations of 'Persia' in England, was arguably one of the earliest examples of its kind; what we may define as the 'Sherley effect' appears to be present in the conception of every major work of Persian nature or origin in nineteenth-century Britain. In what follows, I give an account of the Sherleys' connection with Persia, before moving on to discuss the nature of the literature that was produced in England during and in the aftermath of their travels.

The Sherleys arrived in Persia by accident. Anthony was the leader of a group of twenty-five or so English, Dutch, French, and Italian adventurers who set out, in 1598, with the support of the Earl of Essex, to assist the illegitimate son of the Duke of Ferrara, Cesare d'Este, in his conflict with the Pope.[56] Their excursion, however, turned out to be futile, since by the time they reached Ferrara, the quarrel had been settled. Still, Anthony, who wanted to keep his men busy, in a sudden change of course, redirected the attention of his party to Persia. It is also probable that Anthony had learned about Persia's lucrative trade market at some point along the way. The journey to Persia, nevertheless, was long and perilous; the group had to travel through hostile Ottoman territories to reach Qazvin in November 1598. The city was the Safavid capital at the time, though soon to be replaced by Isfahan. In any event, Shah Abbas was not there. He was on his way back from a successful campaign against the Uzbeks. Once he reached Qazvin in December, he had the first of many meetings with Anthony and Robert. The Sherleys appears to have made a good impression on Shah Abbas, as evidenced by these words that are often attributed to the Persian monarch: 'whilst he [Anthony] hath been in these parts, we have eaten together of one dish and drunk of one cup, like two brethren'.[57] Modern scholarship, however, draws a different image of Anthony. Roger Savory calls him 'a plausible rogue', a 'born intriguer'.[58] R. W. Ferrier describes him as 'plausible, though untrustworthy'.[59] There are contemporary narratives that corroborate these modern accounts. In *The English*

Spanish Pilgrime (1629), James Wadsworth, for instance, declares him to be 'a great plotter and projector in matters of state'.[60] It may have been these qualities that charmed Shah Abbas, convincing him to seek alliance with the Christian powers, though it may have also been the timing of the Sherleys' arrival: after the defeat of the Uzbeks, Shah Abbas would have been more open to new initiatives.

For whatever reason, only about half a year after his arrival in Persia, Anthony, together with an entourage of Persians and non-Persians, went on a European mission. The Shah dispatched Anthony with a *farman*, a royal decree, giving 'to all Christian merchants freedom from customs, religious liberty, and the right to trade to all parts of the shah's dominions'.[61] But there was no mention of him being his sole ambassador. A Persian named Hosein Ali Beg was, in fact, purposefully included in the party to curtail Anthony's ambassadorial ambitions. The Safavids were divided over both the necessity of forming alliances with the Christian West and the legitimacy of the men who had been assigned for the task.[62] Still, Anthony set out for Europe in the summer of 1599, leaving Robert behind (both as Shah Abbas's favourite and a hostage for his return).[63] He travelled through Cracow, Prague, Rome, Barcelona, and Madrid.[64] But the presence of Hosein Ali Beg caused constant friction in the group. The 'ambassadors' could not decide which one of them should represent the Persian monarch, and in the autumn of 1600, on their way from Prague to Rome, they parted company. Hosein Ali Beg went to Spain, where he arrived in May 1601; Anthony himself reached Rome in April 1601, and went on to Venice in 1602. By this point, he appears to have abandoned his Persian mission, 'offering his services of espionage (and counter-espionage) instead to the Holy Roman Empire, Spain and England'.[65] From Venice, Anthony continued to write letters to the King of Spain, expressing his devotion to the Spanish monarchy.[66] Some of these letters were eventually seized by the English and brought him accusations of treachery. Anthony was consequently barred from returning to England; he was also excluded by other English ambassadors abroad. He never returned to Persia either.[67]

Now that there was no news of Anthony, it was Robert's turn to leave Persia.[68] Robert departed in February 1608. But unlike that of his brother, the legitimacy of his embassy, and his status as Shah Abbas's sole ambassador, was undisputed, at least until he reached Spain.[69] Robert was Shah Abbas's sole ambassador, at least for much of his lengthy enterprise in Europe. Travelling through the Caspian Sea, he reached Russia and Poland. But while he was received with dignity in these states, he was unsuccessful in his negotiations with them. He then travelled to Florence (August 1609), to Rome (September 1609), and eventually to Spain (January 1610). In his negotiations with the European powers, Robert pursued three objectives: he wanted to solidify the relationship between Shah Abbas and the Christian states; he hoped to terminate the silk trade route via the Turkish empire, establishing instead an alternative path through the Persian Gulf; and lastly, he advocated an invasion of Aleppo, preferably through Cyprus, which would have required an intervention by the Spanish army.[70] But Robert had little success in attaining any of these objectives, particularly in Spain, where he stayed for a year, and where the validity of his embassy was eventually challenged by the arrival of another Persian ambassador, Dengiz Beg, in February 1611.[71]

Angry and despondent, Robert left Spain for England, where he was received as the Persian ambassador, though his first audience with James I at Hampton Court on 1 October 1611 did not go smoothly. The king granted him a hearing but ordered Robert not only to change his Persian attire but to kneel before him to beseech pardon for having accepted office under a foreign monarch.[72] Even so, the monarch did not authorise any Anglo-Persian partnership. Robert hoped to convince the English to divert the silk trade route via the Persian Gulf to Persia. But the Levant Company and the East India Company were against this. The chief merchants in London, many of whom were already involved with the companies, were unwilling to risk their commercial success for an untried trade route.[73] Ultimately, the companies' power prevailed and Robert returned to Persia empty-handed. Robert, his wife, Theresa, and their personal servant, Nazir Beg, left England on an East India Company ship on 7 January 1613.[74]

Not long after, Robert found himself on another ambassadorial mission to Europe. He left Isfahan in September 1615 and reached Lisbon almost two years later. He then spent the next five years in Spain trying to convince the Spanish to establish trading relations with the Persians. But the Spanish were not interested; they already had their own silk and spice trade with India, China, and Japan. Robert's dejected departure from Spain coincided with the Persians' capture of the Portuguese garrison at Hormuz in May 1622 with the assistance of the ships of the East India Company, an incident that gave more security and mobility to the English in the region. Robert arrived in England in December 1623. This time, Persia was in a stronger position, both geopolitically and economically.

Notwithstanding the fall of Hormuz, the Persians' capture of Qandahar in 1622 had brought unprecedented peace to the region; a global trade route was now in order, stretching from the western ports of Europe to the Indian subcontinent, with Persia being at its centre.[75] In England, Robert had a royal meeting with James I in January 1624. But the king died in March 1625, and Robert had to start from scratch with Charles I. The new monarch was, nonetheless, in favour of Robert's proposal.[76] But again despite this royal support, Robert failed in his aim. The companies, especially the East India Company, were already engaged in commerce in the south of Persia and hence in no need of any new partnership. The capture of Hormuz had put them in a comfortable position. They also preferred their own mediators rather than someone like Robert Sherley, who, thanks to his brother, had a perilous reputation.[77]

The arrival of a new Persian ambassador, Naqd Ali Beg, in February 1626, added to Robert's misfortunes. Robert was now in the same predicament as he had been with Dengiz Beg almost ten years before in Spain. To discern the motives behind the Safavids' dispatch of Naqd Ali Beg is beyond the boundaries of our discussion here. The possibility of the East India Company's involvement in Naqd Ali Beg's arrival in England has been refuted; though it is worth noting that it was through the aid and the interventions of the company that the new Persian ambassador was granted a royal meeting.[78] Robert was understandably threatened by this; a Persian who had recently left Persia was likely to be received with more credence than an Englishman who had been absent from the country for almost a decade. Therefore, he tried to meet with Naqd Ali Beg before the latter could meet with the English king. But their meeting turned out badly. After Robert presented his credentials, Naqd Ali Beg, who was 'sitting in a chair on his legs double under him after the Persian Posture, and affording no motion of respect', suddenly rose 'out of his chair, stept to Sir Robert Sherley, snatcht his Letters from him, toare them, and gave a him a blow on the face with his Fist'.[79] The consequence of Naqd Ali Beg's behaviour was that he was received by the king not as an 'ambassador' but as a 'private gentleman'.[80] Ultimately, Charles I, who was confounded by the presence of two Persian ambassadors at his court, sent both back to Persia, so that they could resolved the imbroglio there. But with them, he also dispatched his own delegate, Sir Dodmore Cotton, to further discuss Robert's proposals. The group reached Persia in 1627, but their return was beset by misfortune. Many of them died on their way to Persia. Naqd Ali Beg died of an opium overdose (he might have done this purposefully out of his fear of facing Shah Abbas). Robert died at Qazvin on 13 July 1628; perhaps the shock of being disgraced at home and disregarded in Persia was too much to bear. Cotton died of dysentery ten days after.[81]

Such an ending has a kind of dramatic propriety to it, like a stage filled with corpses at the end of a tragedy. But the events that led to this denouement are less easy to classify. The question of Robert's exact status, as an Englishman who was acting as the ambassador of a foreign power in his own country, is fraught with contradictions. The adventurer-protagonist, who can act as an intermediary between different cultures, finds it hard to operate in a space increasingly defined by corporate entities and institutions, whether those of the nation state or the commercial interests on which the state increasingly depended. At the same time, the individual's status was still conferred by royal decree, at home where Robert was not allowed to fully abandon his English identity, and abroad where Anthony was not allowed to fully embrace the role of a Persian ambassador. Robert's enforced change of costume before he could be granted an audience with James I suggests that he was an ordinary English subject at home, just as the plots of his brother's misadventures in Europe reveals that he was not more than an unscrupulous political schemer.

But things were different in the realm of fiction. To contemporary English audiences, the Sherleys were depicted in a different light; they were shown not as disgraced or 'rogue' ambassadors but as chivalric heroes who had taken upon themselves to acquaint foreign nations with the pre-eminence of the English. The Sherleys, the 'Three Heroes of our Time [. . .] haue so glorified their names by their honourable Actes [. . .] that honour by them hath added to her glory'.[82] These words appear at the beginning of a contemporary pamphlet, Anthony Nixon's *The Three English Brothers* (1607), commending the Sherleys for upholding and expanding the glory of the English across distant lands. Proto-imperialist assertions of this kind were becoming increasingly common within the literary-political discourse of early modern England, gradually moulding the ideological backbone of the British empire in the centuries to come. But the foregrounding of politics in the literature that was produced on the Sherleys was not disinterested; the Sherleys had their own personal agenda in disseminating such populist views.

In general, two types of texts were written on and about the Sherleys with respect to their Persian expeditions; and the Sherleys themselves, particularly Anthony and the elder brother, Thomas, appear to have been involved in the making of them. First, there were the texts that purported to offer first-hand narratives of the Sherleys' voyages. Some of these were written by Anthony's entourage: for example, William Parry's *A New and Large Discourse on the Travels of Sir Anthony Sherley* (1601) and George Manwaring's *A True Discourse of Sir Anthony Sherley's Travel into Persia* (1601), or by Anthony himself: *Relation of Travels into Persia* (1613). There were also narratives that were written by a third party but were still commissioned by Anthony's associates: for instance, Nixon's *The Three English Brothers*, which actually copied a large of part of its content from earlier narratives, and was most likely ordered by Thomas.[83] There were other accounts too, such as *A True Report of Sir Anthony Sherlies Journey* which was published anonymously in 1600, but quickly withdrawn, lest its highlighting of burgeoning Anglo-Persian trade damaged existing Anglo-Ottoman commercial ties.

The second group of texts consisted of the dramas based on these eye-witness accounts. The earliest and most notorious example of them was *The Travailes of the Three English Brothers* (1607) by John Day, William Rowley, and George Wilkins.[84] The Jacobean play drew heavily on Nixon's *The Three English Brothers*, especially the parts where the image of the Sherleys is more agreeable.[85] But such borrowings were driven by a purpose. Day and his co-authors were part of the Sherleys' 'public relations campaign'.[86] They were interventionists, looking to sway the public view of the Sherleys in a positive way through theatrical reinterpretations of their endeavours. At the time of the play's first performance at the Red Bull Theatre, it was no secret to its patrons that in hawking his services across Europe Anthony had, as we would say nowadays, 'gone rogue'.[87] The *Travailes* was thus a dramatic defence of the Sherleys, reframing their enterprise through the mode of romance. Whether this was done fortuitously, or whether the Sherleys were careful in both preparing fitting accounts of their travels and in choosing appropriate imaginative platforms to represent them, the narratives of their journeys fitted well with the structure and thematic patterns of romance. Their voyages were filled, like those of their fictional contemporary, Othello, with 'moving accidents by flood and field', the staple of both writers of romance and books of travel, and readers and spectators might be expected, like Desdemona, to 'devour up' such tales 'with a greedy ear'.[88] And of course, the romances were the right platform for the Sherleys, too. 'By dressing explorers' adventures in the garb of romance', as Laurence Publicover notes, 'one implicitly applauded them, or at the very least condoned them'.[89] Romances enabled the elder Sherleys in particular (Thomas and Anthony), and their comrades, to promote a chivalrous image of themselves that was, to say the least, ill-grounded. My aim here is not to dismantle this image, or to investigate the accuracy of the textual and theatrical representations of the Sherleys in England; both topics have been extensively discussed by Renaissance scholars.[90] Rather, my concern is with the treatment of Persia itself, to show how despite the existence of various references to a contemporary Persia, the Persia of a text such as the *Travailes* was still entangled in fantasies and falsehoods.

We see an example of this in the play's rendition of the Persian army. Early in the *Travailes*, the Governor of Casbin (Qazvin) asks the Sherleys, who are waiting for the shah to return to his capital, to greet him with his 'high tongues of wars, | Whose thunder ne'er was heard in Persia' (1, ll. 21–2).[91] According to this exchange, the Sherleys introduced the Persian to firearms for the first time. Later in the play, the 'Sophy', who is equally stunned by the Sherleys' 'loud tongues that spit their spleen in fire' (1, l. 95), asks the brothers to teach them their 'unknown rudiments of war' (1, l. 126). These exchanges inscribe Persian inferiority and exalt the Sherleys as patrons and benefactors. But the idea that either Anthony or Robert introduced firearms into Persia or that they had any major role in reforming the Persian army is simply false. The Persians, as it is noted by various contemporary commentators including Anthony's own companion, George Manwaring, had access to firearms well before the Sherleys arrived, though firearms were not central to their military operation, at least in the reign of Shah Abbas.[92] 'The Persians', as Savory maintains, 'had an innate dislike of firearms, the use of which they considered unmanly and cowardly.'[93] It is ironic in this light that the image of the Persians in the *Travailes* is that of a morally weak and stagnant nation: 'We have never heard of honour until now', says the Persian shah to Anthony after discovering that the English 'shed no blood upon a yielding foe' (1, l. 104). Again, such a condescending display of moral superiority is unsurprising for a text like the *Travailes*; the Sherleys' reputation demanded that the playwrights portray them as such; next to their Persian hosts, they are of higher moral standards, to the extent that even the great Sophy desires 'to be no other but as he [Anthony]' (1, l. 79). This display of supremacy reaches an absurd point at the end of the play where the Sophy allows Robert to build a house 'Where Christian children from their cradles, | Should know no other Education, | Manners, language, nor religion, | Than what by Christians is delivered them'

(8, ll. 188–91), as if the Persians themselves were bereft of any understanding of such moral values.

Ultimately, the difference between fact and fiction made itself felt for the Sherleys, thanks to the large body of scholarship that came to be written on their travels and on the travelogues, pamphlets, and the imaginative literature that their ventures inspired. But the discourse that the Sherleys created, or that was created around them, was to become a standard model of imaginative engagement with Persia (and the Orient). The Sherleys were not colonialists, at least not in the way that we have come to define the term today. Yet the texts that mediated their engagement with Persia prefigured the ways in which more overt colonial enterprises might be culturally 'constructed', a process in which political and economic exploitation was masked by a projection of the Oriental 'other' as backward, stale, and non-progressive. As we shall see, the nineteenth century evolved a particular version of this in the image of Persia as having declined into sloth, superstition, and tyranny from its once-great imperial past.[94]

Persia after the Sherleys

After the fall of Hormuz in 1622, which coincided with the collapse of Robert Sherley's second ambassadorial mission, the English engagement with Persia took a more current and diplomatic form. The kind of textual appropriation of ancient Persian imperial models which had been practised in the second half of the sixteenth century no longer seemed apt. Safavid Persia, its silk market, and the geopolitical significance of its southern ports, were now of importance to the English.[95] This change of interest inevitably had its impact on the English approach to and perception of Persia. There was for the first time a demand in England for information about contemporary Persia and its people. From the early decades of the seventeenth century, the British thus started to bring back eye-witness accounts of their travels in Persia (a tradition that was kept alive up until the second half of the twentieth century). These 'modern' narratives, although still infused with bias and imprecision, were notable for their detailed and often inquisitive attention not just to Persia's geography or landscapes but also to its arts, architecture, language, culture, and traditions.

One of the earliest of these texts, which became one of the more influential sources for knowledge about Persia in the seventeenth century, was written by a member of Charles I's embassy. After

Robert Sherley's death, and the subsequent death of Dodmore Cotton, the survivors made a slow return to England. Amongst them was a young man, named Thomas Herbert, whose journey took him through cities like Tehran, Qum, Kashan, Qazvin, Isfahan, Shiraz, and Gombroon (the former name of Bandar Abbas, a city in southern Persia). During his travels in Persia in 1627–9, Herbert kept a detailed account of his encounters. He did so because he needed to present a journal of his observations to the people who had sent him to Persia. But what he delivered was so thorough that he was asked to share it with the public. In 1634, he thus published his travelogue under the title of *A description of the Persian Monarchy now beinge: the orientall Indyes Iles and other parts of greater Asia and Africka*. An expanded second edition with a new title (which became the standard name for the following editions), *Some Yeares Travels into Divers Parts of Asia and Afrique*, appeared in 1638, with further augmented editions in 1665, 1675, and 1677. Herbert's narrative contains detailed and vivid descriptions of the peoples and places he had visited in Persia. The book also includes information about Shah Abbas, his court, his administration of the Safavid court, and his mannerisms (Herbert relays numerous anecdotes about Shah Abbas's cruelty).[96] Evidently, *Some Yeares Travels* is not without the attitudes and the errors that one would expect from an early seventeenth-century Western travel account of the Orient. We see it, for instance, in Herbert's comments about the Persians' level of literacy; a sense of Western superiority reverberates through his words: 'few of them can read; yet honours such as can; that Sciences being monopolized by Church-men, Clerks, Santos, and Merchants'.[97] But overall, Herbert's image of the Persians is positive: they are 'generally of a very gentle and obliging Nature; facetious, harmless in discourse'.[98] But what is perhaps most noteworthy about Herbert's description of the Persians is his attention to their appreciation of arts and culture: 'Poetry lulls them', Herbert says; 'that Genius seeming properly to delight it self amongst them'.[99] Such praise had no precedent in English, though it anticipates Sir William Jones in the second half of the eighteenth century.

Herbert, as Farhang Jahanpour rightly notes, was 'one of the earliest British travellers to show some interest in the cultural side of Persian life'.[100] He was, for instance, one of the first Englishmen who left a record of his exposure to Persian as a living language.[101] *Some Yeares Travels* includes a six-page glossary of Persian words and phrases.[102] But Herbert was probably the earliest commentator on Persian poetry too. *Some Yeares Travels* is arguably the first English travel book on Persia with a reference to Sa'di and Hafiz. Both men are mentioned in a chapter on 'Shyraz':

> A little out of the Town is interred that learned Poet and Philosopher *Musladini Saddi*, who wrote the *Rosarium* which is lately turned into *Latin* by *Gentius*: And near him his Brother Poet Hodgee Haier, whose poems are of great esteem in *Persia*.[103]

The spellings of the Persian names may indicate the author's scant knowledge of Persia's poetic culture, but the excerpt is informed in another sense; it shows Herbert's knowledge of not only Sa'di or Hafiz but of contemporary European scholarship on them. '*Rosarium*' is the title for Georgius Gentius's Latin translation (1651) of *Gulistan* (1258). John D. Yohannan notes that the citing of Hafiz as 'Hodgee Haier' is probably from the same source too.[104] The accuracy of Herbert's remarks, or the depth of his knowledge, however, are not my concern here; my aim is to show how a work such as *Some Yeares Travels* can be taken as an exemplar of a change of direction in writings about Persia in the seventeenth and eighteenth centuries, towards a deeper and more nuanced understanding of Persian culture, language, literature, history, and arts. Of course, this change did not mean the abandonment of old ways of thinking. Rather, different approaches co-existed, often within the same text.

The proliferation of translations of Persian poetry in Europe was also a significant development in the seventeenth century. The British, though, had little involvement in these literary-cultural engagements. The only person with a slight interest in the poetry of Persia in this period was Thomas Hyde, the Oxford Professor of Arabic and Hebrew. Today, Hyde is known for his *Historia religionis veterum Persarum* (1700) through which he intended to familiarise Europe with the ancient religion of Zoroaster (as far as he understood it). But amidst his sporadic and often unfinished Oriental endeavours, Hyde also appears to have translated a few verses from Persian. According to Yohannan, Hyde probably made the first Latin translation of Hafiz in England.[105] Hyde is also said to have included the first translation of Omar Khayyám in the second edition of *Syntagma Dissertationum* (1767).[106] Europe, however, had a larger engagement with Persian poetry in this period. One of the earliest and more celebrated translations of Persian poetry in the seventeenth century was Herbert's source for the above excerpt: Georgius Gentius's Latin translation of Sa'di, *Gulistan. Musladini Sa'di Rosarium Politicum*, which had been published in Amsterdam in 1651, following two earlier versions in French

(André du Ryer's *Gulistan, ou l'Empire de Roses Composé par Sa'di*, 1634) and German (John Ochsenbach's *Gulistan. Das ist Königlicher Rosengart: Des Persischen Poeten Sa'di*, 1636).[107] In 1654, the German scholar, Adam Olearius, published another translation of Sa'di, titled *Persianisches Rosenthal*. Olearius claimed to have worked on his translation with a native speaker, named 'Hakwirdi' (who had in 1639 defected from the Persian embassy of Shah Safi I to Gottorf).[108] How much of a help 'Hakwirdi' might have been, we do not know; but the fact that Olearius felt necessary to mention the help of a native informant in translating a work of Persian origin indicates the value he expected his readers to find in this kind of authenticity. And it is at least true that Olearius had first-hand experience of Persia. He refers to both of these privileges in his preface:

> I gladly confess that in translating this book I alone would not have been good enough had I not partly observed the customs of the Persians firsthand, and partly received further information from the previously mentioned old scholarly and knowledgeable Persian Hakwirdi – both orally and from the writings he carried with him.[109]

Olearius had visited Persia as part of the German (Holstien-Gottorf) embassy of 1635–9 to the Safavid court of Shah Safi I, with the aim of convincing the Persian monarch to divert his silk trade route through the Volga, Russia, the Baltic States, and finally Holstien-Gottorf.[110] An account of his delegation to Muscovy and Persia as secretary to the ambassador of Duke Fredrick III, ruler of the Duchy of Holstein-Gottorf, was published in 1647 as *Offt begehrte Beschreibung Der Newen Orientalischen Reise, So durch Gelegenheit einer Holsteinischen Legation an den König in Persien geschehen* ('Revealed Description of the New Journey to the Orient, Often Requested by the Public, which took place when a Holstein Embassy Visited the King of Persia'). An expanded edition under the title of *Vermehrte newe Beschreibung der Muscowitischen und Persischen Reyse* ('Expanded Description of the Journey to Moscow and Persia') came out in 1656. With its various illustrations, descriptive details, and its promise of authenticity, *Vermehrte newe Beschreibung* came to play a huge role in introducing Persia to the West. The book was very well received in seventeenth-century Europe; numerous editions and translations appeared in the years following its publication.[111] *Travels of the Ambassadors sent by Frederic, Duke of Holstein, to the Great Duke of Muscovy and the King of Persia* (1662), by John Davis, was the standard English translation.[112] An indication of the widespread popularity of Olearius's *Vermehrte newe Beschreibung* was that the source text behind Davis's translation was not just the 1656 original German but also a French rendition which had been published in Paris in 1659 by Abraham de Wicquefort.[113]

The French had their share in introducing Persia to Europe too. One of the most notable French writings on Persia in this period was Jean-Baptiste Tavernier's *Les Six Voyages de Jean Baptiste Tavernier, Ecuyer, Baron d'Aubonne, en Turquie, en Perse, et aux Indes* (1675) whose English translation, *The six Voyages of John Baptista Tavernier, a noble man of France now living, through Turky into Persia and the East-Indies* was made available by John Phillips in 1677. Another example was the work of the jeweller Jean Chardin (a Huguenot exile, knighted in England in 1681 as Sir John Chardin), who stayed in Persia for ten years from 1665 to 1677. Chardin, who seem to have known Persian, offered a great deal of information on Safavid Persia in his voluminous travelogues. An edition of Chardin's travels in four volumes was set for publication but only the first volume, *Journal du voyage du chevalier Chardin en Perse et aux Indes Orientales par la Mer Noire et par la Colchide*, appeared with an English translation in 1686. The remaining three volumes were published in Amsterdam in 1711. Another two-volume English translation of Chardin's travels was also being circulated in England as early as 1720; the edition reappeared in the following years under different titles.[114] In whatever language or form, Chardin's writings became 'a veritable mine of information' on Persia in the second half of the seventeenth century.[115] Men of letters such as Voltaire, Edward Gibbon, Montesquieu, and Sir William Jones are amongst those who came to acknowledge the value of Chardin's writings on Persia.[116] Much of Montesquieu's knowledge of contemporary Persia is, for instance, from the writings of Chardin (and Tavernier).[117]

By the turn of the eighteenth century, Europe had access to numerous sources from which it could shape its idea of Persia. A number of valuable travel accounts were now available. Various scholarly editions and translations of Persia's classical poetry had by now been published in Europe. Persia's regions, cities, and geography were no longer entirely unknown to Europe. The importance of Persia's markets in regional and global trades was also by now better recognised. Yet, despite all these modern revelations, one thing had remained unchanged about Persia in the Western imagination: the Persian imaginary was unbreakable. Persia was still seen in the light of the past and as a realm of fantasies and fiction. Neither the narratives of the British Herbert or the German Olearius, nor the burgeoning scholarly interest in men like Sa'di, had been able to detach Persia from its outlandish peculiarity, from myths and legends. The name 'Persia' remained to feed the love for fancy in both writers and readers throughout the seventeenth and eighteenth centuries. In literature, this Persian imaginary manifested sometimes in extreme fashion, with Barthélmy d'Herbelot's *Bibliothèque orientale ou Dictionaire universel contenant généralement tout ce qui regarde la connaissance des peuples de l'Orient* (1697) being the most notorious example of this trend. D'Herbelot's reference book stemmed from the growing contemporary interest in France in systematic knowledge and 'critical, source based historical research'.[118] But while the book's organisation conformed to this pattern (for example in its alphabetical arrangement and the array of Oriental sources that d'Herbelot had consulted), in its representation of the Orient, it was anything but erudite and scholarly. 'All the *Bibliothèque orientale* did', as Edward Said notes, 'was represent the Orient more fully and more clearly'.[119] Instead of appraising Europe's idea of the Orient, d'Herbelot's text confirmed the older perceptions.[120] There was, of course, a duality of purpose to the d'Herbelot compendium: *Bibliothèque orientale* was designed for reference but there was also an imaginative quality to it that seemed to have implanted in it to excite and entertain readers. The book was so fanciful that Charles Perrault, the French collector of fairy tales, applauded it 'for introducing its readers to a new heaven and a new earth'.[121] Nevertheless, d'Herbelot's encyclopaedia came to shape a large part of the Western perception of Persia (and the Orient) in the centuries following its release. Edward FitzGerald's idea of Persia was, for instance, partly shaped by the *Bibliothèque orientale*.[122]

In literary terms, Persia also formed part of a broad domain of Oriental romance, cultivated by writers and translators such as Antoine Galland whose translation of *The Tale of Sinbad the Sailor* (1701) was one of the earliest examples of the genre. Galland had learned Turkish, Persian, and Arabic during his stay with the French embassy in Constantinople (1670–5). He was a friend of d'Herbelot, and wrote an introduction to the first (1697) edition of *Bibliothèque orientale* that was published after d'Herbelot's death. The favourable reception of his first work, *Sinbad*, encouraged him to publish more Arabic tales, making use of new manuscripts sent to him from Syria. The manuscripts were from the fourteenth and fifteenth century, but they could have not been Galland's only sources. Eventually, his translation of fourteen tales (not all of which perhaps had Arabic origin) under the title of *Les Mille et une nuits, contes arabes traduits en français* ('The Thousand and One Nights, Arab stories translated into French') came out from 1704 to 1717.[123] An anonymous English translation of the work, titled *The Arabian Nights' Entertainment*, appeared in 1707. The immense popularity of Galland's work inspired a rash of rival versions and imitations. Ambrose Phillips's *Persian Tales* (1722), for instance, became popular enough to be mocked by Pope in the *Epistle to Dr. Arbuthnot* (1735): 'The Bard whom pilfered Pastorals renown, | Who turns a *Persian* Tale for half a crown' (ll. 179–80).[124] Samuel Johnson's *History of Rasselas, Prince of Abyssinia* (1759) is probably the most celebrated mid-century example of the English Oriental tale. Johnson's use of Oriental characters and settings as a mask for philosophical and satirical reflection on his own culture draws on Montesquieu's *Lettres persanes* (1721), translated by John Ozell as *Persian Letters* in 1722.[125] Later examples include Frances Sheridan's *The History of Nourjahad* (1767), William Beckford's *Vathek* (1786), Jonathan Scott's *Bahár-i-Dánish, or, Garden of knowledge: an oriental romance* (1799), from a collection of Indian tales written in Persian, and Francis Gladwin's *The Seventy Tales of a Parrot* (1801).[126] Persian poetry, too, was gradually gaining prestige in those years: examples include William Collins's *The Persian Eclogues* (1742), John Richardson's *A Specimen of Persian Poetry* (1774), and John Nott's *Select Odes from the Persian Poet Hafiz* (1787). However, the pre-eminent figure in the period was that of the linguist, translator, and poet Sir William Jones, who may be said to have given definitive shape to the 'Persian imaginary' of nineteenth-century English poetry.

Sir William Jones

> Sweet maid, if thou would'st charm my sight,
> And bid these arms thy neck infold;
> That rosy cheek, that lily hand,
> Would give thy poet more delight
> Than all Bocara's vaunted gold,
> Than all the gems of Samarcand.[127]

These are the opening lines of Sir William Jones's 'A Persian Song of Hafiz' (1772), perhaps the most influential translation of Persian poetry in the century following its publication. Today, we remember Jones mostly for his theories on the Indo-European family of languages, which laid the foundation of modern historical linguistics and (later) modern racial theories. But alongside his numerous linguistic breakthroughs, Jones was also one of the first men in Britain who devoted a large part of his career to introduce the West to the wit and the beauty of Eastern languages and literature.

Jones had a gift for languages. He excelled in Latin and Greek at Harrow and soon started to compose verses in imitation of Virgil. He then taught himself French, Italian, Spanish, Hebrew, and the basics of Arabic before leaving the school. Jones pursued his study of languages, especially the Oriental ones, after his admission to University College, Oxford in 1764. There, he studied Arabic with the help of a Syrian Arab, Mirza, whom he had employed to help him with pronunciation. In learning Arabic, Jones also made use of Franciscus Meninski's *Thesaurus Orientaliuim Turcicæ, Arabicæ, Persicæ* (1680–7) and Jacobus Golius's *Lexicon Arabico-Latinum* (1653).[128] But Persian posed a different challenge to Arabic. The alphabet was almost the same but there was no native informant to study with; there was also only one reliable grammar in English: *Elementa Linguæ Persicæ* (1649) written by John Greaves, the Savilian Professor of Astronomy in Oxford (1643) with an 'unusual' interest in Persian.[129] This absence of proper sources drove Jones to make use of Persian poetry.[130] He carefully read through *Gulistan*, again using Meninski's *Thesaurus* as a guide, while concurrently consulting Gentius's rendition of Sa'di.[131]

Jones's reputation as an expert in Oriental languages eventually brought him to the attention of the authorities. He was only twenty years of age when he became the government's official interpreter. Almost three years later, he was asked to translate into French Mirza Mohammad Mahdi's *Tarikh-e Naderi* (the history of Nadir Shah, 1747), which was obtained in 1765 in Shiraz by the Danish explorer, Carsten Neibuhr, and brought to Britain by the King of Denmark, Christian VII.[132] Jones at first refused; the task appeared dull and laborious, and he had reservations about his command of French and Persian. But he later conceded (the Danish king had hinted that if the British did not translate the text, he would take the manuscript to France).[133] And so, in April 1770, *L'Histoire de Nader Chah* was published. Jones was right though: not only was his knowledge of those languages lacking (eighteenth-century Persian was not very similar to the poetic language of Sa'di with which he was more familiar), he also seems to have needed better tools for such a task (no alternative historical accounts of contemporary developments in Persia were available at the time). Consequently, Jones made various mistakes in his translation, particularly in identifying the historical figures in the original text and converting the dates from the Islamic calendar to the Christian one.[134]

But Jones had other reservations for translating *Tarikh-e Naderi*; he was reluctant to work on Mahdi's text because of its sympathies with a despotic warlord. Jones had a strong dislike for unconstitutional power.[135] 'Power', he writes in the preface to the *History of the Life of Nadir Shah* (1773), 'is always odious, always to be suspected, when it resides in the hands of an individual.'[136] Later in the preface, he states that the history of Nadir's life is 'the last manuscript in the world, I should have thought of translating'; he adds that 'out of so many *Persian* books of poetry, ethics, criticism, science, history, it would have been easy to have selected one more worthy of the public attention; and the works of *Hafez* or *Sadi* might have been printed for half the expense, and in half the time'.[137] Jones does speak of this ideological motive behind his rendition of Mahdi's text: 'I would not attempt to write *The Life of a Conqueror*; unless it had been for the sake of exposing a character of all others the most infamously wicked [. . .]'.[138]

And yet, despite his strong distaste for the book's ethics and moral purpose, Jones might have also seen something positive in *Tarikh-e Naderi*. One thing that might have appealed to him was the comparative nature of the book. To praise Nadir, Mahdi compares the Persian ruler with other legendary conquerors such as Alexander; both men, for instance, invaded a country but left the original administration in place.[139] In this, Jones perhaps saw an opportunity to introduce his own unconventional and sympathetic views of the Orientals; the treatment of Nadir in *Tarikh-e Naderi* was an ideal opening for Jones to show that traits such as destruction or slaughter were not the preserve of Oriental leaders.

Not only was Jones keen on introducing Oriental literature and culture to the West (he even appended 'Un traité sur la poësie orientale', including translations of Hafiz, to *Histoire de Nader Chah*), he was also insistent on lessening the 'otherness' of Orientals in the eyes of his readers. An early example of this occurs in *Dissertation sur la littérature orientale* (1771), an essay in which Jones uses as his measure the neoclassical tenets that dominated the literary and poetic culture of the period. To align the poetry of Hafiz with that of Anacreon or Horace borrowed from the prestige of these ancient models and allowed the same 'modern' treatment in translation and imitation. Far from relegating Persian poetry to the category of the exotic, by which, in the end, it could only be diminished, Jones aimed to enhance its status by a kind of creative parallelism. For example, in one of his many notes on Firdausi's *Shahnameh* in 'On the Poetry of the Eastern Nations' (1772), he equates the *Shahnameh* to the *Iliad*, while highlighting the primitiveness of both works and the similarities that exist between ancient Greek and Persian literature:

> The whole collection of that poet's [Firdausi's] works is called *Shahn-âma*, and contains the history of *Persia*, from the earliest times to the invasion of the *Arabs*, in a series of very noble poems; the longest and most regular of which is an heroic poem of one great and interesting action, namely, *the delivery of Persia by Cyrus*, from the oppressions of *Afrasiab*, King of the *Transoxan Tartary*, who, being assisted by the emperours of *India* and *China*, together with all the dæmons, giants, and enchanters of *Asia*, had carried his conquests very far, and become exceedingly formidable to the *Persians*. This poem is longer than the *Iliad*; the characters in it are various and striking; the figures bold and animated; and the diction every where sonorous, yet noble; polished, yet full of fire. [. . .] Whatever elegance and refinements, therefore, may have been introduced into the works of the moderns, the spirit and invention of *Homer* have ever continued without a rival: for which reason I am far from pretending to assert that the poet of *Persia* is equal to that of *Greece*; but there is certainly a very great resemblance between the works of those extraordinary men: both drew their images from nature herself, without catching them only by reflection, and painting, in the manner of the modern poets, *the likeness of a likeness*; and both possessed, in an eminent degree, *that rich and creative invention, which is the very soul of poetry.*[140]

Jones's praise of Homer's, and Firdausi's, originality, especially the emphasis on 'invention', is in one sense conventional in the period, drawing on established eighteenth-century sources such as Pope's preface to his translation of the *Iliad* (1715).[141] But while Homer might provide an analogy for Firdausi, it would not have been politic to suggest that they were equivalent; hence Jones's careful disclaimer: 'I am far from pretending to assert that the poet of *Persia* is equal to that of *Greece*'. Even so, the mere juxtaposition of Oriental literature with classical writings makes the point here. Jones's admiration was sufficiently strong for him to recommend the *Shahnameh* to a modern readership: 'I see no reason why *the delivery of Persia by Cyrus* should not be a subject as interesting to us, *as the anger of Achilles*, or *the wandering of Ulysses*.'[142] Jones's approach was taken up by his European contemporaries such as Goethe, and persisted into the following century. We will see its effects most clearly in the poetry and criticism of Matthew Arnold and Edward FitzGerald.

I have cited 'A Persian Song of Hafiz' from its publication in a volume of poems, but this was not its first appearance in print. It originally appeared, with a different title, in *A Grammar of the Persian Language* (1771), a book with (ostensibly) a quite different purpose, though in fact the two projects were, so to speak, in league with each other. To understand why, we need to remember that there was no tradition of learning Oriental languages in England until the end of the eighteenth century. French, Latin, and Greek were still the lingua francas of the educated elite, with German fast making its way as the language of scholarship; languages like Persian were deemed so foreign that appellations such as 'barbaric' and 'rude' were still being used in reference to them. Persian literature, like all Oriental literature, was also considered to be of little literary and aesthetic value. It was, however, amidst such aversion and disinterests that Jones published *A Grammar of the Persian Language* (1771). The genesis of the *Grammar* went back to 1766 when Jones, from his extensive Persian reading, gathered a set of descriptive formulas for a friend who planned to travel to India.[143] Those notes later formed the foundation of a larger grammar book. Jones's primary objective in the *Grammar* was to teach Persian to those who were in contact with British India. In fact, in his preface, Jones, somewhat optimistically, claims that 'whoever will study the Persian language according to my plan, will in less than a year be able to translate and to answer any letter from an Indian prince, and to converse with the natives of India, not only with fluency, but with elegance'.[144] But this is not quite true: the pedagogical design of the *Grammar* could only enable learners to read and write in Persian, not speak it.[145] Nevertheless, teaching Persian was not Jones's sole purpose for writing the *Grammar*. In the light of neoclassical canons, Jones hoped that his book, with its numerous quotations from classical Persian poetry, would generate a more positive outlook towards Persian literary culture; this would then inspire more translations and accordingly enrich the resources of British literature.

One of the examples in Jones's *Grammar* was the poem quoted at the start of this section, a translation of a qazal by Hafiz entitled simply 'A Persian Song'; the name 'Hafiz' was appended when it was reprinted in *Poems* the following year. Jones cannot have envisaged that this rendition of a single lyric poem, with its Romantic turn of phrase and freedom in poetic adaptation, would become one of his most influential works. But the design was clear from the start: the

Grammar gave weight both to the study of the Persian language, and to the rich literary and cultural history that language embodied. 'A Persian Song of Hafiz' was especially well chosen for this purpose because it could be represented as analogous to English lyric verse in the same way that the *Shahnameh* bore comparison with classical epic. It reintroduced and infused a set of familiar images and literary motifs into British poetry, freshened by their being in an 'original' costume. Essentially a free rendition and expansion of the original, 'A Persian Song of Hafiz' set a standard model for translating Persian poetry in the following century, balancing the need to adapt the original to the understanding and taste of English readers while remaining attentive to its linguistic and cultural nuances.[146]

Why did Jones choose Hafiz? Partly because he admired him (Hafiz and Firdausi supply many of the illustrative quotations in the *Grammar*) and partly because this particular qazal contained the ideological and aesthetic particles that he might have looked for in a work of Persian origin, lending itself to the kind of adaptation he intended. Jones wanted to acquaint his readers with those thematic and material features of classical Persian poetry that he believed to be unusual (exotic) but also agreeable. But the introduction needed to be done in a subtle way, so that the 'foreignness' of the original would attract readers, not repel them. The novelty of Hafiz, in other words, needed to be retained but also refashioned in a way that would not seem too outlandish. We see an example of this in the opening lines, which only bear a trace of the original. This is Hafiz's verse:

> If that Shirazi turk would take
>   My heart within his loving hand,
> I'd give for his dark mole the towns
>   Of Bokhara and Samarqand;[147]

اگر آن تُرک شیرازی به دست آرد دل ما را

به خال هندویش بخشم سمرقند و بُخارا را

And this, as cited above, is Jones's version:

> Sweet maid, if thou would'st charm my sight,
> And bid these arms thy neck infold;
> That rosy cheek, that lily hand,
> Would give thy poet more delight
> Than all Bocara's vaunted gold,
> Than all the gems of Samarcand.

Jones's poem is a manifestation of Eastern sentiments glossed with Western imagery. The 'Sweet maid' is his addendum. Jones knew that the description *Turk e Shirazi* ('Turk of Shiraz') would seem odd and unclear to his readers; hence, to avoid confusion and erase the possibility of any homoerotic reading, he altered the conceptual framework of the poem, readdressing it to a woman, a 'maid', rather than the *Turk e Shirazi* or a *saki* (who appears in the following lines and is conventionally identified as a young man in Persian poetry). But Jones's ingenuity and inventiveness in translating Hafiz becomes more noteworthy in light of a grammatical peculiarity that seems to always puzzle those who are unfamiliar with Persia's classical poetic diction. The lack of gender markers for personal pronouns in Persian makes translating Persia's lyric verse a vexing task; there is usually no indication in classical Persian poetry as to whether a poem is addressed to a man or a woman. The convention is that the speaker is addressing a boy; it is, in fact, unusual if he is not.[148] Both Hafiz and Sa'di are frequently speaking to young men in their poetry; 'such verse', as Dick Davis explains, 'was rarely translated in the nineteenth century, because it was thought offensive, or, if it was translated, it was usually quite altered, as in Jones's "Sweet maid if thou wouldst charm my sight"'.[149] It is curious though that such a quality would bring an unexpected affinity between the Greeks and the Persians; the issue of same-sex poems in Greek and Latin writings caused similar anguish to commentators and translators in the eighteenth and nineteenth centuries.

Another difficulty in translating Persian lies in rendering its symbolism. Persian literature has its own distinctive imagery for conveying beauty and sensual desire, and such imagery does not easily cross national and cultural boundaries. As such, any literal (direct) translation of Persian symbolism is likely to lose all or part of its aesthetic charm or semantic splendour in a new language. Thus, regardless of how resourceful or adept a translator may be, it is very difficult to translate Persian imagery without it seeming strange, unconventional, or even foolish. One way to solve this is to 'domesticate' these culturally specific expressions, to replace them with descriptions that are well established in the target language and that bear comparison with the imagery in the original work. This is what Jones has done in his 'Persian Song of Hafiz'. A locution such as 'Hindu mole' (خال هندو) has been replaced with familiar expressions such as 'rosy cheek' and 'lily hand'. But familiarity must not go too far. The 'foreignness' of Hafiz has to be maintained; we see this in the rendition of the name of the locations that are mentioned in the original verse. In the second verse of 'A Persian Song of Hafiz', we read:

> Boy, let yon liquid ruby flow,
> And bid thy pensive heart be glad,
> Whate'er the frowning zealots say:
> Tell them, their Eden cannot show
> A stream so clear as Rocnabad,
> A bower so sweet as Mosellay.

Again, the translation itself only bears an echo of Hafiz's line:

> Come boy, and pour the Wine's last drop –
>   Since heaven's court will not provide
> The gardens of our Mosalla
>   Or Roknabad's garden riverside.

بده ساقی می باقی که در جنّت نخواهی یافت

کنارِ آبِ رکن آباد و گلگشتِ مُصلّا را

Eden (*adan*) is a common image in Persian poetry. But in this case, it does not translate a term in the original. Jones has replaced the river in paradise with Eden, a more familiar metaphor for paradise for Christian readers. On the other hand, Rocnabad and Mosellay are both transliterations of words that actually appear in the original. Jones likens Eden to the stream of Rocnabad (the name of several villages in Persia including one in Fars province) and Mosellay, by which he probably meant *mosalah*, a garden in Shiraz. But Jones's juxtaposition is not a mere comparison; in his Perso-biblical association, he favours these Oriental localities to their Western parallel: Eden has neither a stream as clear as 'Rocnabad', nor a bower as sweet as 'Mosellay'.

In terms of impact, 'A Persian Song of Hafiz' did not have the reach of the *Grammar*. The latter marked a shift in the perception of Persian literature more clearly than Jones's translation of Hafiz in itself, which modern readers may see as compromised by his lack of fidelity to the diction and tropes of the original. But a distinction needs to be made between Jones's desire to give the users of his *Grammar* more direct access to Persian literature, and his desire to transmit that literature to a non-specialist readership. The former aim required exactness; the latter required assimilation. Asking to what extent the true Persian 'Hafiz' survives in Jones's version may be the wrong question; we may better understand Jones's achievement if we ask how many British readers, by the end of the nineteenth century, took it for granted that Persia had produced a lyric poet as great as any in the classical tradition. Overall though, Jones's scholarship made large changes in the British perception of Persia. His linguistic and literary endeavours, most importantly, provided a scholarly picture of Persia to set against the more ancient ideas of the country. Access to Persian before Jones had to come through grammars and dictionaries that were mostly in Latin (and French and German). Jones's scholarship changed this pattern of engagement; it established a different kind of approach to Persian, based on actual knowledge of the language; the *Grammar* also standardised English as the intermediary for learning Persian in Britain. In 1784, Jones also founded the Asiatic Society of Bengal (later the Royal Asiatic Society of Bengal) with the aim of expanding British academic interest in the literature and culture of the Orient. Britain hereafter saw the appearance of direct translation of Oriental works (as we have seen, the familiar and frequently imitated tales previously reached the country through French translations).

On a more practical level, the fact that Persian was the official language of the Indian judiciary gave more significance to Jones's studies. Persian was the language of the educated elites and courtiers in India, while Hindustani was the language of the people. The military and civil servants of the East India Company were as a result obliged to have knowledge of the Persian language, at least until 1835, after which, and with the introduction of the English Education Act by India's governor-general, Lord William Bentinck, Persian ceased to be the official language in India. The teaching of Persian to the British in India had nevertheless begun before the nineteenth century. In Britain itself the language was being taught in the East India Company Military Seminary at Addiscombe in Surrey as early as 1809. Persian, alongside other Hindustani vernaculars, was also being taught at University College from 1826, and a little later at King's College, London. The repercussion of this growing interest in Persian was also evident in the press of the time. Within half a century, a number of special gazettes, dedicated entirely to the study of the Orientals appeared in London (and Calcutta). These publications included *The Asiatic Miscellany* (1785–6), *Asiatick Researches* (1788–97), *Oriental Collections* (1797–9), *The Asiatic Annual Register* (1799–1811), *The Asiatic Journal and Monthly Register for British India and its Dependencies* (1816–29), *The Oriental Herald and Colonial Review* (1824–9), and *The Oriental Quarterly Review* (1829–30). Although literature and culture were ancillary to politics and commerce in these periodicals, knowledge of them was deemed necessary for a more effective colonial presence in the subcontinent. Persian poetry and its translation, therefore, received particular attention in these publications, although the contributions were varied: there were learned commentaries, such as Jones's notes on the medieval Persian poet Nizami in *Asiatic Miscellany* (II, 1786), or translations of Persian poetry, such as his 'Persian Song of Hafiz' (Jones's translation was republished in monthlies such as *The Asiatic Annual Register* (XV, 1772), *Gentleman's Magazine* (LVI, 1786), *Town and Country* (XVIII, 1786) and *The Monthly Review* (LXXVII, 1787)). There were also translations of Persian poetry by amateur Orientalists such as Thomas Law's 'Yusef Zelikha' of Jami, published in *The Asiatic Miscellany* (II, 1786), and translations of Persian texts of lesser renown such as Sir William Ouseley's 'Account of Cashmere, translated from the Persian of Rafieddin' in *Oriental Collections* (I, 1797), which is likely to have inspired Thomas Moore's *Lalla Rookh*.[150] There was an interest in Persian studies in non-Oriental periodicals too: reviews of recent works on Persian literature were at times included in these journals, for example the article in *The Monthly Review* (LI, 1774), which was a review of Stephen Sullivan's *The Select Fables from Gulistan* (1774), a rendition of Sa'di's *Gulistan* (1258). Translations of Persian poetry were also published in non-Oriental magazines: for example, 'A Persian Ode to Spring' by Isaac D'Israeli in the *Scots Magazine* (LXI, 1799). Dozens of travel books on Persia, and the Orient, were also being published in Britain in this period, effect and cause of a fascination for the literary representation of the Orient. But more importantly, Persia itself was slowly becoming a crucial political entity for Britain.[151]

Persia and Britain in the Nineteenth Century

The turn of the nineteenth century marked another watershed in the history of Anglo-Persian contacts. The colonial activities of the French and the Russians in the Near East at the dawn of the nineteenth century embroiled Persia in the politics of the Great Game; Persia became a potential buffer state that could impede Britain's imperial rivals' encroachment on India. The first indication of a possible threat to British India was Napoleon's conquest of Egypt in 1798. Napoleon's campaign in the Middle East seemed worrying to the British who were expecting a French invasion of India since the passing of Pitt's India Act in 1784.[152] Russia's interventionist military operations in the south east of the Caucasus also seemed alarming. The Russians were closing in on Persia; they annexed Georgia in December 1800 and seized Erivan in 1804.[153] Regardless of their eventual outcome, these displays of European imperialism prompted London and Calcutta to incorporate Persia into their defensive strategies. The British had no colonial or territorial interest in Persia itself.[154] Rather, they were concerned that an invasion of India could become more viable if any of their rivals gained influence in Persia. Hence, from the early years of the nineteenth century, they approached Persia with the intention of preserving its independence and integrity; although there were doubt and indecisions too, as Britain's political stance towards Persia throughout the nineteenth century was impacted and constantly altered by larger colonial developments in Europe and Asia. As an example, take the British handling of the Russo-Persian conflict over Persia's northern frontiers at the start of the nineteenth century. Despite the precepts of the Definitive Treaty of Tehran (1814), Britain offered no military aid to Persia in its struggles against Russia. The British did not want to upset the Russians by intervening in their colonial affairs because they needed their alliance against France; at the same time, they needed to end the Russo-Persian conflict so that Russia might exert its full military strength against France.[155] This strategic uncertainty continued until Persia lost its distinctive geopolitical position and Russia was perceived as a greater threat. After the signing of the Treaty of Turkmenchay (1828), Persia could no longer be a buffer state: Russia's gains weakened its northern frontiers. Persia's trust in Britain was also largely damaged. Turkmenchay dissolved the barriers between Russia and Afghanistan and as such the frontiers between Russia and British India were pushed back from Caucasus to the eastern shores of the Caspian.[156]

Persia's strategic importance in the defence of British India was recognised only fitfully in the nineteenth century: as George N. Curzon put it in *Persia and the Persian Question* (1892), the principle that British diplomacy needed to engage with Persia 'has prevailed at intervals of greater or less frequency, and with greater or less earnestness [. . .] throughout the present century'.[157] The aim of Curzon's monumental study was to explain the 'true bearing in its many and momentous ramifications of the Persian question'.[158] It is not my purpose here though to follow his example; an examination of these 'ramifications' would be beyond the scope of this study.[159] What I intend to do in the remaining part of this chapter is to focus, briefly and selectively, on a few notable diplomatic contacts during the first decades of the nineteenth century, and to comment on one major literary consequence of these contacts, in order to show how the British perception of Persia was altered and enriched.

Despite reservations in London and Calcutta about Persia's contribution to the defence of India, the British approached the Qajars' royal court with gravity and respect. An indication of the serious nature of the British renewed diplomatic interest in Persia at the start of the nineteenth century could be seen in the attention that they gave to diplomatic protocols and formalities in the dispatch of their first mission. In 1799, the governor-general of India, Lord Wellesley, sent Britain's first official envoy, Sir John Malcolm, to Persia. Malcolm was dispatched to negotiate an alliance that would ultimately require Britain and Persia to support each other against foreign threats including the Afghan ruler, Zaman Shah, who, the British suspected, might invade Punjab, and 'those villainous but active democrats the French'.[160] Regardless of the conclusions of these diplomatic pacts, the procedure of Malcolm's arrival with regard to form and ceremony, and the extent of his entourage, prove how important Persia had come to be for the British by the turn of the nineteenth century. Malcolm arrived in Bushehr on 1 February 1800 with more than 500 assistants and servants, though his party did not leave the city for almost four months; certain diplomatic arrangements needed to be made in Tehran for the reception of the British diplomatic party.[161] Malcolm returned to Persia twice after this: once in 1808 and once in 1810. His second visit, which I will come back to later in the chapter, was in response to the French growing diplomatic presence in Persia; curiously, his third mission was in response to how the British had managed to counter the French threat in Tehran in those years. In March 1809, the Home Government's mission, Sir Harford Jones, managed to sign a treaty of friendship and alliance with Fath Ali Shah; all previous treaties with European powers including France as a result were declared null.[162] But Lord Minto, India's governor-general, thought the precepts of the treaty of Tehran would involve Calcutta more than it would involve London; so, he sent Malcolm to Persia on his third mission. Yet amidst these hasty political manoeuvres, London decided to send its first official ambassador, Sir Gore Ouseley, to Persia.[163] Ousley arrived in Persia on 10 January 1810 as Britain's first Ambassador Extraordinary and Minister Plenipotentiary. Malcolm returned to India by way of Baghdad in 1810. Jones left a year after in June 1811.[164]

What is noteworthy, for my purpose, about these early nineteenth-century political contacts is the extent and the range of their literary-cultural repercussions. Almost every diplomat who visited Persia in the opening decades of the nineteenth century produced work of a scholarly nature on Persia. The contemporary intellectual impact of some of these works were immense, and their legacy long-lasting. Malcolm himself wrote two books: *History of Persia, from the most early period to the present time* (1815) and *Sketches of Persia: From the Journals of a Traveller in the East* (1827). As the first comprehensive study of Persia's history in English, Malcolm's first book was widely read and for long considered as the standard work on Persia's history.[165] Sir Walter Scott, for example, wrote to Malcolm: 'I cannot refuse myself the opportunity of thanking you for the information and amusement I have derived and am deriving from your very interesting account of Persia; a history so much wanted in our literature.'[166] Malcolm's peers wrote on Persia too: in 1813, Harford Jones published *The Dynasty of the Qajars* which was a 'Translation of a MS. compiled by order of the Sovereign of Persia'.[167] Ouseley compiled *Biographical Notices of Persian Poets* which came out two years after his death in 1846.[168] Despite their differences in theme, focus, or the quality of scholarship, these writings had one thing in common: they were all labours of love. The British who visited Persia in the opening decades of the nineteenth century had a sort of passion for Persia; they were deeply interested in its history, culture, and tradition. This is not to suggest that they were unmindful of the colonial nature of their mission; quite the opposite, they strove to ensure that Britain's imperial objectives were met and maintained in Persia. But alongside their political objectives, they were driven by a passion for culture and a natural intellectual curiosity. 'I employ every leisure hour in researches into the history of this extraordinary country, with which we are but little acquainted', writes Malcolm to his father in a letter of 17 August 1800; 'I shall, I trust', Malcolm continues, 'collect materials that will either enable myself, or some one better qualified, to give much information on this subject.'[169] The outcome of such cultural investigations appealed to British officials and traders but also to a wider public who were by now familiar with Oriental romance and literature and could be expected to extend their interest to living history. In the early decades of the nineteenth century, and with increasing British involvement in the East, there were both pragmatic and ideological reasons to be curious about a place like Persia, to wish to know more about it, and to want that information to be both factual and imaginatively suggestive.

But something else also ensued from the nineteenth-century British contacts with Persia. For the first time in the history of Anglo-Persians contacts, the British had a chance to observe Persian life up close, to experience a country that, so far, they had only seen through the lenses of the authors and travellers of the previous centuries. And in such direct encounters, the writings of the Greeks, the narratives of the Bible, or even the more recent, early modern travel literature on Persia were not of much use. The real Persia was at hand; it was there to be seen, explored, and described. Naturally, certain aspects of nineteenth-century Persia shocked some observers, and some aspects of it charmed others. But one impression appears to have been shared by all commentators: nineteenth-century Persia bore little resemblance to the Persia that they had in mind. There was little left of that supposed ancient country in the Persia of the Qajars. Modern Persia was no longer the realm of Cyrus or Darius; it was an Islamic country whose people had little understanding of their pre-Islamic national identity. The sense of unity for the Persians now lay in their shared religious beliefs, not in their ancient pre-Islamic past. An average nineteenth-century Persian, as David Morgan explains, 'would not have defined himself as a Persian with a pedigree stretching back to Cyrus and Darius, of whom he would have never heard. He would probably have thought of himself, first and foremost, as a Muslim.'[170] These changes came as a great shock to the British. What they encountered seemed a backward culture, a non-progressive society, out of touch with its own history, marked by social conservatism and religious superstition, and ruled by despotic and ruthless elites with whom they had to engage with in order to advance their political objectives. This seeming collapse of nineteenth-century Persia led to the emergence of a common paradigm in the travel literature of the time, a narrative that rendered modern Persia a state in decline, fallen from its ancient glory into decay and stagnation.

Arguably, the earliest manifestation of the narrative of Persia's decline appears in Malcolm's *History of Persia*. Malcolm's text is largely a historical survey but ideologically it is loaded with the narrative of waning cultural and political vitality. This is particularly notable in the book's second volume, which traces the history of Persia from the fall of the Safavids until the beginning of the nineteenth century. The history itself takes up six of the eleven chapters in the book. The rest are dedicated to the study of Persia's religion, royal court, government, military, and national character. Here, Malcolm appears as a critic rather than a historian, providing a comprehensive account of his impression of Persia and the Persians in the nineteenth century. But nowhere in the book does he specify the causes of Persia's decline; his treatment of the topic occurs within the context of his discussions of other aspects of nineteenth-century Persia such as its religion and its ruling elites. As regards the latter,

Malcolm states that 'there is, perhaps, no country in which so much of the immorality of its inhabitants can be referred to a bad system of internal administration as Persia'.[171] This administrative depravity, Malcolm remarks, has had an inexorable effect on the people: the vice of the Persians 'appertains to the government, and is the natural consequence of the condition of the society in which they live: [. . .] when rulers practise violence and oppression, those who are oppressed will shield themselves by every means within their power'.[172] But the government, Malcolm argues, is callous because of the ethos that Islam imposes; according to Malcolm, the belief of 'the prophet of Arabia' has this inevitably damaging effect on its adherents: 'there is no example, during more than twelve centuries, of any Mahomedan nation having attained a high rank in the scale of civilisation'.[173] Malcolm accordingly sees Islam as the key reason for the venality of Persia's leaders: 'the inhabitants of all those countries who have adopted this religion, have invariably been exposed to the miseries of an arbitrary and unsettled rule'.[174]

There is no denial that Malcolm's rhetoric is charged with anti-Islamic prejudice. However fond of Persia he may have been, Malcolm was still a nineteenth-century Christian with his own set of beliefs and values. To him, as he writes in his personal journal, Islam was 'a religion adverse to all improvement and general diffusion of science [. . .] debilitated and shackled by the chains of Bigotry, Superstition and Prejudice'.[175] I do not intend to dwell on such remarks, which no longer require refutation; by now we know well that denigration of Oriental beliefs and social practices justified, at the ideological level, the intervention of more 'advanced' civilisations. Malcolm's treatment of Persia fits this paradigm; yet within the colonial framework of his approach, and despite the condescension of his rhetoric, he also conveys a sense of sympathy for the Persians, a desire for liberating them from the causes that he understood to have deterred their growth and prosperity. We see this, for instance, in his correspondence: 'If this country ever again enjoys repose', Malcolm writes from Shiraz to Neil Edmonstone, the Persian translator to the Supreme Government of India, in a letter of 26 July 1800, 'it will overflow, as usual, with poetical productions. The men appear to me all poets.'[176] We also see it in his book: on Persian historiographers, for example, he writes: 'it will appear that the defects of eastern history are not to be ascribed to any want of talents in its authors, but to the condition of the society in which they lived, and to the subjects of which they treat'.[177] Or, on Persia's intellectual growth, he says: 'knowledge in Persia has hitherto ebbed and flowed with the changes in the political situation of that empire, and must continue to do so as long as its inhabitants are under the depressing influence of a despotic, and unsettled government'.[178]

The dichotomous set of attitudes with which Malcolm treats Persia and its people in *History of Persia* persists throughout the nineteenth century, providing, in an indirect fashion, a template for later commentators. Many of those who visited Persia later the nineteenth century seems to have formed similar impressions; they interpreted what they saw in the false light of the past and were disappointed to discover that Islam held such sway over the descendants of Cyrus or Darius. We see this, for instance, in Robert Binning's *A Journal of Two Years' Travel in Persia, Ceylon, etc* (1857): 'Persians of modern days are greatly changed from what their fire-worshipping predecessors were, in the time of Cyrus, when a strict adherence to veracity formed a characteristic of the nation.'[179] Views of similar nature were being expressed even in the early decades of the twentieth century, by someone like Edward G. Browne, for instance: 'truly it seemed that a whole nation had been transformed [after the introduction of Islam], and that henceforth the Aryan Persian must not only bear the yoke of the Semitic 'lizard-eater' whom he had formerly so despised, but must further adopt his creed, and almost, indeed, his language'.[180] Browne's bigoted disposition, which, by modern standards, would be considered repellently racist, is an after-effect of the nineteenth-century British and Continental preoccupation with the 'scientific' analysis of racial characteristics, whose methodology was indebted to that of comparative philology. This 'genealogical' movement owed its inception to Sir William Jones's linguistic findings at the end of the eighteenth century. With the advent of Jones's postulations on the relationships between primordial languages and ancestors, the study of linguistic genealogies became key to the study of the genealogies of peoples.[181] The idea of an Indo-European family of languages was subsequently formed and ultimately construed in ethnological terms. One outcome of such linguistic discoveries was that the Persians came to be identified as Europe's Aryan kinsmen, because their language was believed to be of the same origin as a language like German. 'It ought not to be difficult to interest Englishmen in the Persian people', writes Curzon in his *Persia and the Persian Question*; these people, he continues, 'have the same lineage as ourselves. Three thousand years ago their forefathers left the uplands of that mysterious Aryan home from which our ancestral stock had already gone forth.'[182] Curiously, Curzon happens to be a leading proponent of the narrative of Persia's decline, which by the end of the nineteenth century had become a received idea, incorporated into a more general theory of the rise and fall of nations.[183]

Curzon, who was the viceroy of India and British foreign secretary, had a short but first-hand experience of Persia in 1889–90. Being a Machiavellian politician, the main impetus behind Curzon's Persian concerns was the defence of British India: 'the preservation, so far as is still possible, of the integrity of Persia must be registered as a cardinal precept of our Imperial creed'.[184] Yet for that to be attained, he believed the inadequacy of the 'existing sources of knowledge about Persia' needed to be redressed.[185] So, after his first and only visit, he wrote *Persia and the Persian Question* which, as Christopher Ross's rightly says, 'sometimes reads like an elegy for the decline of a once glorious nation'.[186] To Curzon, Persia, in its current state, was the epitome of a fallen nation, a country that could only be rescued by the hands of Western powers. Curzon carried this argument forward in his introduction to a reprint, in 1895, of one of the most remarkable Oriental works of the nineteenth century, James Justinian Morier's *The Adventures of Hajjî Baba of Ispahan* (1824). Though written over half a century before the publication of his own book, Morier's immensely popular fiction to Curzon seemed to fit his narrative of Persia's decline and decay. In Curzon's view, Morier's book is a 'delineation of [Persia's] national character', a 'picture of actual personages, and a record of veritable facts' – and these facts, however lively their presentation, all point to Persia as socially and intellectually backward, oppressed by superstition and governed by despotic caprice and Oriental intrigue.[187] True, *Hajjî Baba* may indeed have a good deal to say about the flaws and foibles of Persian society; but Curzon's suggestion that it does so within the framework of the ideological scheme he was promoting is misleading. The book's subversive comedy may indeed be viewed as opposed to this scheme, and to the hierarchy of civilisations and races that underpinned it.

Two important parameters are first needed to be taken into consideration regarding the depiction of the Persians in Morier's novel. The first concerns the genre of Morier's fiction. *Hajjî Baba* is a descendant of the picaresque tradition that thrived in Europe in the seventeenth and eighteenth centuries. Compared to some of the more notable picaresque novels of the eighteenth century, such as Henry Fielding's *Joseph Andrews* (1742) or Tobias Smollett's *Roderick Random* (1748), the Persia of Morier is not nearly as wicked as the England of these works. The eighteenth-century England of *Joseph Andrews*, for instance, is a monstrous landscape of violence and corruption:

it is a country filled with rapists, thieves, unjust judges, oppressive local landowners, and people who are 'Christian' in name only. This, however, did not mean that Fielding saw no good in his country, only that the conventions of the genre allowed him the licence of a satirist. And the success of the book depended on the pointedness, the verisimilitude of its observations. In the same way, Morier's representation of Persia, filled with comic exposure of its failings, is animated by the linguistic, literary, and cultural knowledge with which he crafted the book. This brings us to the second point: the book's 'depth of field', its use of Persian settings, characters, idioms, and proverbs. Morier's familiarity with Persian culture has a relish to it that goes beyond mockery; the book's detailed cultural and linguistic awareness bears witness to its author's fascination with Persian life. Again, like many of those who visited Persia in the period, Morier found certain aspects of Persian society distasteful, but not everything that was strange repelled him, and he, too, saw the fundamental commonality of human nature whether operating in Qajar Persia or Regency England.

To understand the depth and the accuracy of Morier's treatment of Persia requires a closer look at his *Hajjî Baba*. But before that, let us see how he came up with the idea of writing a novel on Persia. Morier was part of the official diplomatic mission that was dispatched by London to Tehran under Sir Harford Jones. Jones met Morier in Constantinople (where Morier was living with his father) and offered to make him his Private Secretary. Jones had been dispatched to counter the burgeoning French influence in Persia. The diplomatic interest that the British at the start of the nineteenth century had in Persia waned soon after Malcolm's first mission. The threat from both the Afghans and the French receded, and the English did not support the Persians in their ongoing struggle with Russia. This inevitably drew Persia close to France. In 1808, Napoleon sent missions to Persia, and in May 1807, the Treaty of Finkenstein was concluded in Poland between Persia and France. This concerned the British, although 'whether or not India was endangered by a Franco-Persian alliance, and whether a French army could invade overland, were subjects of acrimonious debate in Great Britain'.[188] Still, the British were worried enough that London and Calcutta each sent their own envoy to Persia. London dispatched Jones in 1807. Jones had a good understanding of Anglo-Persian diplomatic relations; he was the British Resident in Baghdad from 1798 to 1806 (the Persians in January 1805 had actually contacted him with the hope of resuming negotiations with the British Government in London).[189]

But it took Jones so long to reach Persia that in January 1808 Calcutta decided to dispatch its own mission, that of Sir John Malcolm, for his second visit.[190] Malcolm left Bombay on 17 April 1808 but he failed in his mission; Fath Ali Shah in Tehran was untroubled by Malcolm's threats from Bushehr, exhorting him to dismiss the French envoy and all the Frenchmen from the country. The shah declined, and Malcolm thus returned to India.[191]

But with the arrival of Jones on 14 February 1809 things changed: the British convinced the Persians to replace the Franco-Persian Treaty of Finkenstein with the Anglo-Persian Treaty of Friendship and Alliance. The signing of the latter, however, was largely prompted by the conclusion of the Treaty of Tilsit between France and Russia in July 1807. The French had promised the Persians to help them in their wars with Russia. But the signing of the Treaty of Tilsit (when Napoleon's Minister Plenipotentiary, General Claude-Mathieu de Gardane, and another French envoy, the First Secretary at the French Embassy in Constantinople, M. de La Blanche, were still in Persia and engaged in negotiations with the court of Fath Ali Shah) ended Persia's hopes. To consolidate his hold over Europe, Napoleon was willing to cede control over the whole of Asia.[192] This became a source of great disappointment for the Persians who had thought to end their struggle with Russia with the aid of the French.[193] The alliance with Britain was now the right move for the Persians. So, to transform the treaty that was signed in Tehran into a 'definitive Treaty', the Qajars decided to send an emissary, a Persian named Mirza Abul-Hasan Shirazi, to England. Morier was appointed to accompany him.[194]

It was Mirza Abul-Hasan that sparked something in Morier.[195] His company seems to have prompted, or facilitated, Morier's shift from travel writing to fiction. Morier established a close relationship with Mirza during his short stay in England, but he was able to observe Mirza's conduct and character more closely in their eight-month-long return journey from London to Tehran. This time Morier was returning to Tehran as secretary to the ambassador, Sir Gore Ouseley. It was during this second mission, which lasted longer and was less troubled than Jones's, that Morier gained the opportunity to observe and study Persian customs, history, antiquities, language, and dress.[196] The extent of Morier's understanding of Persian life is shown by his two substantial travel books, *A Journey through Persia, Armenia and Asia Minor to Constantinople* (1812) and *A Second Journey* (1818), both greeted with critical acclaim and welcomed by a public which knew little of Persia and the surrounding regions. In the third decade of the nineteenth century, and after the publication of his two travel narratives, Morier could claim to be an authoritative writer on Persia and Persian affairs. By the time *The Adventures of Hajjî Baba of Ispahan* (1824) and its sequel *The Adventures of Hajjî Baba of Ispahan in England* (1828) came out, his reputation was established in Britain and the subcontinent. So renowned was he that many took his fictitious account of Persian life as fact.[197]

Hajjî Baba tells the story of his hero's rise from a young boy in his father's barbershop in 'Ispahan' to the point when he becomes the chief secretary to the Persian ambassador to the court of England.[198] Hajjî embodies Persian speech, behaviour, and way of thinking in the novel. His character allows Morier to capture the life of the people whom he perceived to be, in Terry Graber's words, 'a whole nation of picaros'.[199] Hajjî is also a figure of fun, a picaroon who fails repeatedly throughout the story, but who bounces back after every failure. Yet he is not devoid of complexity. Although he seems to have no moral boundaries (he is congenitally selfish, a habitual liar, a thief, a charlatan, or a despot when the opportunity arises), he is not evil by nature. His most distinctive and endearing quality is, in fact, his innate decency, something that distinguishes him from the rest of the characters in the book. Hajjî is also capable of real feelings: compassion, sympathy, sorrow. This 'deeper' note is sounded on at least two occasions in the book: once in Chapter XXXI when Hajjî tragically loses his beloved Zeenab, and once in Chapter XXXVI when he meets and helps a young Christian (Armenian) couple in distress, even though Hajjî at that point is an executioner by trade.

Hajjî's occupation and life change rapidly and repeatedly throughout the story. He has to constantly change his dwelling, because of his frequent misdeeds and mishaps. And with each change of setting, he encounters new people. Yet Hajjî barely meets a single decent character in his adventures. Even his own mother (in Chapters XLVIII–LII) appears to be unfeeling and callous; she has found a new partner only a few days after her husband's death, shows no affection at seeing her long-lost son, and even tries to steal her son's inheritance. The reader acquainted with Persian culture would find Morier's picture unorthodox, as it completely contradicts the classic image of the mother as a sacred, unselfish angelic being in the Persian cultural tradition. Whether Morier was consciously poking fun at a Persian stereotype, or based the character on personal experience, we do not know. But such experience does inform some of his depictions. The most obvious example is the shah, who, though he makes few appearances, greatly impacts Hajjî's life. The shah of Morier's account is based on Fath Ali Shah, the second of the Qajar dynasty, whom Morier had personally met in his missions to Tehran with Jones and Ouseley.[200] Like Fath Ali Shah, Morier's shah has an admiration for poetry. In Chapter VII, for instance, we are told about the history of the courtly poet, Asker, and how the shah has rewarded him in an extravagant fashion. Both shahs are also religious. The shah in *Hajjî Baba* visits the holy city of Qum. Morier himself relates in his *Second Journey* that Fath Ali Shah 'frequently visits the Tomb of Fatemeh, and makes costly offering there'.[201]

The poet, Asker, whose fortunes are woven into Hajjî's adventure in early parts of the novel when both are kept captive by the 'Turcomans' is also based on a real-life person. In a footnote in Chapter VII, Morier reveals that 'in sketching the history of the poet Asker', he has 'attempted to record part of the life of the late Fath Ali Khan, poet-laureate to the shah, a most ingenious and amiable man, well known to the British who were at Tehran in the years 1812 and 1813'.[202] In *A Journey through Persia*, Morier speaks of the court poet who declares himself 'superior to Ferdousi, the Homer of their country'.[203] A similar comparison appears in Morier's fictive account of Asker: at one point, the shah permits Asker to write '*Shahin Shah Name*' ('The history of the king of the kings') to outshine Firdausi's *Shahnameh*.[204] The shah of Morier's book sees himself as superior to all shahs, and he calls himself the '*Shahin Shah*' ('the king of the kings'). Another example of Morier's use of people he knew personally or by repute is Mirza Ahmak, the shah's physician. We are introduced to Mirza in Chapter XIX when Hajjî becomes his employee. Mirza Ahmak parallels Fath Ali Shah's personal physician. According to various travel books including those of Morier, the chief physician (*hakim bashi*) was called Mirza Ahmad ('Achmed' in Morier's spelling). Fath Ali Shah's *hakim bashi* was an old-fashioned and orthodox physician whose methods were based on calculations of the patient's destiny rather than empirical knowledge and who naturally distrusted his British rivals. In *A Second Journey*, Morier describes Achmed as someone who would 'attribute all to fate; and, like his compeers, said, when it is decided by God that a man is to die, no human aid can be of avail'.[205] On one occasion, Mirza Achmed even forbade the child of a high official to take the seemingly unfamiliar medicine that was prescribed by a British doctor. The child died not long after.[206] It is no surprise that Morier did not have a high opinion of him, and why he would openly poke fun at him. The physician in Morier's novel is purposefully called 'Mirza Ahmak', instead of 'Mirza Achmed'. 'Ahmak' (or *ahmagh*) in Persian means stupid.

Morier's understanding of the Persian language is indeed a remarkable aspect of his text and emblematic of the extent of his familiarity with Persia. The pages of *Hajjî Baba* are permeated with transliterations of Persian words such as '*khanum*' (lady), '*darogah*' (policeman), '*Jehanum*' (hell), and '*tobeh*' (repentance). Religious (Islamic) phrases, all part of Persia's everyday discourse, such as '*Barîk Allah!*' (praise be to god!) or '*Staferallah!*' (God forgive!) are also frequently spoken by Morier's characters. While many of these words and expressions are self-explanatory (the reader unaware of the Persian language can contextualise their meanings), the more puzzling ones are rendered by Morier in the footnotes (a pattern that may remind us of FitzGerald's endnotes to his *Rubáiyát*). '*Anderún*', an old Persian word, is for example glossed as 'the *inner*, or women's apartment'.[207] '*Banou*' is glossed as 'a female head or chief'. Here, though, Morier showcases his deeper knowledge of the wider context of Oriental writings; he mentions '*Pari-banou*' as one of the main characters in 'The History of Prince Ahmed and Fairy Peri-banou' in the *Arabian Nights*.[208] There are also familiar elements of classical Persian poetry in *Hajjî Baba*. The Persia of the novel is associated with love and romance, a typical motif of Persian tales. There are references to legendary Persian love symbols: for instance, in Chapter XXXI, where Hajjî loses his beloved, Zeenab, he compares himself to 'Majnoun' and Zeenab to 'Leilah'. In a footnote, Morier glosses 'Leilah' and 'Majnoun' as personages whose love has been treated by 'various Oriental writers'.[209] He also mentions that 'Majnoun is looked upon as the model of a lover, and Leilah as the most beautiful and perfect of her sex'.[210] The Persian fondness for poetry is also shown in repeated quotations from Hafiz and Sa'di (for example, page 249 and page 344) and other poets, as well as the account of Asker and the admiration with which he is held in the Persian royal court.

The discourse and demeanour of Morier's characters bear a stamp of authenticity. The Persians in the novel exhibit social traits such as religiosity, superstition, and traditionalism, some of which are still identifiable in modern Iranian society. For instance, like many Persians in today's Iran and certainly most in Qajar Persia, Morier's characters are immersed in their religion. Islam and its values are their primary point of reference. Hence, a strong sense of Islamic consciousness drives their language and actions. At the same time, their verbal communication in many cases is limited to short sayings in Arabic such as 'Allah Karim' (God is great!),

Barîk Allah!' or '*Mashallah*' (praise be to god!) or '*Staferallah*'. It is a reductive technique, suggesting a kind of perfunctory religiosity rather than genuine religious feeling. As noted earlier, Islamic Persia to most British appeared oppressed with a static and oppressive religion, full of ritual that generates sloth and makes people lazy and intellectually decadent. Morier was no exception and his negative projection of Islam testifies to that. The Muslims of his novel are deluded by their religious convictions. They can be swayed by anything associated with their religion; they are a prey to absurd superstitions, as in the black comedy that surrounds the death of Hajjî's father in Chapter XLVIII, in which the sick man's sneeze is deemed an omen so bad that no one dares look at him, or administer the medicine he needs, for two hours, after which he is found to have died.[211] In Chapter LI, when Hajjî decides to become a '*Sahib Calem*' (man of the pen), he admits that his 'foolish' sayings will be counted as 'wisdom', if he holds a 'mortified-looking face', covers his head with a '*mollah's*' shawl, and especially if he exclaims '*Allah ho Akbar!*' or '*Allah, Allah il Allah*'.[212] Morier here is consciously poking fun at Islamic clerics; he is mocking the credibility of their sayings and doings. Through Hajjî's guileless claim, Morier implies that '*mollahs*' are typically impudent shams.[213]

From the Sherleys to James Morier, the sociopolitical interactions between Persia and Britain always caused literary repercussions in Britain. The general picture though was almost always of very heavy mediation so that the historical events and actualities were absorbed into a strong pre-existing paradigm for thinking about Persia. This Persian imaginary, shaped by a long tradition of biblical and classical reading, proved very hard to shift, and literary representation was often the result of a difficult 'negotiation' between ancient and modern perspectives. Poetry was especially subject to this process, even in the progressive nineteenth century, as we will see in the following chapters. The illusory image of Persia persists in the nineteenth century, although Persia itself, as a country, was no longer undiscovered. Quite a lot of information about its language, literature, history, culture and, of course, political relations with the British was being circulated in Britain at the time. But nineteenth-century poetry, perhaps deliberately, was catching up with these 'modern' understandings at a much slower pace, so slow that an examination of the poetic depiction of Persia in the nineteenth century implies a disconnection between historical reality and poetic representation.

Notes

1. Several of the great 'Persian' stories, such as the biblical book of Esther, involved all of these categories. On Esther see below, pp. 21–2.
2. For a discussion of the veracity of the books of the Old Testament, see Provan, 'The Historical Books of the Testament', pp. 198–211.
3. See Thomas, 'The Intellectual Milieu of Herodotus', p. 60.
4. Flower, 'Herodotus and Persia', p. 278. For an overview of the relations between the Greeks and the Persians, including the Greco-Persian wars, see Burn, *Persia and the Greeks*; Grundy, *The Great Persian War*.
5. Accounts of Persian life and affairs were available to the Greeks before Herodotus; for example, those of Hectaeus (550–c.476 BCE) on the Achaemenids which are believed to have been used by later writers such as Stephanus of Byzantium (sixth century BCE); see Cook, *The Persian Empire*, p. 14.
6. See, for example, Fehling, *Herodotus and his Sources*.
7. Flower, 'Herodotus and Persia', p. 275.
8. Irwin, *For Lust of Knowing*, p. 13. For more on Herodotus' formation of *Histories*, see Lateiner, *The Historical Method of Herodotus*. As an example, see Chapter 2, pp. 79–80.
9. For an account of the failed military expedition of Cyrus the Younger, see Burn, 'Persia and the Greeks', pp. 349–55.
10. For Xenophon's sources, see Gera, *Xenophon's Cyropaedia*, pp. 1–13 and pp. 13–23; also see Due, *The Cyropaedia*, pp. 117–46.
11. Gera, *Xenophon's Cyropaedia*, pp. 6–8.
12. Ibid. p. 2.
13. In writing this section, I have relied on Gera, *Xenophon's Cyropaedia*, pp. 1–25.
14. Lockhart, 'Persia as Seen by the West', p. 320.
15. Aeschylus waited six or seven years after the battle to write his play. He probably knew about Phyrynichus's fate; see Lockhart, 'Persia as Seen by the West', p. 320.
16. In writing this section, I am indebted to Hall, *Aeschylus: Persians*, pp. 1–28.
17. On the Greeks' perception of as 'Others', Vlassopoulos, *Greeks and Barbarians*; Harrison, *Greeks and Barbarians*.
18. See Hall, *Aeschylus: Persians*, pp. 7–10. For more information on the ideological construction behind Aeschylus' play, see Broadhead, *The Persae of Aeschylus*; Harrison, *The Emptiness of Asia*.
19. In alphabetical order: Ahasuerus (the biblical name of Khashayar Shah or Xerxes I) in Ezra 4: 6; Esther *passim*; Daniel 9: 1. Artaxerxes I (the biblical name of Ardashir Shah) in Ezra 4: 7–23, 6: 14, 7 *passim*, 8: 1; Nehemiah 2 *passim*, 5: 14. Cyrus in 2 Chronicles 36: 22–3; Ezra 1 *passim*, 3: 7, 4: 3, 5: 13–17; Isaiah 44: 28, 45: 1–4; Daniel 1: 21, 6: 28, 10: 1. Darius in Ezra 4: 5, 4: 24, 5–6 *passim*; Nehemiah 12: 22; Daniel 5: 31, 6 *passim*, 9: 1, 11:1; Haggai 1: 1, 1: 15, 2: 10; Zechariah 1: 7, 7: 1.

20. See Lockhart, 'Persia as Seen by the West', p. 326.
21. As narrated in Ezra, Darius issued a decree confirming that of Cyrus, and the rebuilding of the Temple was finished in the sixth year of his reign.
22. Modern scholarship treats Esther as a form of historical romance, but its origins and place in the biblical canon were not questioned in the nineteenth century. To most Victorians, it was as true as anything else in scripture. For more on this subject, see Tucker's entry on 'Esther' in *The Oxford Companion to the Bible*, pp. 198–201.
23. No historical original for Vashti has been identified. Xerxes' queen was known as Amestris.
24. The role of Mordecai in the Persian court is unclear in this part of the book. He is described in Esther (2: 5) as follows: 'Now in Shushan the palace there was a certain Jew, whose name was Mordecai, the son of Jair, the son of Shimei, the son of Kish, a Benjamite.' This attests only to Mordecai's presence in the king's palace, not his status.
25. Esther's 'catchphrase', so to speak, was her declaration 'and if I perish, I perish' (4: 16), which was taken up by Christina Rossetti (see next chapter); later nineteenth-century feminists also recuperated the figure of the disobedient Vashti.
26. For an account of European travellers to Persia in the middle ages, see Lockhart, 'European Contact with Persia', pp. 373–9; Javadi, *Persian Literary Influence*, pp. 6–13.
27. Higgins, *Writing East*, pp. 2–4; Irwin, *For Lust of Knowing*, pp. 50–3.
28. Irwin, *For Lust of Knowing*, pp. 62–6.
29. On Eden, see Gwyn, 'Richard Eden: cosmographer and alchemist'; Kitching, 'Alchemy in the reign of Edward VI'.
30. On Willes, see Parker, *Books to Build an Empire*, pp. 77–81.
31. On Hakluyt, see Quinn, *The Hakluyt Handbook*. On Purchas, see Pennington, *The Purchas Handbook*.
32. The text of *The Faerie Queene* is from Roche's edition, p. 80.
33. The text of the play is from *The Norton Shakespeare*, p. 1787.
34. 'Sophy' in its many variant forms ('sophie', 'sophi', 'sofi', 'sophia') is first recorded by *OED* in 1539.
35. On the Safavids' attitude towards Sufism, see Zarrinkoob, 'Persian Sufism in Its Historical Perspective', pp. 165–6.
36. Irwin, *For Lust of Knowing*, p. 47. The British were considerably late in the study of Oriental languages. Salamanca and Paris had their first chair by 1131. See Yohannan, *Persian Poetry*, p. xxii.
37. Irwin, *For Lust of Knowing*, p. 97.
38. Ibid. p. 109.
39. For more information on the study of Oriental languages in Europe, see Watson, 'Oriental Education in Great Britain', pp. 1232–6; Watson, 'Scholars and Scholarship, 1600–1660', p. 345.
40. The original letter was written in Hebrew, Italian, and Latin. An English rendition of it was included in Hakluyt's *The Principal Navigations*

(1589); part of the letter is printed in Grogan, *The Persian Empire*, pp. 1–2.

41. Foran, 'The Making of an External Arena: Iran's Place in the World-System, 1500–1722', p. 76.

42. The Safavids did not seek to validate their rule through highlighting pre-Islamic Persian ties; see Katouzian, *The Persians*, p. 112. On the significance of Achaemenid iconography in the Safavid monarchical thinking, see Mitchell, *The Practice of Politics in Safavid Iran*.

43. For a list of these contacts, see Lockhart, 'European Contact with Persia', pp. 388–401; Grogan, *The Persian Empire*, pp. 20–1.

44. For a list of other European travel writings on Persia that appeared in the later years of the sixteenth century and early decades of the seventeenth century, see Houston, '"Thou glorious kingdome, thou chiefe of Empires": Persia in Early Seventeenth-Century Travel Literature', pp. 142–3.

45. Grogan, *The Persian Empire*, p. 2.

46. Ibid. p. 5.

47. Ibid. p. 13.

48. The text is from Duncan-Jones's edition, p. 218.

49. Ibid. p. 217.

50. Lockhart, 'European Contact with Persia', pp. 388–9. On Shah Abbas's attitude towards non-Muslims, see Roemer, 'The Safavid Period', pp. 272–4; Matthee, 'The Safavids under Western Eyes: Seventeenth-Century European Travelers to Iran'; Houston, 'Turning Persia: The Prospect of Conversion in Safavid Persia'.

51. On the British perceived racial affinities for the Persians in the nineteenth century, see below, p. 56.

52. Grogan, *The Persian Empire*, p. 10.

53. There were three Sherley (or Shirley) brothers: Sir Thomas Sherley (1564–c.1634); Sir Anthony Sherley (1565–1635); and Sir Robert Sherley (c.1581–1628). I will mainly be concerned with the activities of the two younger brothers, though Thomas also played a part (see pp. 32–4). The *Oxford Dictionary of National Biography* uses the spelling 'Sherley' for Thomas and Anthony, and 'Shirley' for Robert; I use the spelling 'Sherley' for all three, for the sake of convenience.

54. There were earlier British visitors to Persia, such as Geoffrey de Langley who was dispatched by Edward I at the end of the thirteenth century; see Wright, *The English*, p. 2.

55. Ghani, too, notes the Sherleys' lack of interest in social history; see Ghani, *Shakespeare Persia*, p. 89.

56. For more on the motives behind the Sherleys' journey to Persia, see Steensgaard, *The Asian Trade Revolution*, p. 213; Ghani, *Shakespeare Persia*, pp. 67–77; Savory, 'The Sherley Myth', pp. 79–80; Andrea, 'Lady Sherley', p. 281.

57. Quoted in Javadi, *Persian Literary Influence*, p. 16, from an anonymous pamphlet, *True Report of Sir Anthony Sherley's Journeys* (1600).

On the Sherleys' relationship with Shah Abbas, see Ross, *Sir Anthony Sherley*, p. 95; Chew, *The Crescent and the Rose*, p. 262; Ferrier, 'The European Diplomacy of Shah Abbas', p. 76.

58. Savory, 'The Sherley Myth', p. 80.
59. Ferrier, 'The European Diplomacy of Shah Abbas', p. 75.
60. Quoted in Savory, 'The Sherley Myth', p. 80.
61. Ibid. p. 80.
62. Ferrier, 'The European Diplomacy of Shah Abbas', p. 76.
63. The hostage thesis is maintained by Savory (p. 76), Andrea (p. 282), and Javadi (p. 17), and many others.
64. The exact date of Anthony's departure is unclear; see Ross, *Sir Anthony Sherley*, p. 12. A detailed summary of Anthony's itinerary is given in Chew, *The Crescent and the Rose*, pp. 298–339.
65. Grogan, *The Persian Empire*, p. 154.
66. Chew, *The Crescent and The Rose*, p. 291.
67. For an account of what happened to Anthony and Hosein Ali Beg after the collapse of their ambassadorial party, see Steensgaard, *The Asian Trade Revolution*, pp. 227–30.
68. After Anthony, Shah Abbas sent a number of Persian envoys to Europe too, men like Zainal Khan Shamlu (1604), Mahdi Quli Beg (1604), and Fath Ali Beg (1605). But none had any greater success in their diplomatic mission.
69. Stevens, 'Robert Sherley: The Unanswered Questions', p. 117.
70. Steensgaard, *The Asian Trade Revolution*, pp. 275–7; Javadi, *Persian Literary Influence*, p. 16; Ferrier, 'The European Diplomacy of Shah Abbas', p. 75; Stevens, 'Robert Sherley: The Unanswered Questions', pp. 118–20.
71. For an account of the presence of Dengiz Beg in the Spanish court, see Steensgaard, *The Asian Trade Revolution*, pp. 283–7.
72. Wright, *The English*, p. 4.
73. Steensgaard, *The Asian Trade Revolution*, p. 299 and p. 324; Wright, *The English*, p. 4; Ferrier, 'The European Diplomacy of Shah Abbas', p. 79.
74. Ferrier, 'The European Diplomacy of Shah Abbas', p. 80.
75. Ibid. p. 82.
76. Robert's proposal is detailed in Ferrier, 'The European Diplomacy of Shah Abbas', p. 82.
77. For a detailed account of the East India Company's commercial and political interests in Persia in the seventeenth century, see Steensgaard, *The Asian Trade Revolution*.
78. See, for example, Ferrier, 'The European Diplomacy of Shah Abbas', p. 82.
79. Quoted in Stodart, *Journal; being the account of a sea voyage from 1626 to 1629 to the East Indies, Persia, etc*, p. 14.
80. Ferrier, 'The European Diplomacy of Shah Abbas', p. 85.
81. Ibid. p. 92.

82. Nixon, *The Three English Brothers*. Nixon's pamphlet is not numbered. Note that Thomas features alongside Anthony and Robert in this account.
83. See Chew, *The Crescent and The Rose*, p. 504; Grogan, *The Persian Empire*, p. 159; Burton, 'The Shah's Two Ambassadors', p. 33. For a list of contemporary narratives of the Sherleys' travels, see Burton, 'The Shah's Two Ambassadors', p. 32.
84. Other seventeenth-century plays included William Cartwright's *The Royall Slave* (1636), Sir John Denham's *The Sophy* (1642), and Robert Baron's *Mirza: A Tragedie* (c. 1647).
85. The similarities between the texts is explored in Parr, *Three Renaissance Travel Plays*, pp. 7–9.
86. Burton, 'The Shah's Two Ambassadors', p. 33.
87. Casellas, 'the Textual Construction of Early Modern Identities', pp. 258–9.
88. For more on the thematic and structural design of the romances, see Robinson, *Islam and Early Modern Literature*, pp. 3–5. Othello relates his wooing of Desdemona by telling her the 'story of [his] life' in *Othello* I, iii, 128ff. The play is usually dated 1603/4.
89. Publicover, 'Strangers at home', p. 694.
90. See, for example, Parr, 'Foreign Relations in Jacobean England: The Sherley brothers and the "voyage of Persia"'; Burton, 'The Shah's Two Ambassadors'; Publicover, 'Strangers at home'; Casellas, 'the Textual Construction of Early Modern Identities'; Houston, '"Thou glorious kingdome, thou chiefe of Empires": Persia in Early Seventeenth-Century Travel Literature'; also see, Grogan, *The Persian Empire*, pp. 150–79.
91. All references to the play are from Parr's edition, pp. 55–134.
92. Steensgaard, *The Asian Trade Revolution*, p. 259. For a list of contemporary accounts on the Persians' use of firearms, see Savory, 'The Sherley Myth', p. 78. It is noteworthy that the Sherleys themselves seem never to have made such claims.
93. Savory, 'The Sherley Myth', p. 74.
94. On the British nineteenth-century perception of Persia as a fallen nation, see below, pp. 53–7.
95. On the fall of Hormuz and its commercial and geopolitical importance, see Grogan, *The Persian Empire*, pp. 180–4; Awad, 'The Gulf in the Seventeenth Century'; Foran, 'The Making of an External Arena: Iran's Place in the World-System, 1500–1722'; Good, 'The East India Company's *Farmān*, 1622–1747'.
96. Herbert, *Some Yeares Travels*, pp. 177–80. I am using a 1677 edition of the book throughout this section.
97. Ibid. p. 305.
98. Ibid.
99. Ibid.

100. Jahanpour, 'Western Encounters with Persian Sufi Literature', p. 34.
101. Perry, 'Persian in the Safavid Period', p. 270.
102. Herbert, *Some Yeares Travels*, pp. 315–20.
103. Ibid. p. 129.
104. Yohannan, *Persian Poetry*, p. xxi.
105. Ibid. pp. xvi–xvii.
106. Ibid. pp. xxiii and p. 265.
107. See Brancaforte, *Visions of Persia*, p. 73.
108. Ibid. p. 67 and pp. 70–1.
109. Ibid. p. 71.
110. Ibid. pp. 8–9.
111. For a list of these editions and translations, see Poe, '*A People Born to Slavery*'; Kollmann, 'Tracking the Travels of Adam Olearius'.
112. For more on Olearius, see Brancaforte's *Visions of Persia;* Emerson, 'Adam Olearius and the Literature of the Schleswig-Holstein Missions to Russia and Iran'.
113. Kollmann, 'Tracking the Travels of Adam Olearius', pp. 137–9.
114. For more on this edition, see Penzer, 'Preface', pp. 14–18.
115. Lockhart, 'European Contact with Persia', pp. 400–1.
116. Baghal-Kar, 'Images of Persia in British literature', pp. 100–1.
117. Dabashi, *Persophilia*, p. 55.
118. Dew, *Orientalism in Louis XIV's France*, p. 170.
119. Said, *Orientalism*, p. 65. All references to Said's *Orientalism* are from the 2003 reprint of the book.
120. Ibid.
121. See Irwin, *The Arabian Nights*, p. 15.
122. For more on d'Herbelot's treatment of the Orient, see Said, *Orientalism,* pp. 63–7; Irwin, *For Lust of Knowing*, pp. 113–17. Examples of the influence of d'Herbelot's text on FitzGerald's translation are highlighted in Karlin's *Rubáiyát*; see, for instance, p. 67, p. 140, and p. 149.
123. The first two volumes appeared in 1704, the twelfth and final posthumously in 1717; see Irwin, *Arabian Nights*, p. 16.
124. The text is from Rogers's edition, p. 342.
125. For more on the construction of *Lettres persanes* and its critique of contemporary French society, see Dabashi, *Persophilia*, pp. 52–5.
126. For more on the advent of Oriental literature in the eighteenth century, see Javadi, *Persian Literary Influence*, pp. 57–9; Clifford, *The Predicament of Culture*, pp. 255–76; Baghal-Kar, 'Images of Persia in British literature', pp. 100–39.
127. The text is from Jones's first (1772) edition of *Poems, Consisting Chiefly of Translations from the Asiatick Languages*.
128. Other material comprised the twelve-volume edition of Antoine Galland's *Les Mille et une nuits* together with the Arabic manuscript that Edward Pococke, the first professor of Arabic in 1636, had given

to the Bodleian. On Jones's sources, see Mukherjee, *Sir William Jones*, p. 23; Javadi, *Persian Literary Influence*, p. 49; Cannon, 'Sir William Jones and New Pluralism Over Languages and Cultures', p. 129; Cannon, 'Sir William Jones's Persian Linguistics', p. 264.

129. Irwin, *For Lust of Knowing*, p. 92.
130. FitzGerald, almost one hundred years after, tried a similar approach in his study of Persian. He used the second edition of Jones's *Grammar* which he 'had a sort of *Love* for'. He also went through two-thirds of Hafiz with the help of a Persian lexicon and Joseph Von Hammer-Purgstall's *Der Diwan des Mohammed Schemsed-Din Hafis* (1812–13). See FitzGerald's letter of 5 January 1854 to E. B. Cowell in Terhune and Terhune, *Letters*, vol. 2, p. 118.
131. Cannon, *Oriental Jones*, p. 10.
132. See Lockhart, *Nadir Shah*, p. 295.
133. Cannon, *Oriental Jones*, pp. 14–15.
134. See Lockhart, *Nadir Shah*, p. 296; Cannon, *Oriental Jones*, p. 16.
135. Franklin, *Orientalist Jones*, pp. 65–6.
136. Jones, 'Preface' to *The History of the Life of Nadir Shah*, p. 314.
137. Ibid. p. 341.
138. Ibid. p. 316.
139. The comparison between Nadir and Alexander is found in in earlier writings too: for instance, in Jean-Pierre de Bougainville's *Parallèle de l'expédition d'Alexandre dans les Indes avec la conquête des mêmes contrées par Tahmas-Kouli-Khan* (1752), or in James Fraser's *The History of Nadir Shah: formerly called Thamas Kuli Khan, the present Emperor of Persia* (1742); see Mukherjee, *Sir William Jones*, pp. 40–2 and p. 154.
140. Jones, 'An Essay on the Poetry of the Eastern Nations', pp. 354–5.
141. More than half a century later, Charles Augustin Sainte-Beuve speaks of Firdausi in similar terms. See Chapter 3, pp. 126–7.
142. Jones, *Poems*, p. vi.
143. See Cannon, 'Sir William Jones's Persian Linguistics', p. 264.
144. Jones, *Grammar*, p. 180.
145. Cannon, 'Sir William Jones's Persian Linguistics', p. 266.
146. The fact that Jones supplied transliterations of the Farsi text along with his English version signals his willingness to expose his technique to linguistic scrutiny.
147. The translations of Hafiz in this part are from Davis, *Faces of Love*, pp. 128–9.
148. On homoeroticism in the qazal verse form in Persian poetry, see Davis, *Faces of Love*, pp. xxi–xxiv; also see Murray, 'Corporealizing Medieval Persian and Turkish Tropes'; Southgate, 'Men, Women, and Boys: Love and Sex in the Works of Sa'di'.
149. Davis, 'Persian', p. 334.
150. See Javadi, *Persian Literary Influence*, p. 66.

151. In writing this section, I have relied on Javadi's commentary on Oriental periodicals and Persian studies (pp. 63–71) and Yohannan's exploration of the same topic (pp. 15–18).
152. Ingram, *In Defence of British India*, p. 9.
153. Ingram, 'An Aspiring Buffer State', pp. 511–12.
154. Lambton, *Qajar Persia: Eleven Studies*, pp. 198–9.
155. Ingram, 'An Aspiring Buffer State', pp. 509–18.
156. Britain's imperial policy towards Persia in the nineteenth century was unreliable because it was constantly changing, and the Persians had to learn this the hard way. After Turkmenchay, Persia lost two of its northern provinces, Erivan and Nakhichevan. It also no longer had control over the passes from the Caucus to Azerbaijan. Turkmenchay also took away Persia's rights to navigate across the Caspian. See Ingram, *The Beginning*, p. 22, pp. 38–43, and p. 50; Davis, 'The Great Game', p. 6.
157. Curzon, *Persia and the Persian Question*, vol. 2, p. 605.
158. Ibid. vol. 1, p. 2.
159. A large number of critical studies have been written on the Great Game. Throughout this section, I have relied on David Ingram's seminal treatment of this topic in *In Defence of British India*; *The Beginning*; 'An Aspiring Buffer State'; 'Great Britain's Great Game: An Introduction'; and 'Approaches to the Great Game in Asia'. For more on the Great Game, also see Savory, 'British and French Diplomacy in Persia, 1800–1810'; Yapp, 'British Perceptions of the Russian Threat to India' and his other essay, 'The Legend of the Great Games'.
160. See Malcolm's letter of 10 August 1799 to General Ross, in Kaye, *The Life and Correspondence of Major-General Sir John Malcolm*, vol. 1, p. 90.
161. Wright, *The English*, p. 4. For an account of ceremonial complications that Malcolm was faced with upon his arrival in Persia, see Kaye, *The Life and Correspondence of Major-General Sir John Malcolm*, vol. 1, pp. 110–14.
162. Wright, *The English*, p. 7.
163. Lambton, 'Major-General Sir John Malcolm (1769–1833) and "The History of Persia"', p. 100.
164. Wright, *The English*, p. 8.
165. Before Malcolm, the history of Persia was only available in partial form to English readers. The history of ancient Persia was accessible through the writings of the Greeks, that of medieval Persia through the writings of early modern travellers, and the preface and introductions that were later added to these writings; notable examples are L. Langlès's standard ten-volume edition of Chardin's *Voyages . . . en Perse et autres lieux de l'Orient* (1811), or earlier works such as Judas T. Krusinski's *The History of the Late Revolutions of Persia Taken From the Memoirs of Father Krusinski* (1733). Other works included

Louis André de La Mamye Clairac's *Histoire de Perse, depuis le commencement de ce siècle* (1750) and Jonas Hanway's *The History of the Revolutions in Persia* (1753). See Lambton, 'Major-General Sir John Malcolm (1769–1833) and "The History of Persia"', p. 105.

166. See Kaye, *The Life and Correspondence of Major-General Sir John Malcolm*, vol. 2, p. 94.
167. Jones, *The Dynasty of the Qajars*, 'To the King' (n.p.).
168. For a list of these writings, see Yarshater, 'The Qajar Era in the Mirror of Time', pp. 187–8. For an account of Ousely's life, see Gail, *Persia and the Victorians*, p. 59.
169. See Kaye, *The Life and Correspondence of Major-General Sir John Malcolm*, vol. 1, p. 124.
170. Morgan, *Medieval Persia*, pp. 6–7.
171. Malcolm, *History of Persia*, vol. 2, p. 638.
172. Ibid. p. 631.
173. Ibid. p. 621.
174. Ibid.
175. Ibid. i, pp. 169–70.
176. See Kaye, *The Life and Correspondence of Major-General Sir John Malcolm*, vol. 1, p. 123.
177. Malcolm, *History of Persia*, vol. 1, p. 276.
178. Ibid. vol. 2, p. 543.
179. Binning, *A Journal of Two Years' Travel in Persia*, p. 326.
180. Browne, *A Year Amongst the Persians*, p. 123.
181. It was however in Germany, not in Britain, that these ideas proliferated. Fascinated by Georg Forster's 1791 rendition of Jones's translation of Cálidás's play, *Sacontalá* (1789), which was a book of mystic Hindu teachings, Johann Georg Hamann and Johann Gottfried Herder were the first German scholars to announce India as the birthplace of the Indo-European (or Indo-Germanic) languages and people. See Stietencron, *Hindu Myth, Hindu History, Religion, Art, and Politics*, p. 212; Benes, 'Comparative Linguistics as Ethnology: In Search of Indo-Germans in Central Asia, 1770–1830', p. 122.
182. Curzon, *Persia and the Persian Question*, vol. 1, pp. 5–6.
183. Lord Salisbury's famous speech in 1898 articulates this vision of the decline of nations, consequent on their own moral corruption: 'Decade after decade they are weaker, poorer and less provided with leading men or institutions in which they can trust, apparently drawing nearer and nearer to their fate and yet clinging with strange tenacity to the life they have got.' Lord Salisbury's Speech to The Primrose League, 4 May 1898, reprinted in *The New York Times*, 18 May 1898.
184. Curzon, *Persia and the Persian Question*, vol. 2, p. 605.
185. Ibid. vol. 1, p. vii.
186. See Ross, 'Lord Curzon and E. G. Browne Confront the "Persian Question"', p. 396.

187. Curzon's 'Introduction', in Morier, *The Adventures of Hajjî Baba of Ispahan* (1895), p. 21.
188. Ingram, *In Defence of British India*, pp. 131–2.
189. See Ingram, 'An Aspiring Buffer State', p. 516.
190. See Wright, *The English*, p. 5. See Lambton, 'Major-General Sir John Malcolm (1769–1833) and "The History of Persia"', p. 100.
191. Wright, *The English*, p. 6.
192. Amini, 'Napoleon and Persia', p. 114.
193. Ibid.
194. Wright, *The English*, p. 7; Wright, *The Persians*, p. xv.
195. Not everything about Hajjî reflects or was taken from Mirza Abul-Hasan. For instance, the name Hajjî Baba is likely to have been borrowed from Hajji Baba Afshar, who was one of the first students who left Persia (Tabriz) with Harford Jones in 1809 for London. For more on Hajji Baba Afshar, see Wright, *The Persians*, pp. 70–86.
196. Morier stayed in Persia as chargé d'affaires until 1814.
197. Morier's other novels are *Zohrab the Hostage* (1832), *Ayesha, The Maid of Kars* (1834), and *The Mirza* (1841).
198. All references to *Hajjî Baba* are taken from a 1899 edition of the book, with Beckett's introduction. The transliterations of the Persian words in inverted commas are Morier's.
199. See Grabar, 'Fact and Fiction: Morier's Hajji Baba', p. 1224; Javadi, *Persian Literary Influence*, p. 123.
200. Grabar's essay gives a comparative analysis of *Hajjî Baba*'s characters and the real-life people whom Morier's met and knew from his visits to Persia. See Grabar, 'Fact and Fiction: Morier's Hajji Baba', pp. 1225–6.
201. Morier mentions that 'such acts' brings the Persian shah 'a great reputation, which, when at Koom (Qum), he keeps up by going about on foot, an act of great humility in Persian estimation'. See Morier, *Second Journey*, p. 166.
202. Morier, *Hajjî Baba*, p. 30.
203. Morier, *A Journey through Persia*, pp. 188–9.
204. Morier, *Hajjî Baba*, pp. 28–9.
205. Morier, *Second Journey Through Persia*, p. 192.
206. See Grabar, 'Fact and Fiction: Morier's Hajji Baba', pp. 1228–9.
207. Morier, *Hajjî Baba*, p. 10.
208. Ibid. p. 129.
209. Morier, *Hajjî Baba*, p. 27.
210. Ibid. 'Leilah and Majnoun' (*Leili o Majnoon*) are equivalents of Romeo and Juliet in Persian popular and literary culture.
211. Despite the fact that everyone in the room already knows that the man is dead, an old '*mollah*' foolishly orders him (a dead body) to rise: 'In the name of Allah, arise.' But even Allah cannot be of any help at this point, since 'life had entirely fled'.

212. Morier's transliteration is wrong here. He is probably referring to the well-known Islamic invocation: *la ilaha illa allah*, meaning there is no god except the God (Allah).
213. Here, too, the parallels with English fiction are striking. Many of the 'Christian' preachers and their gullible followers who appear in novels from Fielding to Dickens would be thoroughly at home in Morier's Persia.

Chapter 2

Persia and Nineteenth-Century English Poetry

The image of Persia in nineteenth-century English poetry was mul-tifarious. It proliferated in a variety of contexts and was associated with a variety of thoughts. My purpose in this chapter is to chart this diversity, exploring the ways Persia figures in nineteenth-century English poetry. In doing so, I engage with the more dominant catego-ries of knowledge behind the nineteenth-century English perception of Persia; these are the strands of thoughts that I have attempted to outline through my historical exploration and textual analysis of the previous chapter. My aim is to draw on these environments of knowl-edge to map out the ways Persia was perceived and re-presented in English poetry of the nineteenth century. My corpus consists of poems included in Literature Online (LION), with additional data from the British Library catalogue; though I only engage with the lat-ter to gauge the number of times the works of Persia's classical poets were translated in the nineteenth century. Poems have been identified primarily through the use of certain keywords: alongside 'Persia' and its cognates, searches have been made for the names of individuals (such as Cyrus, Sa'di, or Khayyám) and places (Shiraz, Isfahan), together with a selection of words commonly associated with Persian history and culture (nightingale, bulbul).

Persia and its Cognates

A search on LION for the word 'Persia' and its variant spellings in poems published in the long nineteenth century (1780–1920) gen-erates a list of 370 poems. A preliminary examination reveals that these texts, based on the degree and the intensity of their engagement with Persia, are of two kinds: first, poems that are written specifically on Persia and bear direct reference to it; second, poems in which

Persia appears, not in the fore, but in the scenery behind the main object of contemplation. The latter group can be further divided into two smaller categories: first, poems in which the mention of Persia is inevitable, such as poetic retelling of the history of ancient Greece; second, poems in which Persia appears minimally, only once or twice, though, even in this category of texts, brevity does not necessarily mean insignificance. We see this, for instance, in the poetic manifestations of 'Iran', the modern denomination by which the people of Persia (Iran) have always referred to their country. There are thirty-seven poems on LION in which the name 'Iran' is cited. But again, not all of these poems are about Persia. There is, for example, an allusion to Iran in James Gates Percival's 'Expand your snowy wings, ye swans of Helicon!' (*The Poetical Works*, 1859), but the reference is very brief:

> Expand your snowy wings, ye swans of Helicon!
> And bear me to some paradise
> On India's verdant mountains, or on Iran's plains;
>
> (ll. 1–3)

In its only mention in the poem, Iran is represented by a flat land-mass, whereas India, the symbol of another Eastern landscape, represents an expanse of green uplands. Despite these implied geographical differences, Iran and India are, however, brought together to signify space and distance. The levelness of 'Iran's plains' and the height of 'India's verdant mountains' affirm the skill of the swans to hover as low as Iran's deserts and soar as high as India's mountains. The remoteness associated with these Oriental landscapes is also drawn upon to indicate the span of the swans' flight, metaphorically the power of poetry to range from its Greek homeland (Helicon, the home of the Muses) to the most far-flung, exotic places. But then Iran and India are not compara-ble only in concept; they are close in cadence too. The alliterative symmetry in the first syllable of these words is also a reason why Percival has chosen the name Iran over Persia. Iran and India are both far, foreign, and almost homophonous.

In contrast to Percival's fleeting mention of Iran, there are a num-ber of texts with reference to Iran, such as Edmund Gosse's *Firdausi in Exile* (1885) or Edwin Arnold's *With Sa'di in the Garden* (1888), that offer a deeper understanding of the Persian theme. A notable example among these is Grant Allen's short poem, 'For a Special Occasion', subtitled 'Boulge Churchyard, Oct. 5, 1893' – the occasion being the planting of a rose tree on Edward FitzGerald's grave ten years after his death by a group of literary enthusiasts including William Simpson who had brought the seed to England from Iran:

> Here, on Fitzgerald's grave, from Omar's tomb,
> To lay fit tribute pilgrim singers flock.
> Long with a double fragrance let it bloom,
> This rose of Iran on an English stock.[1]

A curious duality runs through Allen's verse. The stanza beautifully, and indeed mournfully, celebrates the Anglo-Persian essence of the *Rubáiyát*. The rose embodies FitzGerald's poem, which is also partly Khayyám's. It has come from 'Omar's tomb' but remains to flower 'on Fitzgerald's grave'. The twofold nature of the rose or, metaphorically speaking, the *Rubáiyát*, is the cause of its double fragrance; the seed is from Iran, but the soil is English.

The word 'Persia' appears in the title or as part of the title in only eleven poems in LION's list of 370 poems. But even among these small number of texts there are poems that are not necessarily concerned with Persia. Take Henry Kendall's 'Persia' (*Poems of Henry Clarence Kendall*, 1890) as an example; the poem is written on the poet's newly born child who is 'christened' Persia:

> I have given my darling the name
> Of a land at the gates of the day,
> Where morning is always the same,
> And spring never passes away.
> With a prayer for a lifetime of light,
> I christened her Persia, you see;
>
> (ll. 9–14)

The above passage is a fine example of the incessant presence of some of the more established notions associated with Persia in the nineteenth century. Persia here stands as a heavenly garden of undying natural beauty, embodying the poem's subject matter and theme. It is ironic in this light though that Kendall's description of this imaginary Persian landscape is brief; it is only four lines in length, despite Persia's conceptual significance in this context (after all, the child and the poem are both named Persia). But there is a reason to this cursory treatment. Kendall's vision of Persia, however pithily constructed, is made with solid imaginative elements, remembering and reverberating a well-established image of the country that takes it to be a charming landscape of natural marvels. No context is thus needed here because Kendall's 'Persia' is wholly shaped by a cliché; many in the nineteenth century, especially after Jones's rendition of Persia in 'A Persian Song of Hafiz', would have been familiar with his romanticised vision of the country.

In contrast to Kendall's poem, there are imaginative writings with Persia as, or in, their title, such as Alfred Tennyson's 'Persia' (*Poems by Two Brothers*, 1827) or Edward Henry Bickersteth's 'A Lament for Persia' (*Poems and Songs*, 1848) that engage more attentively with the Persian theme. And some of these texts, instead of celebrating and perpetuating a familiar Persian imaginary, lament the demise of an ancient, amiable Persia that is no more. Tennyson, for instance, does so by recalling Alexander's conquest of Persia:

> Oh! Iran! Iran! had he known
> The downfall of his mighty throne,
> Or had he seen that fatal night,
>   When the young king of Macedon
>   In madness led his veterans on,
> And Thais held the funeral light,
> Around that noble pile which rose
> Irradiant with the pomp of gold,
>   In high Persepolis of old,
> Encompass'd with its frenzied foes;
>   (ll. 24–34)

These lines retell the burning of Persepolis in the year 330 BCE. After the conquest of the Persian capital, Alexander left the city to his soldiers to ransack with the exception of the royal palace. But one day, when the Greeks were indulging in feasting and drinking, Alexander 'In madness led his veterans on' (l. 28); and Thais – whether she was Alexander's lover or the lover of the Macedonian commander, Ptolemy – persuaded Alexander to set fire to the royal palace: 'And Thais held the funeral light' (l. 29). But is 'Persia' a simple reiteration of an episode in the history of Alexander? No. The poem does indeed relay an ancient historical incident and is built upon a core of classical references; but there is more to its ideological conception than it being a mere glorification of the history of classical antiquity. Tennyson's 'Persia' is a reverberation of the nineteenth-century British perception of Persia as a fallen nation, a paradigm that took Islam as a foreign imposition responsible for the decline of a once glorious nation. Such ideological condemnation is, of course, not expressed explicitly in Tennyson's verse, but the poetic reiteration of the defeat that Alexander forced upon the Persians does recall such modern sentiments, particularly in light of the way the poem's narrative moves forward. Tennyson's verse begins with a standard description of Persia as a 'Land of bright eye and lofty brow!'; this is a garden of 'blossoms, ever young and new' (l. 12). But there is something peculiar about the poem's following lines; while the name Cyrus is never mentioned, a number of covert references to him, such as the evocation of the battle of Thymbra (ll. 14–18) or the battle of Cunaxa (l. 47), are embedded in the subsequent parts of the poem. The references to Cyrus, although obscured, are to create a dichotomy: Alexander, as the emblem of a foreign conqueror, is set against Cyrus, as the embodiment of Persian splendour. One symbolises ancient glory, the other foreign invasion and destruction. But the apposition is also to create a sense of sorrow: the memory of Persia's glorious past under the rule of kings like Cyrus still lingers: 'lives there yet within thy soul | Ought of the fire of him [. . .]' (ll. 13–14). But, then, even Cyrus 'would have wail'd, he would have wept' (l. 21) had he seen 'The downfall of his mighty throne' (l. 25). The repetition of the word, 'Iran', marked by exclamation points, in line 24 is the apex of the anguish that Tennyson aims to convey in his poem: 'Oh! Iran! Iran!' (l. 24) is a wailing for the devastation that Persia has endured since the foreign invasion, whether we take that invasion as a military incursion with immediate effect or an ideological intrusion with gradual but foreboding repercussions.

Only twelve poems in LION's list have a reference to Persia in their first line. But the multiplicity of connotations associated with Persia in the nineteenth century is evident even amongst this small number of texts. William Cox Bennett's 'Sperthies and Bulies' (*My Sonnets*, 1843) is, for instance, a poetic retelling of the encounter between Xerxes' general, Hydarnes and the Spartans, Sperchias and Bulis. These Greeks are celebrated for their bravery and self-sacrifice; they were, as we read in Herodotus, the Spartans who 'volunteered to offer their lives to Xerxes in atonement for Darius's messenger who had been killed in Sparta'.[2] The altruistic nature of their action was enough for the Victorians, with their obsession with ethics and the history of Hellas, to applaud them in their imaginative writings. But something about the poem is not right: Xerxes, as we read in *Histories*, does not execute these men at the end because he did not 'want to behave like the Spartans, who by murdering the ambassadors of a foreign power had broken the law which all the worlds hold sacred'.[3] Yet there is no mention of that in 'Sperthies and Bulies'. One may argue that there is no need for Xerxes' goodwill to be mentioned here, that what happens to these men at the end lies beyond the historical context that the poem intends to encapsulate. That may be true, but only if the poem's exaltation of these Spartans did not occur at the expense of the Persians. Bennet's purpose in adopting this historical incident as his poetic subject is to commend the Greeks; this is particularly evident in his rendition of the conversation between Hydarnes and Sperchias and Bulis:

> 'O Spartans, why the friendship of our king
> Reject ye? Look around, all that your eyes
> Behold is mine; nor will your service bring
> Less pomp or power.' 'Satrap, thou slave, be wise!
> Go, learn how sweet a thing is liberty.
> Life then too wilt thou spurn: the dead are free!'
>
> (ll. 9–14)

This altercation is the embodiment of the nineteenth-century partisan view of the Persians that had the history of ancient Greece as its basis: the Persians are almost always degenerate and tyrannical, while the Greeks are enlightened and free. Of course, the mention of Xerxes' magnanimity would have weakened the ideological force of Bennet's narrative and the legitimacy of the nineteenth-century British view of the Greeks, which was usually conveyed through a condemnation of the Persians.

Another example of Persia in the opening line is Paul Hamilton Hayne's 'The Enchanted Mirror: From the Persian' (*Poems*, 1882). Hayne's poem is not a retelling of a historical incident but, rather, a fictional tale:

> What time o'er Persia ruled that upright Khan
> Khosru the Good, in Shiraāz lived a man,
> A beggar-carle, to whose rough hands were given –
> I know not how – a mirror clear as heaven
> On beauteous, vernal mornings, and more bright
> Than streamlets sparkling in midsummer's light;
>
> (ll. 1–6)

'The Enchanted Mirror' relates the story of a magical mirror in whose reflection everyone 'Grew comely as the loveliest shapes' (l. 9), even if they are 'uglier than a nightmare dream of sin' (l. 8). The poem has the typical elements of an Oriental tale: the phrase 'From the Persian' in the title is a claim to authenticity, purporting the text to be a translation; although there is no mention of an original Persian source in the text. The poem's narrative is also typically anecdotal;

it focuses on an uncanny, magical object, and ends with the delivery of a moral lesson. The exotic backdrop of the poem is also communicated at the outset; the reader learns early on in the poem that the story takes place in Persia and, specifically, in Shiraz. Paradoxically though, the poem's historical background is unspecified, but that too is characteristic of an Oriental tale; Western representation of the Orient is usually ahistorical.

Persian Landscape

The most recurrent theme in LION's list of 370 poems is the representation of Persia as a charming garden of roses and rivers. Like all Eastern localities, the image of Persia's landscape in nineteenth-century English poetry is highly Orientalised: it is picturesque, sumptuous, splendid, and above all, imaginary. This Oriental imaginary has both a positive and a negative facet to it. In *Exotic Memories* (1991), Chris Bongie defines two types of nineteenth-century exoticism (his replacement for Said's term of reference): 'Imperialist' and 'Exoticizing' exoticism. 'Imperialist exoticism', Bongie states, 'affirms the hegemony of modern civilization over the less developed, savage territories', while 'Exoticizing exoticism privileges those very territories and their people, figuring them as a possible refuge from overbearing modernity.'[4] A confluence of both modes of exoticism is behind the imaginary construction of Persian geography in nineteenth-century English poetry. We see this, for instance, in Thomas Moore's *Lalla Rookh* (1817), where Persia is depicted as a heavenly garden; but this delightful landscape, to use Patrick Brantlinger's words, is also 'a sensual paradise of luxury, tyranny and erotic decadence'.[5]

Persian poetry itself supplied some of the materials for the formulaic portrayal of the country's exotic landscape. Take, for example, the common image of Shiraz, identified in Persia's literary culture as a cradle of romance, revelry, and poeticism. Persian poetry celebrates Shiraz as a nourishing ground for verse, love, mirth, wine-drinking, and natural beauty. Shiraz in Hafiz's verse is, for example, where the water is pure and the breeze is pleasantly mild. He describes it as the precious gem of 'seven territories', underlining its special qualities:

Shirāz (Hāfiz's existence) and the water of Ruknabād (love, life-giving), and the breeze of pleasant air (the soul's breathing), –
Them, contemn not; for (though contemptible) they are the lustre of adornment of seven territories of the world.[6]

The image of Shiraz in English poetry echoes that of its counterpart in Persian poetry. It appears as a splendid garden, a landscape of ardour, and a city of wonders. To find out why though, we need to return to 'A Persian Song of Hafiz', which we look at in the previous chapter.[7] If we take Sir William Jones's poem as one of the earliest English renditions of Hafiz, we may see why Shiraz came to be envisioned in such a sentimentalised fashion in English poetry of the nineteenth century. Jones's Shiraz is a fictitious landscape, incomparably beautiful: no 'stream [is] so clear as Rocnabad', no 'bower so sweet as Mosellay' (ll. 11–12). Of course, Jones's poem is a loose translation of Hafiz's qazal, but its description of Shiraz became what many in the following century strove to capture in their works.

There are thirty-nine poems in LION with a reference to Shiraz. In twenty-five of them, the allusion to Shiraz does not amount to more than a few lines, though however short, the conventional pattern of thought still persists. Shiraz in these poems stands as an imaginary garden of carnal joy, an illusory space replete with natural marvels. In George Boker's poem 'Prince Adeb' (*Poems of the War*, 1864), we read of 'mossy floors, | Flowered with the silken summer of Shiraz' (ll. 76–7); in the Sixth Book of Robert Southey's 'Thalaba the Destroyer' (*The Poetical Works*, 1838), Shiraz is a place with 'delicious juice' of 'golden grape' (ll. 329–30). There are also twelve poems in the list in which Shiraz has a greater presence. One is Henry Alford's 'Henry Martyn at Shiraz' (1851). The poem is founded on historical fact: Martyn (1781–1812), an Anglican priest and missionary, and a translator of the Bible into Persian and Arabic, spent eleven months in 1811 amongst the Persians. But unlike the poem's factual subject matter, its portrayal of Shiraz remains fantastical:

> A vision of the bright Shiraz, of Persian bards the theme:
> The vine with bunches laden hangs o'er the crystal stream;
> The nightingale all day her notes in rosy thickets trills,
> And the brooding heat-mist faintly lies along the distant hills.
>
> (ll. 1–4)

Alford's language here is markedly similar to that of Jones: the stream in his Shiraz is as 'clear' as the 'Rocnabad' of Jones's poem. Alford's Shiraz is also 'the City of the Rose' (l. 8), resembling Jones's Shiraz 'where living roses blow' (l. 22). However, not everything in this imaginary representation of Shiraz comes from Jones; there is, for example, no mention of singing nightingales in 'A Persian Song of Hafiz'. As Alford's footnotes reveals, part of the setting has been derived from *Life of H. Martyn* (LION does not identify the book's author, but it is likely to be John Hall).[8] For example, footnote 2: 'The bed of roses on which we sat, and the notes of the nightingales warbling around us, were not so sweet to me as this discourse from the Persian' (p. 417 in *Life of H. Martyn*) appears to have formed the essence of stanza VI:

> Far sweeter to the stranger's ear those Eastern accents sound,
> Than music of the nightingale that fills the air around;
> Lovelier than balmiest odours sent from gardens of the rose,
> The fragrance, from the contrite soul and chastened lip that flows.
>
> (ll. 21–4)

The influence *Life of H. Martyn* (1831) notwithstanding, Alford's appropriation of certain symbols, which are commonly featured in classical Persian poetry, bears a level of sophistication that suggest a more substantial understanding of the original context in which these elements are deployed. We see this, for instance, in the poem's penultimate stanza:

> The nightingales have ceased to sing, the roses' leaves are shed,
> The Frank's pale face in Tocat's field hath mouldered with the dead:
> Alone and all unfriended, midst his Master's work he fell,
> With none to bathe his fevered brow, – with none his tale to tell.
>
> (ll. 25–8)

At its end, the tone of Alford's poem becomes noticeably grave. No explanation is, however, given for this sudden change of mood. The only suggestion is that Martyn is left 'Alone and all unfriended' (l. 27). But regardless of the reason behind Martyn's sorrow, what is most pertinent to our discussion here is Alford's handling of this change through his fitting appropriation of a set of visuals that are uncommon in English poetry. With the poem's change of tone, the imagery becomes similarly sombre: the nightingale no longer sings; the rose starts to wither. A reader acquainted with the more paradigmatic aesthetic images in Persia's classical literature can discern how Alford's deployment of these elements mirrors their manifestations in Persian poetry. In classical Persian verse, the emblematic representation of nature typically agrees with the general temperament and theme of the poem; in times of grief, the nightingale, the rose, the moth (the butterfly) are hushed, faded, dead. But in times of joy, they are mobile, buoyant, exuberant. It is difficult to determine the exact

sources behind Alford's knowledge of Persian poetry, but the translations and imitations of Hafiz that were available in the nineteenth
century are likely to have provided him with an understanding of
these practices.

Isfahan, another notable Persian (Iranian) city of historical and
cultural pedigree, finds its way into nineteenth-century English poetry
too. Much of Isfahan's golden age was spent during the reign of Shah
Abbas. The representation of Isfahan in European travel literature,
particularly in relation to Shah Abbas, made the city a symbol of
Oriental splendour, a notion that was taken up by nineteenth-century
English poetry.[9] We see this in our catalogue. There are twelve poems
in LION's list with a mention of the word 'Ispahan' – an old spelling
of the current name. In some of these poems, the image of Ispahan
appears to have been affected by its historical past as a royal capital,
a city of wealth and extravagance. Take, for example, Godfrey Saxe's
'The Gardener and the King' (*The Poetical Works*, 1889). The poem
is a fictional tale of a gardener from 'Erivan' (l.1) who is persuaded
by a neighbour to take his fruits to Ispahan, in the hope that the king,
who 'Cares more for luxury than gold' (l. 12), would give him 'many
a shining golden piece' (l. 14). The gardener is cast as a naive visitor
from a distant province, ignorant of cities and courts, while the king
is a generic Oriental monarch, but his munificence and good humour
may recall Shah Abbas. The mention of 'Erivan' also implies an historical knowledge; the region, now in central Armenia, was subject to
the Safavids until ceded to the Russians in 1828.

In almost half of LION's poems, the name Ispahan also represent
a majestic Oriental city. This is the case even with poems where the
city also carries other connotations, as it does, for example, in Emme-
line Stuart-Wortley's 'The Wanderer's Return' (*Hours at Naples, and
Other Poems*, 1837). Ispahan here symbolises something greater
than a geographical entity; it is a treasured land, a place that encap-
sulates the speaker's youth and delight:

> Ispahan! do I breathe thy spiced Zephyrs once more?
> Long, long, have I wandered o'er far foreign shore,
> But again through thy fields paved with Jonquilles I roam,
> And I claim thee my City – my Country – my Home!
>
> (ll. 1–4)

Phrases such as 'spiced Zephyrs' belong to the repertoire of Oriental
cliché – though it is also an incongruous phrase to place in the
mouth of a native Persian, given the Greek derivation of 'Zephyr'.[10]

The poet cannot, evidently, claim to be a native of the city; she projects an 'authentic' Persian identity for her speaker, and in that sense, too, 'Ispahan' may seem no more than an exotic costume for a commonplace sentiment. Yet the triple phrase 'my City – my Country – my Home!' carries more conviction, and as the poem proceeds we discover that there is more to the Oriental stage-set of Ispahan than we might have thought. For though the speaker is returning 'home', home is also a foreign place, marked by loss and the presence of the dead. Among the poem's conventional images, a single 'realistic' detail stands out, though it derives more from Turkish than Persian funerary custom: the gravestones where 'Clustered flowers mark the feet, and carved turbans the head' (l. 71). The facile Orientalism in one dimension of the poem is countered by this greater seriousness in another:

> And thou – my Nouzhetos! – like winged Perii fair,
> Thou art still at my heart – still thy deep home is there,
> Though I know thy dark eyes have lost all their glad light,
> That thy beauties are Nothing – thy dwelling is – Night!
>
> (ll. 85–8)

'Nouzhetos' is clearly intended as a Persian name, though it is, in fact, Arabic, and may appear here by courtesy of an episode of *The Arabian Nights*; and the 'winged Perii' are stock figures of Oriental romance.[11] Yet the lines also anticipate, however faintly, the tone of FitzGerald's *Rubáiyát* with its emphasis on 'Nothing' and 'Night'; and the speaker who claimed Ispahan as his 'home' represents his own heart as the 'deep home' of his beloved. In returning to Ispahan the speaker is returning to his own past self.

Persian Poets

Hafiz in the nineteenth century was celebrated as one of Persia's greatest lyricists. His distinctive verse form, qazal, with its erotic nature, vitality, and disciplined elegance, was associated with romance, melancholy, hedonism, and mysticism, to name a few classical Persian tropes. We find Hafiz's name in seventy poems on LION. In six of these, his name appears with a reference to Sir William Jones; in ten it comes in relation to Shiraz; in thirty-five it is associated with wine, in fifteen with the nightingale, in six with the bulbul, in twenty-five with the rose, and in eight with the 'ghazal', a variant spelling of qazal. There are also twenty translations of Hafiz, or critical texts on him, in this period in the British Library catalogue. While these numbers are not conclusive and in no way representative of the extent of British familiarity with Hafiz in the nineteenth century, they can still be taken as an indication of the range of understanding that the British had towards Hafiz.[12] Take for example 'Song' (from *The Dutt Family Album*, 1870), a short poem written by members of the Dutt family, an Anglophile Indian family, renowned for its cultural achievements.[13] The 'Song', as its footnote suggests, is translated 'from the Persian of Mirza Schaffy', by whom is probably meant Mirza Shafi' Vazeh (1794–1852), the poet-philosopher in Persian and Azerbaijani of the Qajar era. In the second stanza, the speaker alludes to the poetry of Hafiz, comparing it with the delicacy of the beloved:

> O, what are all the tender songs by gentle Hafiz sung,
> To the silver accents of thy words, the music of thy tongue?
> What is the chalice of the rose, from which the Bulbul sips,
> Compared with thy soft rosebud mouth, thy dainty, coral lips?
>
> (ll. 5–8)

The 'Song' is a sequence of questions asked in the commendation of the beauty of the beloved. But this adoration is communicated through a language that is deliberately evocative of Hafiz (the choice of 'Song' as the title of the poem recalls Jones's 'A Persian Song of Hafiz'). For instance, in the opening two lines in the above stanza, the beauty of the beloved is said to rival natural elements such as the rose and the bulbul, both of which frequently occur in Hafiz's verse. The 'tender songs by gentle Hafiz', too, pale in significance when compared to the melodic voice of the addressee. The exaltation of the beloved is clearly taking place through the depreciation of Hafiz. But then for these hyperbolic comparisons to hold force, they must rest on the premise of Hafiz's lyrical reputation.

Hafiz dominated the first half of the nineteenth century and his status never really declined; but from 1860, he had a competitor in FitzGerald's Omar Khayyám, whose vogue was more widespread, and more intense, if ultimately less enduring.[14] LION lists fourteen poems in which the complete name of 'Omar Khayyám' (or its variant spelling, Khayyám) is cited. The British Library catalogue has a total of forty-four texts in whose title there is mention of the name Omar Khayyám. But going back to LION, all fourteen of its poems have one thing in common: they are all written in praise of Khayyám (and FitzGerald). While some of these poems, like Aldrich's 'Omar

Khayyám', which we read earlier, are made, so to speak, with FitzGeraldian ingredients, others depart from the model they praise. A group of these poems relates to the convivial gatherings of the Omar Khayyám Club (the English club was founded in 1892, the American in 1900). These include Austin Dobson's 'Verses Read at the Dinner of the Omar Khayyam Club March 25, 1897' and 'Verse Written for the Menu of the Omar Khayyam Club May 17, 1901' (*Collected Poems*, 1913), and William Watson's 'Stanzas Read at the Dinner of the Omar Khayyam Club, March 21st, 1902' (*New Poems*, 1902). These poems do not imitate the form of the *Rubáiyát*, and though they pay tribute to FitzGerald's representation of Khayyám's ideology in his book, they do not always reproduce it accurately. For example, in the second stanza in Dobson's 'Verse Written for the Menu of the Omar Khayyam Club', we read:

> Salaam to Omar! Life in truth is short,
> And mortal Man of many Ills the Sport;
> Yet still th' Oasis of the Board commends
> Its Vantage-Ground for cheerful Talk of Friends,
> And brings Oblivion, like an Eastern Balm.
> Therefore to Omar once again – Salaam!
>
> (ll. 7–12)

This stanza opens with a reiteration of the *carpe diem* belief that was perceived as to be fundamental to Khayyám's philosophy: 'Life in truth is short'. But the *Rubáiyát* contains no mention of the 'cheerful Talk of Friends', and its interpretation of 'Oblivion' is certainly not that of an 'Eastern Balm'. The message of the stanza is bookended between two 'Salaams' (a Persian greeting) to Omar. The opening 'Salaam' is an expression of gratitude to Khayyám for his cheering lesson and an acknowledgment of his prominence. It is also part of the Persian poetic tradition to open a verse by addressing the highest divinity, whether this greatest is the god, the prophet Mohammad, or any other divine being. The only footnote in Dobson's poem quotes from FitzGerald's 'Preface' to the 1872 edition of the *Rubáiyát*: 'It does not appear that there was any danger in holding and singing Súfi Pantheism, so long as the Poet made his Salaam to Mohammed at the beginning and end of his Song.'[15] But it is strange to cite the *Rubáiyát* as an authority here, since part of FitzGerald's argument suggests that Sufism is fundamentally insincere and that it merely pays lip service to Islamic religious forms; 'I must say', FitzGerald remarks in his response to J. B. Nicolas's Sufi rendition of Khayyám, *Les quatrains de Khèyam traduits du Persan* (1867), in the preface to the third (1872) edition of the *Rubáiyát*, 'that I, for one, never wholly believed in the mysticism of Háfiz. It does not appear there was any danger in holding and singing Súfi Pantheism, so long as the Poet made his Salaam to Mohammed at the beginning and end of his Song.'[16] Is Dobson accusing himself of insincerity then? Probably not! But he is indicating, almost without realising it, that he has appropriated FitzGerald for his own purpose. Oddly enough, there is a 'Salaam' at the end of Dobson's poem too with a similar purpose to that of the beginning; it is uttered to acknowledge Khayyám for his timeless philosophy. But the concluding 'Salaam', which this time is preceded by a pause, highlighted by the dash, can also be taken as a drinking toast. 'Salaam' is an attenuation of *salamati*, meaning 'health'. In colloquial Persian, 'Salaam' is an expression of good wishes before drinking, an equivalent of 'cheers' in English. For the lovers of Khayyám, who would assemble not only to praise his poetry and thought, but also to drink in his honour, the concluding stanza forms an injunction, a command urging the listeners (and readers) to drink to commemorate Khayyám.

Despite the scarce number of poems in LION with a mention of Omar Khayyám's complete name, a search for the word 'Omar' generates 100 results (it was FitzGerald who set the fashion for referring to Khayyám by his first name). About half of these poems on LION's catalogue refer to Khayyám, and again the range is great, from the solemn to the trivial or burlesque.[17] Guy Wetmore Carryl's 'The Mysterious Misapprehension Concerning a Man in Our Town' (*Mother Goose For Grown-Ups*, 1900), for instance, has a terrible pun on stanza XI of the *Rubáiyát*:

> Here with a Book of Verse beneath the Bough,
> A Loaf of Bread, a Flask of Wine – and Thou
>   Beside me singing in the Wilderness
> And Wilderness were Paradise enow.
>
> (ll. 47–50)

These lines had become famous by the time Carryl appropriated them for the last lines of his skit, in which we are advised to bear ignorant gossip without making a fuss:

> I beg you treasure no displeasure:
> Bow and hold your peace.
> Like Omar, underneath the bow
> You'll find there's paradise enow!
>
> (ll. 47–50)

Carryl expected his readers to get the joke. Bliss Carman, in 'A Thanksgiving' (*Last Songs from Vagabondia*, 1900) similarly takes Omar for granted as an established figure of the *carpe diem* philosophy, though his poem, unlike Carryl's, is not frivolous:

> I thank thee, Earth, for water good,
> The sea's great bath of buoyant green
> Or the cold mountain torrent's flood,
> That I may keep this body clean.
>
> I thank thee more for goodly wine,
> That wise as Omar I may be,
> Or Horace when he went to dine
> With Lydia or with Lalage.
>
> (ll. 5–12)

Khayyám, too, could fulfil this role of a pure figure of hedonism, as in Eugene Lee-Hamilton's 'A Golden Drop' (*Forest Notes*, 1899):

> You ask me for a drop of golden wine:
> Perchance from Lethe grapes in Circe's cup?
> Or Samian that Anacreon held up
> In his last toast, all crowned with rose and pine?
> Or is it from Khayyâm's great dreamy vine?
>
> (ll. 1–5)

Khayyám here takes his place in a sequence that runs from myth and epic (Circe, in Homer's *Odyssey*) to the Greek lyric poetry of Anacreon. He has been assimilated to a non-Persian tradition, in other words, very much as FitzGerald saw him aligned with Lucretius, or with the Preacher of Ecclesiastes. The Persia to which 'Khayyám's great dreamy vine' belongs is one of the most powerful fantasies projected about the country in the nineteenth century, although, as we shall see, it was a fantasy for which Edward FitzGerald was only partly responsible.

The interest in Omar Khayyám can also be seen in the poems with the mention of the name of the ancient, and well-known, city of 'Naishabur' (or commonly spelt in English, and in the nineteenth century, Nishapur).[18] There are eight poems on LION that refer to Nishapur. The city owed much of its fame to the *Rubáiyát*. FitzGerald's introduction of Nishapur as Khayyám's birthplace and a cradle of many of Persia's great thinkers played a big role in popularising the city. Robert Browning, for example, took FitzGerald's word and placed Nishapur in a similar context: Browning's Ferishtah sets up his school there.[19] In a later poem, John Payne's 'Thought and Speech' (*The Way of the Winepress*, 1920), Khayyám is associated with the province of Khurasan, where Nishapur (as FitzGerald had mentioned) is located. 'Thought and Speech' is a dialectic poem, in the form of an exchange between the speaker and 'the Sage of Khorasan', named at the outset of the poem: '"My long thought," saith the Sage of Khorasan, | "Briefly I cannot tell"' (ll. 1–2). Immediately the speaker replies:

> How often, bard,
> Despairing, must thou curse the Fates ill-starred,
> That branded thee, for birthmark, with the ban
> To be of those, Earth, Hell and Heaven who scan
> For answers to Life's riddle, – all yet marred
> By lack of speech to interpret them! So hard
> It is for man to speak to other man.
>
> (ll. 2–8)

The speaker's addressing of the listener as a 'bard' confirms that the sage is FitzGerald's poet-philosopher, Omar Khayyám. In his response to Omar's disbelieving world view, which is not articulated vaguely in the poem, the speaker turns Omar's hopelessness in finding an 'answer to Life's riddle' against him; the sage of Payne's poem is one of those who are inherently incapable of interpreting divine signs; and since these signs such as earth and heaven are unable to interpret themselves, it is the speaker's responsibility to enlighten his audience. One's bewilderment and failure in reading the divine phenomena should not lead to the denial of soul: 'Yet, soul, despair not' (l. 9). The answer to the sage's thoughts lies in the 'voices of the earth, the air, the sea, | The winds and rains of Heaven' (ll. 10–11).

In all eight poems in LION, Nishapur features as a place of knowledge and sagacity, although other notions such the *carpe diem* that the *Rubáiyát* ascribes to Khayyám are also evident in these poems. Thomas Bailey Aldrich's short poem, which is actually named after Omar Khayyám, is a good example. The poem announces its lineage in its epigraph, '*(After Fitzgerald.)*':

> Sultan and slave alike have gone their way
> With Bahrám Gúr, but whither none may say;
>   Yet he who charmed the wise at Naishápúr
> Seven centuries since still charms the wise today.

Aldrich's verse looks and sounds strikingly similar to the *Rubáiyát*. Not only does it follow FitzGerald's *aaba rubáiy* form, it is also made with FitzGerald's substance. The first line echoes stanza X in the *Rubáiyát*, where Omar speaks of a desert 'Where name of Slave and Sultan scarce is known', and the second line recalls stanza XVII. The mention of Bahrám Gúr, the fifth king of the Sasanian Empire, highlights the transience of human life and worldly supremacy. In the following two lines, the poem turns to Khayyám himself as a counter-example: the impermanency of power, wealth, and physical prowess is contrasted with the enduring appeal of poetry. Khayyám's poetry, thanks to FitzGerald, has the same effect on 'the wise' of today as it had on its original audience. Aldrich takes for granted that Khayyám was the author of the *rubáiyát* translated by FitzGerald, and so he assigns him a reputation that the historical Khayyám never had in his time. During his lifetime, Khayyám was known as an astronomer and mathematician and not a poet. But it would be many years before the authenticity of FitzGerald's version of Khayyám was seriously challenged.

Sa'di, another notable poet of Shiraz, looms large in English poetry of the nineteenth century, with particular attention paid to two of his works, *Bustan* (1257) and *Gulistan* (1259). There were numerous attempts by scholars and enthusiasts to translate Sa'di's writings into English in the nineteenth century. A title search on the British Library catalogue for 'Sa'di' and its alternate 'Sa'dī' generates fifty-eight results, all books written in English during our target timespan.[20] Surprisingly though, there are only five poems associated with Sa'di in LION's catalogue. But although few in number, these poems are all built upon a core of literary knowledge. They are attributed to Sa'di, and claim to be translation of either *Bustan* or *Gulistan*. Two of these poems: *With Sa'di in the Rose Garden* (1888) and 'A Rose of the "Garden of Fragrance" (From the Persian of Sâdi's "Bostan")', published in *Potiphar's Wife* (1892), are by Edwin Arnold, one of the more notable translators of Persian poetry in the second half of the nineteenth century; and the others, despite their authors' lesser fame in poetry or translation, still offer remarkable authenticity and accuracy in their treatment of Sa'di.[21]

As an example, take Edward Robert Lytton's 'The Roses of Saadi' (*Chronicles and Characters*, 1865). Lytton, poet and Viceroy of India, gathers three of Sa'di's anecdotes in one poem. These three segments, as the title of the poem implies, are from *Gulistan*. 'Moses and Dervish', the first of these poems, is a translation of narrative 14 in Chapter 3 of *Gulistan*. The translation is in verse, and consists of twenty-eight lines. But the original Persian is an arrangement of prose and verse, a conventional feature of Sa'di's writing. Only eight lines in 'Moses and Dervish' are in verse, as there are only four *baits* (distichs), eight *mesra'* (hemistichs), in the original Persian. But it is actually in these lines that the extent of Lytton's knowledge of Persian, and his skill as a translator, become notable. We see this, for instance, in lines 4–5:

> If to the creeping cat were given wings
> No sparrow's egg would be a bird.

These lines convey the parable's lesson. Moses, after seeing a dervish, meaning a scrounger, and not a mystic, in this context, prays to God to endow the beggar with financial ease. But after God's blessing, the dervish, who is no longer destitute, turns into a drunkard, a dissident, and a murderer: '"He hath drunk wine, and, having slain a man, | Is going to the death"' (ll. 23–4). Upon discovering this, Moses repents his earlier misjudgement and learns a lesson: 'God to every living soul sets forth | The circumstance according to the worth' (ll. 27–8). There are additions and omissions in Lytton's 'Moses and Dervish'; for instance, the quotation from the Qur'an: 'Had God expanded His provision to His servants, they would have been insolent in the earth; but He sends down in measure whatsoever He will; surely He is aware of and sees His servants' (Chapter 42, verse 26), is missing in Lytton's translation, whereas the original Persian narrative is founded upon these verses. Also, in the English version, Moses' discovery of the dervish's wicked deeds, which happens nine days after he returns 'from Mount Sinai in bliss', has no counterpart in Persian. Lines 4 and 5 also appear in the concluding part of Sa'di's episodes, after Moses' discovery of the incident, whereas in Lytton's, they appear in the opening stanza. So, in contrast to Sa'di's poem, in which the message is delivered at the end of the parable, Lytton opens his poem with the moral lesson, and then delivers the main story. Despite this divergence, Lytton's lines still mirror Sa'di's, and not just in meaning but also in form. The use of animal symbolism in the Persian original, a common feature of Persian literary culture, serves to carry and clarify the story's moral point. God has distributed his blessings in correct measure; any alteration to this celestial design is, accordingly, doomed to fail. In the vein of Sa'di, Lytton retains the thematic and structural design of the original, offering the same note in his verse; the cat-and-sparrow analogy, however foreign, appear almost the same as in original Persian counterpart.

Two other major Persian poets receive relatively short measure, although one of them was the subject of a prolonged attempt at translation by FitzGerald, arguably greater than the effort he devoted to the *Rubáiyát*. This is Faird ul-din Attar, whose name, like that of Khayyám, is linked to Nishapur. Attar was a twelfth-and thirteenth-century Sufi poet, who wrote six major works of poetry and one of prose. None of these, however, earned him much fame outside Nishapur during his lifetime. It was, in fact, not until the fifteenth century that his fame as a mystic and a master of teaching through parables began to spread in the Persian world. The entire corpus of Attar's writing is devoted to Sufism: 'throughout all of [Attar's] genuine collected works, there does not exist even one single verse without a mystical colouring; in fact, 'Attār dedicated his entire lit-erary existence to Sufism', say Leonard Lewisohn and Christopher Shackle in their introduction in *Attār and the Persian Sufi Tradition*.[22] But despite the heavy presence of Sufi thoughts in his works and despite the emerging interest in Sufism in the nineteenth century, no complete translation of Attar's writings appeared in Britain until the twentieth century (the earliest comprehensive work on Attar was Reynold Alleyne Nicholson's two-volume edition of *Tazkirat al-awliai* ('Memoirs of the Saints') which came out in 1905–7).[23] The nineteenth century was either less aware of Attar or less enthusiastic about him. There is, for example, only one poem in LION with a connection to Attar, though the connection itself is dubious. Richard Chenevix Trench in 'The Eastern Narcissus' (*Poems*, 1885) retells a well-known parable in Persian folklore in which a fox, seeing his reflection in a well, jumps into the water:

> But there no fox beside himself he found.
> Upward again he now would gladly spring,
> But to ascend was no such easy thing:
> He splashes, struggles, and in sad voice cries,
> 'Fool that I was! I deemed myself more wise.'
>
> (ll. 12–16)

First, let us look at Trench's choice of title. There are similarities between 'The Eastern Fox' and the story of Narcissus; the death of both is self-inflicted and caused by seeing the reflection of one's self in the water. But the motivations are different in each story. Narcissus becomes the victim of his self-love. He falls in love with the reflection of his self. But the fox becomes the victim of his credulity. He takes the reflection in the water as another fox: '*Another* fox did in the

water show' (l. 6, my emphasis). The attribution of the fable to Attar
is also debatable. In the only footnote to the poem, Trench comments
that 'The fable is Feridoddin Attar's'. But scholars are divided as to
whether *Johar ul-Zat* ('The Essence of Self') the book in whose first
chapter the fable appears was written by Attar or another poet of the
fifteenth-century with a similar name.[24] Trench furthers his note with
the narration of a watershed incident in Attar's life, but again the
validity of the anecdote, though repeated in various biographies and
anthologies, has not been verified either. Before devoting himself to
mysticism, Attar is said to have been 'a rich merchant of spices'. One
day, a pious but unpleasant-looking dervish visits his shop. 'Ferid',
as Trench reports, orders 'him to be gone', but the 'dervisch' replies:

> 'That can I do easily, for I possess nothing save my hood; but thou, with
> so many heavy sacks, how wilt thou contrive to be gone, when the hour
> of thy departure has arrived?' These words made so deep an impression
> on Ferid, that, from that moment, he gave up his worldly strivings, and
> dedicated himself to the spiritual life.[25]

Like Khayyám, the scarcity of biographical information on Attar has
led to the reiteration of numerous fabricated narratives. But regardless of the question of legitimacy, which was probably not of great
concern to Trench, the mention of the anecdote in the footnote suggests that, however limited and flawed, some knowledge of Attar
existed in Britain in the second half of the nineteenth century.

The earliest nineteenth-century English translation of Attar, one
of a very few in the century, was John Hindley's translation of *Pandnameh*, entitled *Pendeh-i-Attar. The Counsels of Attar, Edited from
a Persian Manuscript* (1809).[26] Ironically, the attribution of *Pandnameh* ('The Book of Counsel') to Attar has also been disputed, but
this was yet to be known in the nineteenth century, as the critical
examination of Attar's literary corpus, which disproved the authenticity of many of the texts that were formerly attributed to him, took
place in the following century.[27] Nevertheless, whether it was the
didactic tone of the *Pandnameh* or its humble narrative, the book
seems to have caught the attention of nineteenth-century Europe
more than other works of Attar. In 1819, Paris saw the publication
of Silvestre de Sacy's *Pend-namèh, ou Le livre des conseils de Ferid-
Eddin Attar*. The book, which had a wider distribution than that of
Hindley, probably because of de Sacy's reputation, contained extracts
from Attar's most celebrated work, *Mantiq ul-Tair* ('The Conference of the Birds'). But this was not the first European translation of

Attar's celebrated text. Excerpts from the *Mantiq ul-Teyr* (c. 1178) had been included a year before in Joseph von Hammer-Purgstall's *Geschichte der schonen Redekiinste Persiens*.[28] For the next thirty years, European scholarship on Attar stalled until the publications of Garcin de Tassy's works on *Mantiq ul-Tair*. A pupil of de Sacy, de Tassy was one of the few European scholars who worked profusely on Attar in the nineteenth century. His first publication on him was an 1856 prose translation of the tale of Sheikh San'an, one of most celebrated episodes in the *Mantiq ul-Teyr*. Later in the same year, he wrote an introductory essay on the *Mantiq ul-Teyr*, titled *La Poésie philosophique et religieuse chez les Persans. Le Langage des oiseaux*. De Tassy produced two further works on *Mantiq ul-Teyr*: a Persian edition of the poem that came out in 1857, and a complete French translation that appeared in 1863.[29] While de Tassy was busily engaged with his works on Attar in France, FitzGerald in England was working on the 'Bird Epic'. FitzGerald worked, at intervals, for almost two decades on *Mantiq ul-Tair*, but never managed to convince himself, or Edward Byles Cowell, to publish his translation. Today, he is less known for his *Conference of the Birds*, which was published posthumously in 1889 in William Aldis Wright's *Letters and Literary Remains*, than he is for his *Rubáiyát*.[30]

The second of our less well-represented poets is Firdausi, the author of the *Shahnameh*, Iran's national epic.[31] Despite his paramount role in Persian literary culture, Firdausi did not feature greatly in nineteenth-century poetry. He never had the place that he deserved, or which poets like Khayyám and Hafiz were able to reach. Like Attar, a complete translation of Firdausi's *Shahnameh* did not appear until the twentieth century; Arthur and Edmond Warner released a nine-volume translation of *The Shahnama of Firdausi* over a span of twenty years (1905–25).[32] But the translation history of 'Sohrab', the most renown episode in Firdausi's book, is of a different nature. 'Sohrab' is one of the earliest episodes from the *Shahnameh* to have been translated into English in the nineteenth century. James Atkinson's translation of 'Sohrab', *Soohrab: a Poem, freely translated from the original Persian of Firdoosee*, came out as early as 1814. Samuel Robinson, almost ten years later, published a *Sketch of Life and Writing of Ferdusi* (1823). William Robertson published *Roostam Zaboolee and Soohrab, From The History of Persia, Entitled Shah Namuh: Or Book of Kings, By Firdousee* in 1829. Three years later, Atkinson's *Shāhnāme: Abridgment and Selections* (1832) was published by the Oriental Translation Fund. None of these works, however, gained the popularity of Matthew Arnold's adaptation of the story.[33]

There was, in fact, something anomalous about Firdausi in the nineteenth century. The *Shahnameh*, as a poetic entity, was deemed dreary, lacklustre, and with little artistic value. Western enthusiasts, as Dick Davis explains, saw it as 'an unreliable chronicle that happens to be versified (perhaps best typified by A. V. Williams Jackson's comparison of the *Shahnameh* to Layamon's *Brut*, probably the most tedious long poem in the whole corpus of medieval English verse)'.[34] E. G. Browne was the most notorious practitioner of this trend. He was well acquainted with Persia's literary culture and with the cultural significance of the *Shahnameh*, but he was not necessarily impressed by it:

> It is on the *sháhnáma*, of course, that Firdawsi's great reputation as a poet rests. In their high estimate of the literary value of this gigantic poem Eastern and Western critics are almost unanimous, and I therefore feel great diffidence in confession that I have never been able entirely to share this enthusiasm.

Browne goes on to add that the *Shahnameh* cannot 'compare for beauty, feeling and grace with the work of the best didactic, romantic, and lyric poetry of the Persians'.[35] But the argument was not exclusive to him. We see a similar objection in the brief preface that was attached to the 1886 edition of Atkinson's *Abridgment of the Sháh námeh* by his son, J. A. Atkinson: 'the great length, and in many respects tediousness, of the entire Sháh námeh, renders it little likely that a translation of the whole poem would ever be acceptable to an English public [. . .]'.[36] The length of the *Shahnameh*, the monotony of its metre, and the cultural exclusivity of its contents may help to explain such contentions, though one can also argue that almost all national epics are prone to such criticism. The *Iliad*, for instance, is extremely long and written in simple metre.[37] But the main issue here is that of translation and cross-cultural appropriation, that the substance of the *Shahnameh*, in Percy Sykes's language, 'entirely loses its sonorous majesty in a translation'.[38] This may well be a legitimate dispute: it is an arduous task to render the *Shahnameh* or, in fact, any other epic that stands as the repository of the folklore of an entire nation into another language. Having said that, not every scholar of Persian literature in the nineteenth century saw the *Shahnameh* in that light. Cowell's opinion of the book was, for example, polemically against that of Browne. Cowell believed the *Shahnameh* was 'a poem that all succeeding poets could only imitate and never surpass, and which, indeed, stands as alone in Asia as Homer's epics in Europe'.[39]

Still, what we may call a 'Browne view' of the *Shahnameh* seems to have predominated: only a few nineteenth-century English translations of Firdausi exist. There are also only seven poems in LION with a reference to Firdausi. One of them appears in the 'First Book' of *The Pleasures of Benevolence, A Poem* (1835) by William Hamilton Drummond, although the reference is not actually Drummond's; it is taken from Sir William Jones. In a long footnote, Drummond quotes an excerpt from Jones's speech in 'The Tenth Anniversary Discourse', which was delivered to the Asiatick Society on 28 February 1793. As part of his speech, Jones recites the following verse:

> Ah! spare yon emmet, rich in hoarded grain;
> He lives with pleasure and he dies with pain.[40]

Before reading these lines, Jones speaks of their origin and author: 'nor shall I ever forget the couplet of Firdausi, for which Sadi, who cites it with applause, pours blessings on his departed spirit'.[41] Jones is right: the original Persian lyric appears in the second chapter of *Bustan*, and is one of the most repeated lines in Persian poetry. Part of the couplet's fame is due to its attribution to Firdausi; Sa'di respectfully alludes to Firdausi as the original author of the line.

Another allusion to Firdausi amongst LION's poem comes in Philip James Bailey's *The Age; A Colloquial Satire* (1858):

> Firdausi; you'll not master in the Persian,
> If unassisted by an English version,
> His sixty thousand couplets in a trice;
> Let Atkinson's abridgment then suffice,
> Though base beyond forgiveness in the sample,
> He oft-times gives of the bard's genius ample;
> To whom his native land's religious mystery,
> Traditions, laws, wars, and primæval history,
> The orb supply whereon his creatures move
> 'Mid fairies, fiends, and kings; heroic love;
> Adventures age may blame, but youth defends;
> Just arms; and labours virtue must approve.

(ll. 2550–61)

The poem offers a baffling juxtaposition of Firdausi's *Shahnameh* and Atkinson's abridged version. The excerpt, which is one long sentence, troubles the reader; it encourages misreading, making the reader to slow down and reread the text.[42] The opening lines, in prose paraphrase, read: one cannot master Firdausi's sixty thousand couplets without the help of an English version for reference; what is not stated is that no such version exists.[43] 'Let Atkinson's abridgment then suffice' has a double meaning: it must suffice, whether we like it or not; in the face of 'sixty thousand couplets', it may in fact be a preferable alternative. Yet, this length is also an indication of the magnitude of the *Shahnameh*; Atkinson's 'sample' cannot do justice to Firdausi's 'genius ample'.[44] Indeed it is so bad, so 'base', that it cannot be forgiven. This is because the true meaning of Firdausi's achievement is that he has created a world: his subject, 'his native land's religious mystery, | Traditions, laws, wars, and primæval history', make up the 'orb [. . .] whereon his creatures move'. Atkinson has implicitly shrunk this 'orb', or flattened it. Yet Bailey's radically compressed summary of the *Shahnameh* has its own problems. He makes Firdausi sound like a confused mixture of Homer, Spenser, and Sir Walter Scott.

Biblical Persia

Nineteenth-century religious poetry ratifies the correlation between Persia and the Bible. There are eighty-two poems in LION in which the name Cyrus is mentioned in relation to the history of the Jews. Francis Wrangham's 'The Destruction of Babylon' (*Poems*, 1795), for instance, refers to Cyrus with his biblical designation, 'th' Anointed of the Lord!' (l. 32). There are also sixteen poems in LION with an allusion to the story of Esther at the court of Xerxes; thirteen of these poems retell the biblical anecdote. But the Bible's image of Persia is inconsistent: at times, the Bible speaks of Persia as a saviour (Isaiah 40–55, Ezra, and Nehemiah), and at times as an oppressor (Esther 1–10). This contradictory nature of Persia's biblical presence resonates in the poetic adaptations of the biblical narratives: where Persia's role is favourable, its poetic representation is dignified; where it appears as a threat, its image is degraded. As an example, take Joseph Hart's 'Captivity in Babylon' (*The Captivity in Babylon and Other Poems*, 1840). Hart's poem relates the story of the fall of Babylon. Persia, Cyrus, and Darius feature in this long narrative poem with an approving image. At the end, and after recounting the sequence of events that leads to the emancipation of the Jews, when 'the band | Of Jews once more their ancient lot should draw, | And in their cherished home again restore the Law' (ll. 7–8, LXXVIII), the poem speaks of the Persians as follows:

Darius sleeps where Media's monarchs sleep,
In monumental pomp, and on his throne
The Persian Cyrus sits, his state to keep,
And rule the subject nations, now his own;

(ll. 1–4, LXXIX)

The allusion to the court of Cyrus as stately may at first seem both clichéd and naive. Cyrus' empire, too, will eventually fall. But in the particular context of the poem, it is like a gesture of gratitude and has a kind of tact to it. After Cyrus replaced the Babylonian Empire (covering today's Iraq, Syria, Lebanon, Jordan, Palestine, Israel, and parts of Turkey) with his own in the sixth century BCE, he allowed the Jews, who were exiled in Babylonia, to return to Judea. The forbearance that the Persian monarch showed towards its Jewish subjects brought gratitude from the Jews and found expression in subsequent generations. Hart's poem is a testimony to the persistence of this understanding in the following centuries.

In contrast to Hart's poem, we can find examples of nineteenth-century religious poetry where the portrayal of Persia seems to have been affected by religious prejudice. Hannah Flag Gould's 'Fragments from "Esther", A Poem' (*Poems*, 1839) depicts the Persians in partial and fantastical language.[45] The Persian court is extravagant and luxurious, an Oriental stereotype with a moralistic edge:

There's wine at the palace, and feasting, and mirth;
In Esther's still chamber there's fasting, and prayer;
While he with the crown, has the homage of earth,
She calls on her God her doomed people to spare.

(ll. 18–21)

Esther stands as a symbol of religious modesty, the Persians of ungodly hedonism. The holiness of Esther is shown in her secluded location; she is righteously engaged in her prayers in a 'still chamber', presumably located in the women's quarters, while the Persians are busy with 'feasting and mirth'.[46] The proximity of 'feasting' to 'fasting' succinctly conveys this contrast. The poem's sense of separation becomes more palpable in the concluding lines, where the focus shifts towards the Persian king. The poet looks at the king from a Persian perspective, and defines him as the Persians themselves might do: the king has 'the homage of earth' (l. 20). He enjoys a false supremacy. Esther puts her trust in the true 'King of Kings'.

Hart's poem is an example of poetry as a supplement to the Bible, but there are poems that deploy the story of Esther in more complex ways. In Sonnet 8 of Christina Rossetti's 'Monna Innominata', for example, the speaker compares herself to Esther, and the image of the Persian monarch here emphasises not his royal power, but his sexual subjection, or rather the undoing of one by the other:

'I, if I perish, perish' – Esther spake:
    And bride of life or death she made her fair
    In all the lustre of her perfumed hair
And smiles that kindle longing but to slake.
She put on pomp of loveliness, to take
    Her husband through his eyes at unaware;
    She spread abroad her beauty for a snare,
Harmless as doves and subtle as a snake.
She trapped him with one mesh of silken hair,
    She vanquished him by wisdom of her wit,
        And built her people's house that it should stand: –
    If I might take my life so in my hand,
And for my love to Love put up my prayer,
    And for love's sake by Love be granted it![47]

My interest in this poem is in its Persian (Oriental) connect. The stereotype of the Oriental despot captivated by female wiles is as ancient as *The Arabian Nights*; Esther is given some of the qualities of an Oriental courtesan, and this is in contrast to her image in the Bible which makes no mention of her 'perfumed hair' or her 'smiles that kindle longing'. The image of the Persians as addicted to luxury, and as effeminate, also hover in the background. Rossetti, of course, would have known that the Book of Esther opens with an extravagant description of the Persian court of Ahasuerus, with its feast lasting 'an hundred and fourscore days', its 'white, green, and blue, hangings, fastened with cords of fine linen and purple to silver rings and pillars of marble', its 'vessels of gold' and its 'royal wine in abundance' (1: 4, 6, 7). It is against this background that Esther plays her dangerous game: she risks her life, but is also a femme fatale, able to subjugate the monarch whom the Bible describes as 'this Ahasuerus which reigned, from India even unto Ethiopia, over an hundred and seven and twenty provinces' (1: 1).

As indicated at the start, the brevity of an allusion to Persia may not correspond to its significance. An example concerning the Book of Esther occurs in the opening of Book X of Robert Browning's *The Ring and the Book*, in which the Pope, about to pronounce judgement on Guido Franceschini and his accomplices, consults a history of the Papacy which records the deeds of his predecessors. In doing so, he invokes another kind of predecessor:

> Like to Ahasuerus, that shrewd prince,
> I will begin, – as is, these seven years now,
> My daily wont, – and read a History . . .
>
> (Book I, ll. 1–3)[48]

The allusion here is to the opening of Chapter 6 of the Book of Esther: 'On that night could not the King sleep, and he commanded to bring the book of records of the chronicles; and they were read before the King.' As with Rossetti, Browning could be sure that many, if not most of his readers would recognise the allusion. In calling Ahasuerus 'that shrewd prince' the Pope may be ironic (since he is manipulated throughout, first by Haman, then by Esther and Mordecai), but it is also a serious comparison because the Pope, like the Persian monarch, has the power of life and death and is, in fact, about to deliver a sentence of death on Guido. It seems only a glancing allusion, but it penetrates deep into the poem's plot, for if the Pope is Ahasuerus, then Guido may be a version of Haman, and Pompilia of Esther.

One last example will illustrate the variety of ways in which the biblical image of Persia was circulated in our period. It comes in William Tennant's 'Anster Fair' (1812), and it, too, concerns the feast given by Ahasuerus at the start of the Book of Esther, but this time done as a comic or mock-heroic parallel to a Scottish rural wedding:

> Not such a wassail, fam'd for social glee,
>   In Shushan's gardens long ago was held,
> When Ahasuerus, by a blythe decree,
>   His turban'd satraps to the bouse compell'd,
> And bagg'd their Persian paunches with a sea
>   Of wine, that from his carved gold they swill'd,
> Whilst overhead was stretch'd (a gorgeous show!)
> Blue blankets, silver-starr'd – a heav'n of calico!
>
> (Canto II, st. lxii)

Tennant has misremembered his biblical text; Ahasuerus does *not* force anyone to drink: 'the drinking was according to the law; none did compel' (1: 8), and of course the 'turban'd satraps' are a historical anachronism. But the point is still that the poet expects his readers to know the original biblical episode, and to appreciate his comic disrespectful treatment of a familiar stereotype. Even this slight example shows the pervasiveness of a certain kind of 'Persianness', associated with luxurious extravagance and supported by the authority of Scripture.

Ancient Greece

The ample influence of ancient Greek writings on nineteenth-century English poetry makes it particularly difficult to identify every poem that is infused, or enthused, by the Greek projection of the Persians. There are, for example, more than 150 poems in LION with a reference or references to Persia and Greece. There are various allusions to various historical figures such as Darius and Xerxes. The name of the former, for example, appears in sixty-four poems in LION, and the name of his son and successor, Xerxes occurs in ninety-three poems. Alfred Gibbs Campbell, in his poem 'Xerxes' (*Poems*, 1883), gives an interesting image of the Persian king:

> 'I, Xerxes, am, beyond all kings, the Great!
> The hills I level, and through mountains carve
> A goodly pathway for my stately fleet,
> And millions come and go at my behest.'
>
> (ll. 5–8)

Extravagance is a common attribute of Persia's kings in nineteenth-century poetry. Xerxes' ostentatious words are no exception; not only is he 'beyond all kings, the Great', but his power is equal to that of a god: hills are levelled and mountains are carved at his will. But in this particular example, the pomposity ascribed to a Persian king appears to be founded on a reputedly authentic historical narrative. Campbell's poem is set before the commencement of the battle of Salamis, the naval clash that took place in the narrow strait between Salamis and Attica between Persia and Greece in 480 BCE. According to Herodotus, the Persians, who outnumbered the Greeks, were being watched by Xerxes who had his throne placed on a hill overlooking the sea.[49] The image that the poet draws in the opening stanza is based on this historical narrative; the King of the Persians 'from the hill-top' (l. 1) sees 'The plains beneath him covered with his troops, | And, on the sea beyond, his gallant ships, | His heart swelled big with vanity and pride' (ll. 2–4). Curiously, the poem does not relate

the battle or reveal its grand finale; rather, it refers to the tragic ending that awaits the Persians. After Xerxes' tirade, the poet takes us to
his mind, where there is no sign of invincibility or supremacy, where
Xerxes is anxiously contemplating his future: "'Where, in a hundred
years, shall all this pomp, | These fleets and armies, and their master,
be?'" (ll. 11–12). This is where Campbell shows his poetic omnipo-
tence: Xerxes could have not worried about defeat before the battle;
on the contrary, he was assured of victory. But Campbell knows
more: he knows that Xerxes' forces are going to be vanquished. Yet
the ending that he chooses is not the defeat that the Persians suffered
at Salamis, but the tragic denouement that befell Xerxes' dynasty
almost 150 years later, when the Persians confronted 'a greater conqueror!' (l. 16), namely Alexander the Great.

A keyword search on LION for the name of some of the major
battles of the Greco-Persian Wars shows the obsession that the nineteenth century had for the Greeks. The name Marathon, for instance,
appears in 171 poems, Salamis in 110, Thermopylae in 134, and
Plataea in 21. Elizabeth Barrett Browning's long narrative poem, *The
Battle of Marathon* (1820), which she wrote at the age of twelve and
which was privately printed by her proud father, is a fine example of
nineteenth-century fascination with the history of the Greeks. The
poem's introductory lines are indicative of its substance and underly-
ing tenets: 'The war of Greece with Persia's haughty King, | No vulgar
strain, eternal Goddess, sing!' (ll. 1–2). The young poet, consciously
imitating Homer, sees Greek history as a worthy epic subject, and
invokes her divine Muse accordingly. But this subject has its own
peculiarities. Greece is set, as a nation, not against Persia as country
or kingdom, but against an individual; the war of Greece is with 'Persia's haughty King', who was Darius, the third Achaemenid king after
Cyrus and Cambyses. His image is fixed in Greek historical myth,
like that of all Persia's kings, as a type of the insatiable, over-reaching
tyrant, whose unimaginable wealth and apparently limitless power
make him blind to his fate. Nineteenth-century Hellenism embraced
this ancient image of Persia. The Persians are almost always barbaric
when they are set against the Greeks; Augustine Hickey's apostrophe
in 'On to Freedom' (*Utterances*, 1865), 'O! thou poor barbarian,
Xerxes!' (l. 17) is a typical instance.

'We are all Greeks', said Percy Shelley in the 'Preface' to *Hellas* (1822), expressing a powerful conceit that deemed many of the
greatest achievements of Western civilisation to be refinements of
classical Greek culture and society. Almost every major nineteenth-
century poet, and a host of minor ones, pay tribute to this notion,

which is often made the vehicle of a kind of transhistorical fantasy, as in Algernon Charles Swinburne's 'Athens: An Ode':

> Sons of Athens born in spirit and truth are all born free men;
> Most of all, we, nurtured where the north wind holds his reign:
> Children all we sea-folk of the Salaminian seamen,
> Sons of them that beat back Persia they that beat back Spain.
>
> (ll. 13–16)[50]

Persia here figures as a matrix from which the Spanish Armada springs; it is an archetype of tyranny. And like Barrett Browning, Swinburne sees this tyranny embodied in a single figure: in an epitome of the Hellenistic view, the Greeks are 'They that had no lord', and these free people 'made the Great King lesser than a slave [. . .] King by king came up against them, sire and son, and turned to flee' (ll. 78, 83). So prevalent is the binary opposition between the freedom-loving Greeks and the despotic Persians that exceptions are striking – even when they come in poems of poor quality. In 'Liberty' (*Songs of the Army of the Night*, 1892), Francis William Adams points out that the opposition looks different from the perspective of the oppressed industrial masses of the late nineteenth century:

> There were Greeks who fought and perished,
>   Won from Persians deathless graves.
> Had *we* lived then, we're aware that
>   We'd have been those same Greeks' slaves!
>
> (ll. 9–12)

It must be admitted that even here the Persians are not really let off. It is just that the Greeks are reduced to their level.

Modern Persia

Most nineteenth-century poets did not think of the state of modern Persia as a subject for poetry, and stuck to older perceptions and images of the country in their works.[51] But those few who did write on it seem to have had different approaches, since no uniformity can be found in their representations. In some cases, a 'modern' understanding of the cause of Persia's decline as a great power may underlie representations of its ancient history, as in Tennyson's 'Persia', which we looked at earlier, and in which the image of the country, as Brantlinger remarks, is 'locked away in a charming past'.[52] There are other works that display political perceptions in a more direct fashion, such as those that were written on contemporary Anglo-Persian diplomatic contacts and exchanges. Such poems are highly politicised, but their tone is variable, ranging from the serious to the satirical. Take 'The Persian Ambassador', as an example. This anonymous poem is written on the occasion of Mirza Abul-Hasan's visit to Britain in 1810–11:

> The Persian Ambassador's come to town;
> Heigh-ho! Says Boney;
> And he is a person of rank and renown,
> Says in Persia they'll knock all French politics down,
> With their *Parlez-vous*, *Voulez-vous*, gammon, and spinach too;
> Heigh-ho! Says Emperor Boney.
>
> (ll. 1–6)[53]

'The Persian Ambassador' is, in one sense, a celebratory poem; the British had good reasons to celebrate the arrival of the Persian ambassador whose presence in Britian implied diplomatic triumph over their long-standing French rival.[54] Other satirical poems use familiar images of Oriental despotism and backwardness as a means of attacking, not just Persia itself, but contemporary Britain. Montesquieu's immensely popular *Lettres persanes* (1721) set the model and the fashion for such works, by which aspects of modern Western society could be either validated or disparaged by contrast with their Oriental equivalents. Thomas Moore's 'Letter VI. From Abdallah in London, To Mohassan in Ispahan', for example, is one of his *Intercepted Letters, or Twopenny Post-Bag*, a collection which originally appeared in 1813 under Moore's pseudonym 'Thomas Brown, the Younger', and which consists of skits on the reactionary politics of the Prince Regent and the Tory ministry, religious hypocrisy, sexual misconduct in high society, and other liberal targets.[55] Moore, in the first footnote to the poem, clearly shows his hand:

> I have made many inquiries about this Persian gentleman, but cannot satisfactorily ascertain who he is. From his notions of Religious Liberty, however, I conclude that he is an importation of Ministers, and he has arrived just in time to assist the P – – e and Mr. L – ck – e in their new Oriental Plan of Reform. See the second of these Letters.

'The P – – e' is, of course, the Prince Regent; 'Mr. L – ck – e' is the now-obscure diplomat and political writer Gould Francis Leckie, whose *Essay on the Practice of the British Government, distinguished from the abstract Theory on which it is supposed to be founded* had been published in 1812 and savagely reviewed by Francis Jeffrey in the *Edinburgh Review*.[56] Leckie's book is a defence of absolute monarchy and an attack on parliamentary government, and not surprisingly Moore associates these political views with Persian or Oriental despotism. Letter II, to which he refers here, purports to be a letter addressed to Leckie by one of the Prince Regent's entourage, who commissions Leckie to compile

> A Plan of radical Reform;
> Compil'd and chos'n, as best you can,
> In Turkey or at Ispahan . . .
>
> (ll. 43–5)

'Letter VI' continues this theme: it opens with Abdallah complimenting his friend on living under such a regime:

> Whilst thou, Mohassan, (happy thou!)
> Dost daily bend thy loyal brow
> Before our King – our Asia's treasure!
> Nutmeg of Comfort; Rose of Pleasure! –
> And bear'st as many kicks and bruises
> As the said Rose and Nutmeg chooses;
> Thy head still near the bowstring's borders,
> And but left on till further orders –
>
> (ll. 1–8)

The subject of this poem, however, is not political despotism but religious intolerance; Abdallah praises Britain for being as 'enlightened' as Persia on this subject. He compares the supposedly mild repression of the Sunni sect in Persia with the treatment of Irish Catholics:

> The same mild views of Toleration
> Inspire, I find, this button'd nation,
> Whose Papists (full as giv'n to rogue,
> And only Sunnites with a brogue)
> Fare just as well, with all their fuss,
> As rascal Sunnites do with us.
>
> (ll. 63–8)

My purpose here is not to examine Moore's polemic from the British side, but to look at the Persian material, so to speak, from which he has made his satirical costume. Abdallah is in some respects a forerunner of Hajjî in Morier's *The Adventures of Hajjî Baba of Ispahan in England* (1828), the sequel to *Hajjî Baba* (1824).[57] Both works follow a first-person narrative, and both mingle familiar stereotypes with shrewd cultural understanding. Abdallah, like Hajjî, pokes fun at the national characteristics and temperament of his people. One quality of the Persians that Morier, through Hajjî, pokes fun at is excessive flattery. Hajjî himself is an epitome of such behaviour (his fawning behaviour towards his superiors is repeatedly displayed, as in his encounters with the chief of Turcoman thieves, 'Mirza Ahmak' or the Persian Shah). Moore's poem opens, as we have seen, with just such an allusion (again, I am not concerned here with the implication that the Prince Regent would like the same kind of servile flattery from *his* courtiers). Although Moore did not have Morier's first-hand experience of Persia, he makes up for it with a series of footnotes referring to learned Orientalist authorities and travel writers. The specific comparison of the Sunnis to the Catholics is attributed to Barthélmy d'Herbelot, author of the *Bibliothèque orientale*. Abdallah's allusion to a trivial difference in religious ritual between the two sects is supported by a quotation from George Forster's *A Voyage round the World in His Britannic Majesty's Sloop Resolution, Commanded by Capt. James Cook* (1777). Abdallah also refers to theological disputes over the authenticity of a chapter of the Qur'an, and Moore's footnote referring to 'Picart's Account of the Mahometan Sects' points the reader to one of the volumes of Bernard Picart's *Cérémonies et coutumes religieuses de tous les peuples du monde* (1723–37).[58] And yet, at the same time, Moore has his speaker caricature Islamic ideas of the afterlife, in which sexual indulgence goes along with abstinence from alcohol: 'A Persian's Heav'n is eas'ly made, | 'Tis but black eyes and lemonade' (ll. 32–3). Such satire is 'eas'ly made' indeed.

The despotic nature of the Persian kings is noticed in other poems of the century. 'The Shah', for example, is a ballad sung by agricultural labourers in England in the 1870s on the occasion of Nasir ul-Din Shah's visit to England in 1873; the ballad criticises him and relates the labourers' own conditions in England to the situation in Persia. Although the public reception of the king was generally good across the country, 'The Shah', unlike 'The Persian Ambassador', does not celebrate the royal visit. On the contrary, it uses it to condemn the king for the current state of his kingdom:

A despot King of a serfdom land is
     The Shah, the Shah.
Where his will is law, dealt out by the hand of
     The Shah, the Shah.

Where filth and pestilence, famine, decay,
Is of small concern, so his will they obey,
And robe with diamonds brilliant and gay,
The Shah, the Shah, the Shah.

(ll. 9–12)[59]

The poem has a lilting rhythmic structure to it, but this does not lessen its critical tone and content. The repetition of 'The Shah, the Shah' may sound as though the crowds are cheerfully hailing, but the repetitions also signal, and accentuate, the shah's guilt for his country's impoverishment and degradation.

The variety of responses to contemporary Persia may be illustrated by a wholly different response to the same visit, 'The Shah', the record of a real conversation with an old Romany woman, according to Charles Godfrey Leland in *English-gipsy Songs* (1875):

'Yes, my master, I've seen the Shah,'
    Said old Dame Petulengro to me.
'And I says to my son, "You needn't talk,
    For I know he's a bit of a Rommany."'

'I've seen all sorts of Gipsy folk,
    Our own and them from beyond the sea;
I knows the eye, and I knows the walk:
    I tell you he's somehow a Rommany.

'Other folks' eyes may be werry good eyes,
    I won't say never how *that* may be;
But this I say, that that Persian rye's
    Have got the shine of the Rommany.'

And as she talked in her Gipsy tongue,
    With just one Persian word in three,
It seemed as if she couldn't be wrong,
    And the Shah were a bit of a Rommany.

Leland was an American humourist (famous in his own day for the *Hans Breitman Ballads*). He was also a pioneering folklorist and historian of the Gipsy people. This odd little poem is also supported by a footnote, in which Leland, after affirming the truth of the incident, comments:

No effort has been made to introduce Persian words in these lines, and it chances that the proportion of them is rather less here than usually occurs. The following, however, belong to that language: Avali, Persian *bali*; rye, Pers. *ray*; rakker, Pers. *rakídan*; kush-ti, Pers. *khush*; shuned, Pers. *shun-ídan*; puri, Pers. *pír*; Ma (prohibitative), Pers. *ma*; Gorgiko (from Gorgio), Pers. *kh'ája*, pronounced *khorja*.

This happens to be one of the rare instances in nineteenth-century poetry in which the Persian language is deployed, if not in the poem itself then at least in its paratext. Whatever the accuracy of Leland's ethnographic or linguistic views (it seems that there are no obvious genetic links between Romany and Iranian ethnic groups according to modern science), the interest of the poem lies in its balancing of an ignorant, intuitive kind of knowledge, belonging to 'Dame Petulengro', with a more informed 'Western' perspective, and the meeting ground between these two is the figure of 'The Shah'. The shah is not represented here as a despot; he is still an exotic foreigner, but is his dignity enhanced or undermined by his being 'a bit of a Rommany'?

The kind of literary-historical investigation that I have undertaken in the first two chapters of this study, whereby I have attempted to divide the Western idea of Persia into its diverse conceptual and thematic constituents, might not have appealed to nineteenth-century British readers and writers. Persia was attractive because the protean nature of its conception allowed various types of intellectual and imaginative engagement; Persia was ancient yet familiar, foreign yet well textualised, nebulous yet demarcated within certain well-established strands of thought. Rather than dismembering it to its key ideological components, the Victorians would have thus preferred to engage with Persia as it was, at an intersection of the multitude of designs and discourses that embodied it. As such, my intention is not to strip Persia of its historic charm; my breakdown of the nineteenth-century perceptions of Persia has been to convey something of the range of its connotation. However, it needs to be noted again that my study of the Persian presence is not conclusive. Completeness, as I note at the Preface, is not possible; Persia in the imagination of nineteenth-century Britain embodied a far too diverse set of ideological, political, cultural, and historical phenomena for that to be feasible. True, it is possible, as I have done here, to provide a representative sample of different nineteenth-century poems, based on their mode of engagement with Persia; but it is very difficult to examine and categorise every nineteenth-century English poem on the basis of its approach to Persia. This is particularly true of the three case-studies that will be studied in the following chapters in this book. There exists behind the conception of each of these works a complex matrix of aesthetic, political, and ideological motives that makes it impossible to boil down their engagement with Persia into one theme or topic. There is, however, one connecting thread that links these works to one another: the Persia of each of them is imaginary in its own way.

Notes

1. The text is from Allen, *The Lower Slopes*, p. 28.
2. Herodotus, *Histories*, Book VII, 134, pp. 458–9. All references to the *Histories* are from de Sélincourt's translation.
3. Herodotus, *Histories*, Book VII, 136, pp. 459–60.
4. Bongie, *Exotic Memories*, pp. 16–17.
5. Brantlinger, *Rule of Darkness*, p. 85
6. Wilberforce-Clarke, *The Dīvān-i-Hāfiz*, p. 95.
7. For more on Jones's poem, see Chapter 1, pp. 45–8.
8. See LION's 1868 edition of the poem from *The Poetical Works*.
9. For Shah Abbas's renown in the West, see Chapter 1, p. 26.
10. Later in the poem we encounter 'the glowing Pomegranate-lined grove, | Where the Bulbul sings still in the Sun-brightened day' (ll. 18–19). The 'spicy zephyr' belongs to the large poetic family of spicy winds, breezes, gales, etc. associated with the East; LION has several occurrences before Wortley; for example, Erasmus Darwin's 'The Loves of the Plants', Part Two of *The Botanic Garden* (1799), vol. 1, p. 399.
11. 'Nouzhetos' appears as the name of a female slave in the episode of 'Ganem, the Slave of Love'.
12. For an analysis of nineteenth-century British translation of Hafiz, see Javadi, *Persian Literary Influence*, pp. 193–208; for a list of references to Hafiz in the nineteenth-century, see Yohannan's *Persian Poetry*, 'Index', p. 359.
13. Toru Dutt (1856–77) is a noted figure in nineteenth-century Anglo-Indian poetry. Her 'The Roses of Saadi' (*A Sheaf Gleaned in French Fields*, 1880) is also amongst LION's Persian poems.
14. For more information on Khayyám's life and poetics, see Chapter 4, pp. 146–50.
15. See LION's edition of the poem.
16. FitzGerald, *Rubáiyát* (1872), p. xxii.
17. There are more than thirty-five poems in LION that deploy the name Omar in an Islamic context (for example the 'Omar' who was a friend of the Prophet Mohammed, mentioned in Robert Southey's 'Mohammed; A Fragment Written in 1799'), but none has a specifically Persian focus.
18. Other Persian cities appear in LION's list: Tebriz in four, Yezd in four, and Tehran in one.
19. For more on *Ferishtah's Fancies*, see Chapter 5.
20. For a list of nineteenth-century translations of Sa'di, see Davis, *The Oxford History of Literary Translation in English*, pp. 333–4.

21. Javadi's *Persian Literary Influence* contains a chapter (pp. 184–93) on Edwin Arnold's poetic treatment of Sa'di; also see Yohannan, *Persian Poetry*, p. 183 and p. 185, and his 'Index' (p. 369) for a catalogue of citations and translations of Sa'di in English.
22. Lewisohn and Shackle, 'Introduction', p. xix.
23. Nicholson's books were the only two notable scholarly works on Attar in the first two decades of the twentieth century. Nicholson was a great admirer of Sufi literature and had studied Persian with Edward G. Browne. See Yohannan's *Persian Poetry* (p. 224) for more information.
24. Ernst, 'On Losing One's Head', p. 331 and p. 336.
25. See LION's edition of the poem. Another version of this tale has often been retold in studies of Attar's biography. In his 'Narratology and Realities in the Study of Attar' in *Attār and the Persian Sufi Tradition* (pp. 57–74) Mohammad Este'lami cites the story, but his account, too, is borrowed from Nur al-Din Abd al-Rahman Jami's Nafahat al-uns: 'one day, Attar was very busy with his patients, when a dervish who was begging in front of his pharmacy asked him to give something in the name of God. Attar was so busy that he didn't have the time to pay attention to the beggar's request, at which the latter became angry with him and said: "Sir you are too attached to the worldly life. How will you ever pass away?" Attar replied: "Just as you will!" The beggar thereupon lay down, invoked "Allah", and died. Suddenly, thereafter, Attar allowed his business to be plundered, and became a devotee to Sufism' (p. 58).
26. Hindley, the author of *Persian Lyrics, or scattered poems, from the Diwani-i-Hafiz* (1800), was an early nineteenth-century scholar of Persian literature from Manchester.
27. On Attar's literary corpus, see Lewisohn and Shackle, 'Introduction', pp. xvii–xxvii and pp. xviii–xix, and Shackle, 'Representations of 'Attar', p. 168.
28. Irwin, *For Lust of Knowing*, p. 151.
29. Shackle, 'Representations of 'Attar', pp. 168–70.
30. For more information on FitzGerald's treatment of Attar's *Mantiq al-tair*, see Javadi, *Persian Literary Influence*, pp. 167–70; Yohannan, *Persian Poetry*, p. 100, p. 165, and pp. 168–70.
31. For more on Firdausi, his *Shahnameh*, and his place in Persia's literary culture, see Chapter 3, pp. 115–17.
32. Warner's translation, according to Davis, 'is based on an inferior text as were, necessarily, the eighteenth- and nineteenth-century versions of parts of the text by, respectively, Champion and Atkinson'; Davis, *Epic and Sedition*, p. xvii.
33. For a detailed analysis of Arnold's translation of Firdausi's 'Sohrab', see Chapter 3.
34. Davis, *Epic and Sedition*, pp. 3–4.
35. Browne, *A Literary History*, vol. 2, p. 142.

36. Atkinson, 'Editor's Preface', p. vii.
37. For further notes on the similarities between the *Shahnameh* and the *Iliad*, see Chapter 3, pp. 124–5.
38. Sykes, *A History of Persia*, vol. 2, p. 62.
39. Cowell, 'Persian Poetry', p. 281.
40. Jones, 'The Tenth Anniversary Discourse', p. 221.
41. Ibid. pp. 221–2.
42. For example, the comma after 'sample' represents a grammatical elision: 'which' needs to be supplied.
43. Bailey ignores Mohl's French (prose) translation, assuming he was unaware of its existence.
44. The phrase 'genius ample' contains, but cannot be contained by, the word 'sample'. Sixty thousand as the number of lines to have been composed by Firdausi was, and still is, very much a myth; discounting those manuscripts that have added verses, most manuscripts of the *Shahnameh* have approximately around 100,000 lines, equal to 50,000 couplets (or *bait* in Persian).
45. For a summary of the biblical narrative of Esther, see Chapter 1, p. 21.
46. There may be an allusion to Ecclesiastes 7: 2–4: 'It is better to go to the house of mourning than to go to the house of feasting [. . .] The heart of the wise is in the house of mourning; but the heart of fools is in the house of mirth.'
47. 'Monna Innominata' was first published in *A Pageant and Other Poems* (1881). The text here is from Crump and Flowers, *Rossetti*, p. 298.
48. *The Ring and the Book* was first published in 1868–9. The text here is from Hawlin and Burnet, *The Poetical Works of Robert Browning*, vol. 9, p. 93.
49. We read in *Histories*: 'Xerxes watched the course of the battle from the base of Mt Aegaleos, across the strait of Salamis'; Herodotus, *Histories*, Book VIII, 90, p. 531.
50. The poem is dated April 1881; text from *The Poems* (1905).
51. For a discussion of the British perception of nineteenth-century Persia, see Chapter 1, pp. 53–5.
52. Brantlinger, *Rule of Darkness*, p. 9.
53. The poem was published in *The Statesman* on 25 January 1810.
54. For more on Mirza Abul-Hasan and the reasons behind his presence in Britain, see Chapter 1, p. 59.
55. Text from Moore's *Poetical Works* (1841–2).
56. For Jeffrey's review, see Jeffery, *General Politics*, pp. 145–80.
57. For more on *Hajjî Baba*, see Chapter 1, pp. 57–63.
58. *Cérémonies et coutumes religieuses de tous les peuples du monde* is a nine-volume folio published in Amsterdam by Jean Fredrick Bernard, and profusely illustrated by Bernard Picart. With its display of the harmful consequences of fanaticism, and its commendations of theological broadmindedness, *Cérémonies* is considered to be of the earliest cultural ventures in Europe towards religious toleration.

59. It is not clear where and when the ballad was first published. The poem appears in Appendix 5 (pp. 229–31) in Wright, *The Persians Amongst the English*. It can also be found in Clayden's *The Revolt of the Field* (pp. 100–3). Clayden gives more background information about the song, though he does not speak of its exact date of publication, nor does he say where it was published. Clayden, however, does mention (p. 99) that the author of the ballad is the 'witty secretary of the Union, Mr. Henry Taylor', who composed the song on the occasion of their 'late illustrious visitor, the Shah of Persia's presence in England'.

Chapter 3

'Sohrab and Rustum'

'Sohrab and Rustum' (1853) is an adaptation of the story of 'Sohrab' in Abu'l-Qasim Firdausi's *Shahnameh* ('the Book of Kings'). Firdausi, however, is transfused in Matthew Arnold's poem indirectly and without consideration of his specific linguistic or poetic traits. Arnold did not know Persian. He read, in French, Charles Augustin Sainte-Beuve's 'Le Livre des Rois, par le poëte persan Firdousi, publié et traduit par M. Jules Mohl', a review of Julius von Mohl's French translation of the *Shahnameh* which featured a synopsis of 'Sohrab'.[1] Arnold did not have access to Mohl's French translation either, though he had indirect access to it through Sainte-Beuve's rendition of Mohl's ideas and, in some cases, his actual phrasing. In this manifold sequence of textual interactions, only Mohl could, in fact, read Firdausi in its original language, and neither Sainte-Beuve, nor Arnold, was in a position to judge the value of Mohl's scholarship or the fidelity of his translation. Sainte-Beuve approved of Mohl because their ideas on epic poetry coincided, and Arnold trusted the fidelity of Sainte-Beuve's judgement and rendition of Mohl for the same reason. This complex process of cultural transmission has conditioned Arnold's appropriation of Firdausi's story, setting, and characters in 'Sohrab and Rustum'. But however secondary and indirect Arnold's understanding of Firdausi and the *Shahnameh* may have been, his rendition of 'Sohrab' remains unusually faithful to its original. There are, of course, diversions and variations, and it is difficult to discern why Arnold's fidelity to Firdausi oscillates through the poem. The explanation must be sought at a more abstract level, which belongs to Arnold's own idea of what he was doing in taking hold of the poem in the first place. But leaving aside psychological explanations, which may reveal that Arnold was perhaps wrestling with his own over-mighty father, my purpose in this chapter is to first reveal, then examine, the processes at work in the conception of 'Sohrab and Rustum'. To do so, I will begin by surveying the sociopolitical developments that led not only to the formation of the *Shahnameh* but to its recognition as a book of epic poetry. Knowledge of the historical context behind the *Shahnameh* is necessary here because it was crucial in Sainte-Beuve's appreciation and identification of Firdausi as an epic poet. By recognising Firdausi as a Homer-like literary figure, and writing on Mohl's translation of his *Shahnameh*, Sainte-Beuve was effectively challenging the authority of any modern poet to rival a primary epic poet such as Firdausi. But Arnold did the opposite: he overlooked the cultural supremacy and singularity that Sainte-Beuve had ascribed to Firdausi, dismissing Sainte-Beuve's ideas on the unrepeatability of the epic moment and epic poetry. Following this, I will focus on 'Sohrab' and a canonical aspect of its conception which appears to have held Arnold's attention. I will subsequently explore Sainte-Beuve's delineation of Firdausi and 'Sohrab', and then conclude the chapter with a comparative reading of the two poems to highlight how and why 'Sohrab and Rustum' stays close to its Persian counterpart at some points and swerves away from it at others.

Not long after his return to Paris in 1849, after spending a year in Belgium as a visiting professor at the University of Liège, Charles Augustin Sainte-Beuve began to write a series of essays and reviews on current literary topics to be published in the newspaper *Le Constitutionnel*. Named after their day of appearance, *Causeries du lundi* ('Monday chats') were published in *Le Constitutionnel* for three years from 1849 to 1852 and later for another six years from 1861 to 1867. One of these essays, published on 11 February 1850, was Sainte-Beuve's 'review' of Julius von Mohl's translation of the *Shahnameh*, the national epic of Iran. The *Shahnameh*, in Persian literary tradition, stands as the single most important source of the formation and definition of Persian Iranian (Persian) identity. Firdausi's book is, at once, a versified chronicle, an epic cycle, and a compendium of historical myths and legends that exalts Iranian national identity by celebrating pride in the institution of the ancient Persian monarchy and the efforts of those who perpetuated the empire. Firdausi saved Persia's collective past through versifying its oral and written traditions, writing over 50,000 lines of poetry in Persian, without using much Arabic, the language of conquest as well as of the new religion of Islam. With the coming of the Muslims in the seventh century, the language of the conquered Persians was threatened by the impending influence of Arabic. Persia was now part of a world where Arabic was the lingua franca; more and more Arabic words were being infused into Persian, and the Middle Persian script was being slowly replaced with the Arabic alphabet. Poetry written in Arabic also becoming more prevalent.[2] But during the reign of

the Abbasid caliphate (750–1258), a rather unanticipated development started to unfold in Greater Khurasan (consisting of today's
Iran, Uzbekistan, Tajikistan, Afghanistan and Central Asia): eastern
provinces in Persia and particularly Khurasan saw a renaissance of
Persian language and culture.[3] Persian began to gradually reclaim its
former political legitimacy under the Tahirids (821–73 CE) and Saffa-
rids (861–1003). These ruling houses claimed to have been of Persian
origin, though culturally they were 'highly Arabicised'.[4] For that,
the growth of Persian identity remained limited under their administration; 'neither the Tāhirids nor the Saffārids', observes A. C. S.
Peacock, 'for very different reasons, promoted Persian literature seriously, with the exception of a few fragments of verse composed as
experiments at their courts'.[5] But during the Samanids (819–999 CE),
Persian eventually flourished as a courtly language, though Samanids' imperial pretensions, too, were driven by political incentives.[6]
They, nevertheless, promoted both poetry and prose in Persian (and
Arabic).[7] Persian poetry, in particular, became a robust cultural force
during their reign with verse such as epic poetry receiving unprecedented attention.[8]

Firdausi's composition of the *Shahnameh* started during the
rule of the Samanids in c. 977 and ended in 1010 in the reign of
the Qaznavids (977–1186), the successors of the Samanids. Sultan
Mahmoud, the Qaznavid ruler, had an interest in Persian poetry,
not only because myriads of panegyrics in Persian were dedicated
to him, but because Persian poetry, especially that which celebrated
Persia's imperial past, could be deployed as a vehicle for monarchical self-validation. To claim legitimacy, the Turkish sultan was at
times even attributed a Sasanian genealogy, though this was not necessarily unique to him; other contemporary dynasties claimed pre-
Islamic Persian roots too.[9] It was against this political background
that Firdausi gained the patronage of Sultan Mahmoud, at least for
the first years of his vast undertaking.[10] There are numerous legends
as to how Firdausi was assigned the task and how the news of his
genius reached the Qaznavid's court.[11] We now know that Firdausi
took up the unfinished work of Abu Mansur Ahmad Daqiqi, a young
poet who had been murdered when only about a thousand lines of
what would have been his version of a '*Shahnameh*' had been completed.[12] But crucial in the formation of Firdausi's *Shahnameh* was
also Firdausi's own social background and the cultural context in
which he had been nurtured. Firdausi was a product of Khurasan: a
centre of national, political, and cultural movements since the eighth
century. He also came from a distinct social background; he was a

dehqan, a member of the 'landed gentry', whose pedigree went back to the Sasanians and whose national consciousness was entrenched in Persia's antiquarian past.[13] What had reached Firdausi through his heritage and what he had learned through living in Khurasan were hugely influential in the development of his national views. Firdausi was conversant in Persia's national folk tales and thus capable of composing a work with the scope and the magnitude of the *Shahnameh*.

'Sohrab'

'Sohrab' is by far the most well-known story of the *Shahnameh*. It is, briefly told, a tragic tale of the accidental killing of a son by his father. In this episode, Rostam, the Hercules-like figure of Iranian mythology, unknowingly kills his son, Sohrab. The youthful, untried hero is the natural son of a brief liaison between Rostam and Tahmine, a princess of a neighbouring state. Raised by his mother, Sohrab longs to be acknowledged by the father he has never seen. He shows early prowess as a warrior and, in the service of Turan, Iran's traditional foe, he leads an invasion of Iran; his secret hope is to provoke Rostam to reveal himself. But Rostam, the man whom Sohrab seeks, is the chief guardian of the Iranian monarchy, and the young Sohrab is unaware that in the scheme of things in the *Shahnameh*, there can only be one outcome if Iran is endangered: the threat has to be eliminated, however tragic the emotional cost. By appearing in the guise of a mighty warrior from Turan, Sohrab thus ensures that his quest will lead to his death. Through a series of misunderstandings and mishaps, Rostam does not discover Sohrab's true identity, nor does he unveil that of his to Sohrab until he has mortally wounded him in single combat.

The murder of Sohrab is precipitated by the weakness of the Iranian shah (Kai Kavus) and mediated by a ruthless fate that is determined to end Sohrab's life at the hand of his father. The accidental nature of Sohrab's death is, in fact, the most excruciating element in the composition of Firdausi's story. The narrative of paternal filicide is by itself a source of great discomfort, let alone when the unfolding of the events that leads to its culmination is discerned by forces that appear to be out of human control. But there is a reason to this; the importance of that which Firdausi, with his cruel arrangement of the narrative, aims to convey to his readers surpasses the value that the life of a young man as extraordinary and as dear as Sohrab may have. Sohrab, in other words, is a victim of the royal grounds of the *Shahnameh*. He is a sacrifice to the nationalistic design of the book. Firdausi's unflinching vision has purposefully placed Sohrab, as a threat to Iran, against his father, as the guardian of Iran, to dramatise the significance of the Iranian monarchy. The *Shahnameh*, as noted at the beginning, is essentially a celebration of Iran (though not a celebration of kingship; only a few kings in the *Shahnameh* are given 'what looks like unalloyed approbation').[14] Firdausi celebrates Iran through an elevated, and at times critical, narration of the sequence of antiquarian Iranian royal houses; 'Fifty reigns', as Dick Davis explains, 'are described [in the *Shahnameh*], and the poem is [. . .] in its most basic sense both a chronicle of rulers and a (largely legendary) genealogy of the ruling families'.[15] But the thematic force that carries forward the narrative of 'Sohrab' opposes, and undermines, this fundamental premise of the *Shahnameh*. Sohrab arrives at the border of Iran with the intention of overthrowing the Iranian monarchy; no other man than Rostam, he believes, deserves to rule Iran; that means Sohrab's search for his father is also a quest to make Rostam king (Sohrab is of the same mind as to his own position at court; he believes he is the rightful ruler of Turan). But Sohrab is young and gullible. We see various manifestations of this during the story: for instance, in his clash with Gordafarid where the Iranian lioness relies on her femme fatale to flee from Sohrab's uncanny physical force. But Sohrab's actions are imprudent and thoughtless within the grand framework of the *Shahnameh*, too; Sohrab, for instance, is credulous to think that he can interfere with the immutable arrangements of Firdausi's royal composition, that he can throne or dethrone kings. With that token, Sohrab can also be taken as the victim of his own youth, which is his foremost feature and the precocity of his heroism. Sohrab dies at the end because his perverse, youthful method of locating his father places him up against not only his father's fatherland, which is also in part his own, but also against the unbreakable structures of the *Shahnameh*.

Firdausi represents this bitter collision as ineluctable, decreed by 'Fate'. But he is, in effect, the man who orchestrates Sohrab's demise. Numerous incidents in the story show how Firdausi's manipulation of events, however improbable, ensures Sohrab's death. Rostam, for instance, cannot see that the mighty Sohrab is his son; not only does he fail to recognise the physical resemblances, his more instinctive paternal feelings also seem to fail him. Firdausi does not reveal why Rostam insists on hiding his identity either, or rather the explanations he offers seem inadequate. But if 'Fate' is to blame, this fate is embodied in a patriotic poet who has made a blind man, a liar, and a heart-broken father of his great and pious hero. Let us not forget that we speak here of Rostam, the most iconic hero of the *Shahnameh*. Rostam is Firdausi's supreme creation. Not only does he represent absolute physical strength, he also amalgamates benevolence and decency, intellect and wisdom, courage and bravery, patience and tolerance.

What, then, is the cause of such a sequence of thoughtless actions which end in the death of his son? This is a vexed question to which there is no certain answer. There are other mythic heroes who are similarly problematic, and their actions can embrace appalling irrational violence as well as magnanimity and moral rectitude. The obvious example would be Hercules, who slaughters his own children in a fit of madness in, for instance, Euripides' *The Madness of Hercules* (c. 416 BCE); though this madness is in one sense inflicted on him by the Gods (or by the Goddess who hates him, Hera, wife of Zeus). In another sense, this external affliction symbolises an internal flaw.

The tragic encounter between Rostam and Sohrab may seem like a single episode in the long and dreadful war between Iranians and their old enemies, the Turanains, but it is not simply one among many narratives of the long-standing struggle between these peoples. 'Sohrab' is an emblematic representation of intergenerational conflict, a conflict that is also a clash of moral and spiritual values. These values are not distributed according to a simple binary opposition between old and young, today and yesterday, wisdom and foolishness, forbearance and ambition. The *Shahnameh* itself is a complex, many-layered work whose concepts of fatherhood, heroism, politics, religion, acceptable social behaviour or attitude towards the Deity and religions cannot be reduced to formulas either within the scheme of the work as a whole, or within any particular episode. The sacrifice of the son by the father resonates in every culture and first Sainte-Beuve then Arnold were quick to seize on some of the parallels offered by the story of 'Sohrab' to their own familiar myths.[16]

'Sohrab' through Sainte-Beuve

Arnold made use of Persian themes in two of his works: first in 'Sohrab and Rustum' and second in 'A Persian Passion Play'. The latter was a prose essay, which he wrote in 1871 for *Cornhill Magazine*, and in which he looked at the Shiite Persians' commemoration of the martyrdom of Imam Husain.[17] But this was nearly two decades since his first attempt at the Persian subject. Arnold wrote 'Sohrab and Rustum' some time between December 1852 and May 1853, although he may have begun working on it at an earlier date. After many interruptions, Arnold eventually corrected and finalised the poem for publication in *Poems. A New Edition*, which came out in November 1853. The volume was a selection from two of his earlier collections: *The Strayed Reveller and Other Poems* (1849) and *Empedocles on Etna, and Other Poems* (1852) with a critical preface and new poems among which was 'Sohrab and Rustum'. We do not know when exactly, but Arnold had come across a summary of 'Sohrab' in Sir John Malcolm's *History of Persia, from the most early period to the present time* (1815). In a footnote in the fourth chapter to the first volume of his *History of Persia*, Malcolm gives a sketch of 'Sohrab'.[18] But however novel Malcolm's note may have appeared to Arnold, his decision to write his rendition of Firdausi's story came after he read Sainte-Beuve. Arnold speaks of this in his letter of 6 January 1854 to Sainte-Beuve:

> [. . .] it is in one of your charming Causeries that I found the information about the episode of the death of Sohrab, which gave me the courage finally to begin my poem. I had read a very brief account of it in a note in Sir John Malcolm's history of Persia, and at that time conceived the plan to put it into verse; but I found myself immediately obliged to desist, for the lack of details which I did not manage to learn until later, on reading your article.[19]

James Atkinson's translation of the *Shahnameh* could have also been a possible source. In his notes reprinted in his *Poetical Works*, Arnold says that he would have used a prose English translation, had he been able to find one. John D. Yohannan takes this as an indication that Arnold might have been 'acquainted' with Atkinson's *Soohrab: a Poem, freely translated from the original Persian of Firdoosee* (1814) or his *Shāhnāme: Abridgment and Selections* (1832).[20] But even if Arnold had come across an English translation of the episode, or even if he could have read Firdausi in Persian, the impetus that he would have gained would have probably been less convincing than that which he obtained from reading Sainte-Beuve's redaction. Arnold was a great admirer of Sainte-Beuve. His critical ideas, particularly with regard to Homer, almost mirrored those of Sainte-Beuve.[21] His views on the role and nature of literature were also largely influenced by Sainte-Beuve: 'every time that I am saddened by considering the literature of our day', Arnold wrote to

Sainte-Beuve in his letter of 6 January 1854, 'I recoil more than ever towards you; and even though you mostly speak of French literature, still, as you consider everything from a universal point of view, everyone can always find instruction in reading you'.[22] It is of no surprise then that Arnold found immediate interest in Firdausi and 'Sohrab' after learning about them in Sainte-Beuve's essay.

Sainte-Beuve's 'Le Livre des Rois' appears to begin with a joke: 'Don't worry: this title, The Book of Kings, has nothing seditious about it.'[23] But not many readers of Le Constitutionnel on 11 December 1850 perhaps found this funny. It was almost two years to the day since Louis Napoleon was elected President of the Second Republic, following the overthrow in February 1848 of Louis-Philippe, the last king of France. History was, of course, waiting to cap Sainte-Beuve's joke, because in another year Louis Napoleon would launch the coup d'état that led to his being crowned Emperor in 1852. But Sainte-Beuve's joke was not really a joke, as he goes on to speak of the Shahnameh, as a work valuable not just for itself, but for what its appearance in France says about recent history:

> This poem, in which he [Firdausi] has given vent to his genius (and this genius is evident), was thought worthy, some years ago, of being published in a luxury edition at Paris, at the Government's expense, in the Oriental Collection of unpublished manuscripts. Three volumes (text and translation) have already appeared, and the learned translator, M. Mohl, is in a position to complete the task. But since February 1848, the vicissitudes which have befallen the management of what was formerly the Royal Printing House have affected the fate of the magnificent book, whose production has been halted without cause. It is high time that printing resumed and continued. It is a great sign that a civilization is restored to stability when no delay is felt in these works of high scholarship, which are the luxury and as it were the crown of the intellect.[24]

By writing on Mohl, Sainte-Beuve was not really reviewing a new work. He was intervening in a work-in-progress, throwing his critical weight behind a project that signified political stability and civilised values. Mohl had been commissioned by the French government to prepare an edition of the Shahnameh, and had been working on the project since 1826.[25] But two revolutions occurred during the course of his work: one in 1830 and one in 1848, and the latter, in particular, which saw the fall of the monarchy and the establishment of the short-lived Second Republic, was accompanied by severe administrative and financial upheavals. Both the

Shahnameh and its translation were born under royal patronage but had to be completed in its absence. Never mind that the *Imprimerie Royale* has become the *Imprimerie Nationale*, the Republic must behave as a kind of surrogate monarch, ensuring that the continuity of civilisation survives revolutionary change. The phrase *la couronne de l'intelligence* ('the crown of the intellect') is no accident; this is a book of kings in more ways than one. France may be once more a republic, but Firdausi's poem represents another form of royalty, of pre-eminent cultural authority.

Everything Sainte-Beuve says about the *Shahnameh*, its author, the history of its composition, and its status as a national epic, comes to him from Mohl. In his long preface to the first volume of his translation, Mohl focuses on two critical points, which later become central to Sainte-Beuve's piece: he first sets the composition of the *Shahnameh* in the political context of tenth-century Persia and, second, he discusses the nature of epic poetry. Accordingly, Sainte-Beuve first surveys Persia's political setting in Firdausi's era. He considers the revival of Persian nationalism in Firdausi's milieu, before moving on to explain how this resurrection of interest in Persia's antiquity became a strong incentive for the composition of a book like the *Shahnameh*. Surprisingly though, there is no mention in Sainte-Beuve's account of the significance of the *Shahnameh* in protecting the Persian language. The role of Firdausi in preserving Persia's cultural identity appears to have been casually dismissed in 'Le Livre des Rois'. Of course, the *Shahnameh* is of importance to Sainte-Beuve, but for a different reason, for its moral purpose (and this is something that is often disregarded in the discussions of the *Shahnameh*). Sainte-Beuve takes the succession of dynasties in the *Shahnameh* as an indication of its didactic design, as the book's attempt to highlight the impermanency of life and material existence. The *Shahnameh* retells tales of kings, heroes, and empires, but these are all unfolded to allow one final conclusion: nothing but a sound reputation lasts in life. Firdausi, in Sainte-Beuve's view, 'has conceived the profound sense of the instability of human things, the fleetingness of life and the years of brightness, the nothingness of all things, except a good name'.[26]

To validate his point, Sainte-Beuve then brings in two of the more celebrated episodes in the *Shahnameh*. The first of these is the story of 'Iraj', which he relays selectively and in brief. But however short, 'Iraj' gives Sainte-Beuve enough materials to showcase the kind of didacticism that he believes the *Shahnameh* conveys. Like 'Sohrab', 'Iraj' is named after an extraordinary young man who falls victim to the ideological design of Firdausi's book. 'Iraj' is also a tragedy that hinges upon familial killing. It is a tale of fratricide in which two brothers of royal descent, Salm and Tur, murder their younger brother, Iraj. The elder brothers are enraged by their father's division of his sovereignty. Salm is given the Western lands. Tur, as his name prefigures, is given Turan. But Iraj has inherited a greater portion of wealth and status. He has been given the lordship of the heartland of Iran. Filled with hate and envy, Salm and Tur ultimately put an end to Iraj's life, despite the young prince's earlier proclamation of his abdication of the Iranian throne. This unassuming attitude of Iraj in response to his brother's heartless scheme, his noble character and, more importantly, his modest views on life are the quintessence of the moral values that, in Saint-Beuve's opinion, are upheld in the *Shahnameh*. Iraj is the embodiment of self-effacement: he is young, but magnanimous and insightful, seeing life as unworthy and ephemeral: *O Roi! Pense à l'instabilité de la vie qui doit passer sur nous comme le vent* ('O King! Think of the instability of life which must pass over us like the wind').[27] This is Sainte-Beuve's rendition of Iraj's final words to his father.

Of course, literary treatment of the themes of territorial legitimacy and tension over dynastic succession would not have been unfamiliar to him; Sainte-Beuve would have known about other, and more familiar, treatments of the topics, including Shakespeare's *King Lear* (1606), which bears a number of resemblances to Firdausi's tale. Both Iraj and Cordelia are, for example, mistreated by their elder siblings in these narratives. The love that Lear has for Cordelia, at least in the opening parts of the play, is akin to Fereydon's love for Iraj. Cordelia and Iraj are also both endowed with a profound understanding of life, which is what makes Iraj relevant to Sainte-Beuve's purpose. Iraj's benevolence, his selflessness, and his unassuming views on life as transient and unworthy exemplify Sainte-Beuve's understanding of Firdausi's book. Iraj is an incarnation of the ephemerality that the *Shahnameh* contains in its heart. He is noble, yet reluctant to accept his royal heritage, because he knows that it ensues needless violence and bloodshed. This is the personification of Firdausi's vision of a true Iranian monarch: nobility is not the only prerequisite to sovereignty; the Shah of Iran has to be judicious and generous, capable of leading his people through troubles and hardship; he needs to have the gift of rule. Iraj proves to have this quality; amongst the chaos caused by his brothers, he proves that his father's assessment of him is accurate. Overall, and in terms of its conceptual design, the story of 'Iraj', like 'Sohrab', is concerned with Iran and nationalism. True, the three brothers are of the same noble bloodline in 'Iraj'; yet at some point in the story the two elder ones become the figure of the 'other', while Iraj stands as the embodiment of 'Iran'. The nobility, fairness, and altruism with which Firdausi has drawn Iraj are in fact meant to make him a symbol of Iran; the story of 'Iraj', as Abbas Amanat explains, is 'one of innate political insight, tolerance, and forgiveness versus the greed, treachery and aggression of the "other", the *aniran* [non-Iranian]'.[28]

After 'Iraj', Sainte-Beuve moves to 'Sohrab'. But while his retelling of 'Sohrab' is considerably longer and more detailed than his summary of 'Iraj', it is still selective, reporting only parts of the original. This, however, was enough to spark Arnold's interest, though, at the same time, it was not the originality of Firdausi's story that prompted Arnold to write his version of it (Arnold would have already been familiar with Western narratives of paternal filicide); rather, it was the intellectual congruity that Arnold had with Sainte-Beuve and what he understood Firdausi to be through Sainte-Beuve's mediation that compelled him to write 'Sohrab and Rustum'. It was Firdausi's Homeric role in Persia's historical culture, the primitive and ancient nature of the *Shahnameh*, and its substantial affinity with Homeric epic that had prompted Sainte-Beuve to write on Mohl's translation. Similarly, a large part of Arnold's attraction to the *Shahnameh*, and especially 'Sohrab', similarly came from its aptness for Homeric (and Miltonic) adaptation. Arnold looked at the *Shahnameh* through Sainte-Beuve's vision, and following his lead, he saw something Homeric in the subject, narrative structure, and rhetorical ornament of the narrative of 'Sohrab'.

The *Shahnameh* and the *Iliad* are indeed analogous on general and specific grounds. They both, for instance, draw on Indo-European sources, as evidenced by the correspondences that we can draw in different episodes in both books. Certain elements in the story of Prometheus, as Dick Davis notes, are, for instance, similar to the story of Jamshid and Zahak that comes early in the *Shahnameh*. Jamshid's idea of himself as supreme is, for example, akin to that of Prometheus. Also, the punishment imposed on Zahak is similar to that which is imposed on Prometheus, so 'what appears as a story about one mythological figure in the Greek sources appears as a story about two associated figures in the Persian sources'.[29] The *Shahnameh* and the *Iliad* share structural and thematic features too. For example, they are both written in simple metrical scheme, though the *Iliad* is unrhymed and the *Shahnameh* rhymed. In both, the chronicles of wars are often followed by episodes of revelry (as well as episodes of debates in councils and parleys); the attention given to details in describing the material aspects of life is in fact particularly paramount in both works. Both poems also feature tales of individuals that arouse extreme sorrow and pathos.[30] They both also have distinctive heroes: these men, and, in some cases, women, have characteristics that are identifiably different from other characters. A clear example would be Rostam and Achilles: both are supreme and almost indestructible, although in terms of invincibility, Achilles is also like Esfandiar. Rostam's retirement from wars in 'Sohrab', in particular, not to mention his initial reluctance to go to Kai Kavus's aid, is also reminiscent of Achilles' dismissive attitude towards Agamemnon (a point which is also raised by Sainte-Beuve). Rostam's condition in 'Sohrab' is also akin to that of Odysseus: both have sons (Sohrab and Telemachus) who are searching for them. There are similarities between other characters in these stories too: Kai Kavus's erratic behaviour, for example, evokes images of Agamemnon; the sagacious Perian Wisa is also reminiscent of Nestor and Odysseus.[31]

Sainte-Beuve most likely did not know about these correspondences between *The Shahnameh* and the *Iliad*, but he knew well, through Mohl's preface, that Firdausi is almost identical to Homer in terms of the primitive and epic nature of his work. The second point that Mohl expounds in his preface is, in fact, the correlation between the earliness of Firdausi's book and epic poetry. Mohl begins his preface with a discussion of epic as a distillation of popular song. He puts forward a manifesto both of Romantic nationalism, and of Romantic primitivism, which identifies true epic with the spirit of the people, even though the content of such epic may be wholly concerned with the actions of gods, kings, and heroes:

> I speak here of true epic poetry, which is wholly historical and national, and represents the history of a people as that people itself has formed it in the oral tradition. All nations have had these traditions, for none can form itself without traversing periods of dangers and heroic actions, and without producing great men who forcibly strike its imagination. The people preserve the memory of these [actions and great men], instinctively clothe them in poetic form, and thus compose a history in which truth and fable are singularly mixed together. A ballad is for it [the people], in barbarous times, what a historical document or a bulletin are in civilised times. The careful study which has for some time been made of popular poetry has cast a vivid light on the nature of these traditions, on the transformations they undergo in oral transmission, and on the real origin of epic poetry. [. . .] The history of all peoples begins there, for story and song come before writing, and the first historians could

only base their accounts on such materials [. . .] but the historian makes use of these traditions only for want of written documents, whereas the epic poet finds in them the only sources he can make use of. He brings them together and makes of them a work of art, while preserving the substance and, as far as possible, the form of his materials.[32]

'The people' is not only the source of epic, but its judge, as Mohl goes on to emphasise:

Certainly it has often happened that a poet has tried to create an epic without being able to give it the foundation of a national tradition; but in this case his poem has always been rejected by the people. The beauty of the language and the conception may have given these poems value in the eyes of the learned and the schools, but it has not sufficed to make them popular, and that is the only true touchstone for any epic poem. If it is adopted by the people and sung in the public square, one can be sure that it rests on authentic traditions, and that it has done no more than give back to the mass of the nation, in a more perfect form, that which it had borrowed. I can give no better example of what I understand by true and false epic poetry than the poems of Homer and the Aeneid. Virgil wanted to supplement the lack of traditions with his imagination; but all his art and all the perfection of his style have not made him popular or made of his book a national work.[33]

The model of epic that Mohl discusses privileges something other than originality. The epic poet is not an inventor of stories, but a collector and editor. Mohl's account of Firdausi goes on to emphasis that he did indeed 'give back to the mass of the nation, in a more perfect form, that which he had borrowed'.[34] The epic poet's genius is formal, not inventive; yet in order to attain perfection of form, he has to incarnate the spirit which gave rise to his material. He is a latecomer, yet he must 'represent' this earliness, in all its primitive energy. There is a historical moment for epic, Mohl suggests: it is the product of a fortunate conjunction of a mass of pre-existing oral legends and stories, the authentic utterance of the people, with the poet able to transform this material into an immortal work of art.[35]

For Sainte-Beuve, Mohl's message was clear: the epic moment is a moment of earliness, and is unrepeatable. Sainte-Beuve directly echoes the exemplary comparison that Mohl offers in his preface: Firdausi, like Homer, is the vehicle of an authenticity, which cannot, by its very nature, be copied.[36] Primary epic, in other words, is unrepeatable: Homer's epic is primary, because it is early; subsequent epic, starting with Virgil, is secondary, forever untimely. Primary epic also draws once for all on popular legend and popular song, generally through oral transmission; once a poetic genius has arisen who gives definitive form to these materials, nothing else can take its place. This is very true in the case of the *Shahnameh*: Firdausi's genius coincided with a historical moment that enabled him to take this primary and immutable role.[37] As such, Sainte-Beuve identifies Firdausi as an ally in an ongoing cultural debate on the value of ancient literature. He aligns Firdausi with Homer. After the joke at the start about the *Shahnameh* not being subversive, the first reference to Firdausi introduces him as *l'Homère de son pays* ('the Homer of his country'): the *Shahnameh* 'concerns a vast poem composed over eight hundred years ago by a great poet, the Homer of his country, and whose name doubtless strikes many readers for the first time'.[38] A few pages later, Sainte-Beuve again likens Firdausi to Homer, stating that they both have created true epic poetry, a poetry whose essence rests on popular roots: 'True epic poetry, if it is to be alive, must rest on popular roots and draw its sap from them, without which it produces nothing but study-pieces, fine enough perhaps, but always a bit frigid.'[39]

In his discussion of 'Sohrab', Sainte-Beuve once again enforces this notion of the primacy of the originary epic poet, thought this time with a dig at modern attempts:

> The most famous episode of the poem, and which is of a kind to interest us still, has as its subject the combat between the hero Rustum and his son Sohrab. It is a beautiful and touching story which has spread throughout the world, which has flowered in many a ballad in every country, and which many poets have reshaped or re-invented in their fashion, up to Ossian in his poem *Cathon* and Voltaire in his *Henriade*. Voltaire had assuredly not read Ferdousi, but he had the same idea, that of a father facing his son in battle, and killing him before recognizing him. Voltaire's thought is wholly philosophical and humane; he wishes to inspire a horror of civil war. Ferdousi, in his story drawn from tradition, is far from having had such an overt intention; but one is not afraid to say that, after reading this dramatic and touching episode, this adventure filled at first with colour and perfume, and at last with tears, if one then comes to open canto VIII of the *Henriade*, one feels the height from which modern epic poetry has fallen, and one has the same impression as if one passed from the river Ganges to an ornamental lake at Versailles.[40]

Sainte-Beuve who knew his literary history would have known perfectly well that Voltaire wrote his ten-book epic in praise of the great king Henry IV and offered to dedicate it to Louis XV. But the dedication was rejected, in part because the poem was suspected of heresy.

It was eventually published, first in a clandestine and mangled form in the French city of Rouen in 1723, and then in England in 1728. The analogy with what happened between Firdausi and Sultan Mahmoud is clear. The Persian poet, too, had been accused of heresy, and had fallen out of favour with the reigning prince. The analogy only works up to a point, needless to say, but that point was far enough for Sainte-Beuve's purpose. The attack on Voltaire is an attack on a perverse modernity, which claims that ancient epic form can serve our turn: the fact that 'Voltaire's thought is wholly philosophical and humane' (*'toute philosophique et humaine'*) is just what Sainte-Beuve has against it.

However, Sainte-Beuve's advocacy of the *Shahnameh* in general, and the 'Sohrab' story in particular, makes no mention of them being models for modern poets to follow. His remark on Voltaire and the decadence of modern 'epic', in fact, should have been enough indication that modern attempts at epic poetry were in his view inherently weak and incapable of recapturing what the classical models possessed. Accordingly, Sainte-Beuve's prescription for remedying what modern writings lack is not to copy the classics; Sainte-Beuve had already discussed this in an earlier essay in *Causeries du lundi* (III):

> Let us be content to know them, to penetrate them, to admire them; but let us, the late-comers, endeavor to be ourselves. Let us have the sincerity and naturalness of our own thoughts, of our own feelings; so much is always possible.[41]

This explains well why Sainte-Beuve's response to 'Sohrab and Rustum' was probably not what Arnold might have expected. A part of Arnold's initial letter to Sainte-Beuve, dated 6 January 1854, is dedicated to 'Sohrab and Rustum'. After a brief discussion of the sources of the story (which we looked at earlier), Arnold refers to 'Sohrab and Rustum' as his 'principal poem' which 'belongs in great measure' to Sainte-Beuve. Ironically, and via Sainte-Beuve's own words, Arnold here admits that his poem is an example of a work that shows 'from what height epic poetry, among the moderns, has fallen'.[42] But this statement is rather too modest. It may have been a precautionary vindication, a premeditated act of humility, because Arnold knew that he had violated Sainte-Beuve's rules.

Unfortunately, Sainte-Beuve's reply to Arnold's first letter has not survived. But there are instances in their further correspondences that suggest there might have been something contentious in Sainte-Beuve's response to Arnold.[43] In his letter of 10 October 1854 to his sister (Jane Forster), Arnold talks about the content of Sainte-Beuve's reply. He is, of course, pleased with Sainte-Beuve's letter: 'You can hardly tell what pleasure Sainte-Beuve's letter gave me, because you do not know how highly I estimate him as a critic.'[44] But he also implies that Sainte-Beuve might not have been impressed with his writing: Sainte-Beuve's 'intention of reviewing me [. . .] arises more from his interest in the question raised in the preface, than from his caring much about the poems'.[45] There also seems to be an ongoing debate in the second letter from Sainte-Beuve, which is the first of Sainte-Beuve's to Arnold that is available to us. The letter, as is typical of their correspondence, is permeated with compliments. But there is a note at the core of it that seems to look back at an earlier disagreement: 'I do believe that we are not far from being in agreement about the choice of the best subjects for poetry.'[46] Following this, Sainte-Beuve actually reiterates part of Mohl's argument: epic poetry only emerges in the right (primal) historical moment, which correspondingly makes modern subjects innately unsuited and irrelevant. True epic poetry cannot be made 'with our wars of the Empire', Sainte-Beuve remarks. At the end, he uses Arnold's own comparison of Virgil and Apollonius of Rhodes (in his letter of 29 September 1854 to Sainte-Beuve), in which he had discussed the merits of Virgil and Apollonius of Rhodes and debated whether the poet has to take his subject from the present or from the past, to highlight the importance of the antiquity of the subject matter for the composition of true epic:

> Accepting your two examples of Virgil and Apollonius of Rhodes, I take hold of them by dividing them. The Aeneid lived, and has continued to live, by appropriating an antique subject for a contemporary time, and by the infusion of a wholly Roman spirit which flows back to the origins; Virgil's representation of the origins of Rome is already 'Roman' in spirit: he does not try to recreate an authentically 'primitive' cultural outlook. The soul of the Scipios breathes through it in places, and we are moved to tears at: 'tu Marcellus eris' – Apollonius, by contrast, despite his admirable song [lyric poem] on Medea which Virgil has wholly made use of, has on the whole composed a learned, dead poem, and not a single Alexandrian heart beat faster at its birth, unlike the young Roman for the Aeneid.[47]

Ironically, Sainte-Beuve here is praising Virgil. The *Aeneid* (19 BCE) has lived because Virgil did not just try to emulate Homer; rather, he adapted epic models to tell the story of his own people and time.

His poem is thus true (not primary) epic because his subject matter is of his present. Apollonius, however, failed because he simply attempted to recreate an earlier epic whose subject matter was a past and did not belong to his contemporary moment – which resembles something that Arnold seems to have done. It is thus fair to say that Arnold's 'Sohrab and Rustum' was an epitome of the kind of poetry that Sainte-Beuve disliked and disapproved. The poem was a modern retrieval of an ancient epic, something to which Sainte-Beuve was opposed in a double sense; first, the modern to him was necessarily inferior to the ancient, as the modern compositions were inherently unable to embody the primitiveness and earliness that were associated with the ancient works. Second, Sainte-Beuve believed that imitating the ancient placed the modern in a false position, unable to be itself yet unable to emulate the past.

But not only does Arnold disregard Sainte-Beuve's views, he also completely overlooks the rationale behind Mohl's style of translation. For Mohl, translating the *Shahnameh* into prose was an act of humility, a way of *not competing* with Firdausi.[48] Had Arnold wanted, he could have taken Mohl's French prose version from Sainte-Beuve's essay, and *translated* it into English verse. But Arnold does not produce a second-hand version of Firdausi's episode. He instead writes a poem about Rostam and Sohrab in which the scaffolding of the action, the plot and the characters are mostly the same as Firdausi's, but in which the spirit and mode of treatment are his own. Arnold, in other words, sets out to emulate Firdausi, despite, so to speak, Sainte-Beuve's warning. For if, as Sainte-Beuve asserts, the *Shahnameh* has the primacy of 'early' epic, what will prevent Arnold from becoming a second Voltaire? One way of answering this question is to set Arnold's confrontation with Firdausi against FitzGerald's approach to Omar. After reading Khayyám, FitzGerald discerned an affinity so strong that he thought of himself as having a kind of privileged access to his precursor's mind. In many of his letters to Cowell, FitzGerald states a strong sense of like-mindedness with 'Omar'. 'In truth I take old Omar rather as my property than yours: he and I are more akin, are we not? You see all [his] Beauty, but you can't feel *with* him in some respects as I do', writes FitzGerald to Cowell in a letter of 8 December 1857.[49] Or in a separate letter, he writes: 'Omar breathes a sort of Consolation to me!'[50] Arnold, on the other hand, had no such affinity with Firdausi, beyond seeing in 'Sohrab' a congruity with classical and Western (Greek) standards of epic poetry, overlaying if not overriding its Oriental nature.

Arnold's 'Sohrab and Rustum' and Firdausi's 'Sohrab'

How does Arnold's appropriation of Firdausi play out in the course of the poem? There is no simple answer to this question. Firdausi is not translated in 'Sohrab and Rustum' but then he is not a mere Oriental mask either. Part of Firdausi's conception of the original story has indeed found its way into Arnold's handling of it, though there are significant deviations in Arnold's poem too. 'Sohrab and Rustum' is, for example, considerably shorter than its Persian counterpart Arnold only covers the epic battle and the death of Sohrab in his episode, notwithstanding the setting and Oriental landscape of the poem that have been moulded mostly by materials that are taken from secondary sources, particularly Alexander Burnes's *Travels into Bokhara; being the account of a journey from India to Cabool* (1834).[51] Firdausi, therefore, does not really predominate in Arnold's poem. He is subsumed as he himself had subsumed the works of his precursors such as Daqiqi. In light of this, it is important to note that fidelity to Firdausi was not Arnold's chief objective. Arnold did not want to translate 'Sohrab'; rather, he wanted to render it into something resembling a Greek (Homeric) episode. This is why 'Sohrab and Rustum', for instance, starts *in medias res*. Like several books of the *Iliad*, Arnold's episode begins at the dawn before the morning of the deadly battle. Sohrab cannot sleep; he gets up and leaves his tent in the early hours of the day to see Peran Wisa, the old advisor of the Tartar army:

> And the first grey of morning fill'd the east,
> And the fog rose out of the Oxus stream.
> But all the Tartar camp along the stream
> Was hush'd, and still the men were plunged in sleep;
> Sohrab alone, he slept not; all night long
> He had lain wakeful, tossing on his bed;
> But when the grey dawn stole into his tent,
> He rose, and clad himself, and girt his sword,
> And took his horseman's cloak, and left his tent,
> And went abroad into the cold wet fog,
> Through the dim camp to Peran-Wisa's tent.

The above sequence is entirely Arnold's creation, as Sainte-Beuve's summary, too, begins where Firdausi's does: 'One day he [Rostam] had gone out alone to hunt wild asses, in the direction of the country of the Turks, mounted on his good horse Raksch, speedy as fire.'[52] Up until this point in the poem, the reader does not know who Sohrab is and why an army of Tartars has camped on the bank of the Oxus. But with the appearance of Peran Wisa, things start to gradually become clear. A long conversation between Sohrab and his counsellor reveals that the young champion has come to the Persian border to find his father, Rustum, whom Peran Wisa happens to know from his younger years when 'Rustum was in front of every fray' (l. 80). It is curious why 'Peran Wisa' (or Peeran Veeseh), the wise Turanian king in the *Shahnameh* appears in 'Sohrab and Rustum'. Of course, his role as an old but experienced advisor has precedence in the *Iliad* and so fits well with the Greek design that Arnold intended for his poem. But 'Peran Wisa' does not figure in the original story. Arnold might have learned about him in Malcolm's *History of Persia* where Peran Wisa is introduced with a Homeric tag as the 'Nestor of the Tartars'.[53]

Since 'Sohrab and Rustum' does not follow Firdausi's order of events, the sequence in which its characters come into play differs from the original (or that of Sainte-Beuve). The metanarrative of the *Shahnameh* comprises of an elaborate and interwoven network of actions and interactions. A large number of characters partake in this composition; they are involved with each other, communicating, interacting, and repeatedly changing the course of the book's overarching storyline. We see the effect of this miniature-like narrative in 'Sohrab', for instance. The tragedy of 'Sohrab' takes place against the backdrop of an ongoing squabble between Rostam and Kai Kavus. Rostam's dissatisfaction with the Iranian shah is discernible in his response to the royal summons: Rostam does not grant any urgency to Kavus's call of duty, instead indulging for three days in drinking and feasting with Geev, the shah's messenger. The cause of this disagreement between Kavus and his chief guardian remains unclarified within 'Sohrab'. But looking back at previous chapters in the *Shahnameh*, we can see that the roots of Rostam's discontent with the shah goes back to their earlier interactions. Up until this point in the *Shahnameh*, Rostam has three times rescued Kavus from, in Davis's words, 'the result of his own folly'.[54] The last of Rostam's intercessions takes place in the story immediately prior to that of 'Sohrab' in the *Shahnameh*: 'The King of Hamaveran and His Daughters Sudabeh'.[55] That means there is precedence to Rostam's discontent with the Iranian shah, but this needs to be extrapolated by reading the *Shahnameh*'s overarching narrative closely and retrospectively.

Arnold's narrative, on the other hand, requires no such engagement as it does not have such an interwoven narrative. In 'Sohrab and

Rustum', Arnold, in keeping with Homeric traditions, uses the 'epic' technique of retrospective narrative, giving his characters the task of unfolding previous developments of the story. It is Peran Wisa, for example, who is given the somewhat awkward task of explaining to the reader who Rustum is and why he has sulkily abandoned the Iranian army:

> For now it is not as when I was young,
> When Rustum was in front of every fray;
> But now he keeps apart, and sits at home,
> In Seistan, with Zal, his father old.
> Whether that his own mighty strength at last
> Feels the abhorred approaches of old age,
> Or in some quarrel with the Persian King.
>
> (ll. 79–84)

The conversation between Sohrab and Peran Wisa lays the foundation of Arnold's episode, not only introducing who Rustum is, but also exposing the nature of Sohrab's quest. Here, however, we also discover that Arnold's Sohrab differs from his counterpart in both origin and intentions:

> Thou know'st if, since from Ader-baijan first
> I came among the Tartars and bore arms,
> I have still served Afrasiab well, and shown,
> At my boy's years, the courage of a man.
> This too thou know'st, that while I still bear on
> The conquering Tartar ensigns through the world,
> And beat the Persians back on every field
> I seek one man, one man, and one alone –
>
> (ll. 42–9)

These words reveal Sohrab's frame of mind: Sohrab knows that he is not a Turani by birth. He has joined the Tartars (Turanians) in 'Ader-baijan' or Azerbaijan, which is located in the north-west of modern Iran, and not in the border city of Samangan, where he was conceived and most likely born in the original story. But there is more to these lines. Sohrab, here, also characterises himself as a faithful Tartar who has already proven his loyalty to Afrasiab, though he also admits to having a mental reservation, so to speak, concerning his motive (his search for his father). Even so, this represents a departure from Firdausi's poem, in which the young warrior is not a devoted Turani.

In Firdausi's poem, Rostam and Sohrab fight each other three times over the span of three days, whereas Arnold's story takes place in one day. Arnold here was influenced by Iliadic models of epic and, of course, Sainte-Beuve, in whose account the champions fight consecutively for two days: 'The duel begins: it is not without vicissitudes and singular changes of fortune; it lasts for two days.'[56] But despite this reduction, Arnold's depiction of both Sohrab and Rustum, especially when they face each other, is very close to the original. Arnold's Rustum is an undemonstrative veteran, his Sohrab an emotional youth. In their first battle, both Rustum and Sohrab show signs of doubts in fighting each another. Rustum is the one who first attempts to persuade his rival to resign:

> O thou young man, the air of Heaven is soft,
> And warm, and pleasant; but the grave is cold!
> Heaven's air is better than the cold dead grave.
> Behold me! I am vast, and clad in iron,
> And tried; and I have stood on many a field
> Of blood, and I have fought with many a foe –
> Never was that field lost, or that foe saved.
> O Sohrab, wherefore wilt thou rush on death?
>
> (ll. 322–9)

These are the words of a wise, experienced warrior. Rustum has already been tried in numerous battles and so knows of their undesirable ends; hence, he warns his adversary about the probable repercussions of his youthful ambitions. This exchange was a rendition of what Arnold had read in Sainte-Beuve's 'Le Livre de Rios': 'O tender youth!' he says to him, 'The earth is dry and cold, the air is soft and warm. I am old; I have seen many a battlefield, I have destroyed many an army, and I have never been defeated [. . .] But I have pity for you and do not wish to tear your life away from you'.[57] But upon seeing a man who corresponds with the image of his unseen father, hope fills Sohrab's heart. Forgetting his status as the leader of an army, he acts impulsively, rushing to embrace his enemy:

> And he ran forward and embraced his knees,
> And clasped his hand within his own, and said: –
>   'O, by thy father's head! by thine own soul!
> Art thou not Rustum? speak! art thou not he?'
>
> (ll. 341–4)

Arnold's image here is again largely shaped by Sainte-Beuve's words: 'Hearing these words which seem to come from a kindred soul,

Sohrab's heart leaps, he has a sudden foreboding; he asks the warrior openly if he is not the one he seeks, if he is not the illustrious Rustum.'[58] And Sainte-Beuve's image repeats those of Mohl and Firdausi. In their first confrontation in the original, after seeing in Rostam all that his mother had told him about his father, Sohrab asks the old warrior to confirm his identity. But Rostam simply evades the question, denying that he is Rostam:

> Rostam replied, 'I'm not Rostam, I claim
> No kinship with that clan or noble man:
> Rostam's a champion, I'm a slave – I own
> No royal wealth or crown or kingly throne.'[59]

> چنین داد پاسخ که رستم نیم
> هم از تخمه‌ی سام نیرم نیم
> نه با تخت و گاهم نه با افسرم
> که او پهلوانست و من کهترم

Arnold's Rustum reacts very similarly to Sohrab's request. He shows no emotion in response to Sohrab's passionate plea, instead coming up with an excuse for himself, and for the reader, as to why he insists on fighting under a feigned name:

> Ah me, I muse what this young fox may mean!
> False, wily, boastful, are these Tartar boys.
> For if I now confess this thing he asks,
> And hide it not, but say: *Rustum is here!*
> He will not yield indeed, nor quit our foes,
> But he will find some pretext not to fight,
> And praise my fame, and proffer courteous gifts
> A belt or sword perhaps, and go his way.
> And on a feast-tide, in Afrasiab's hall,
> In Samarcand, he will arise and cry:
> 'I challenged once, when the two armies camped
> Beside the Oxus, all the Persian lords
> To cope with me in single fight; but they
> Shrank, only Rustum dared; then he and I
> Changed gifts, and went on equal terms away.'

(ll. 347–63)

Rustum here thinks that the mere confrontation with him would bring the young Sohrab much recognition and fame. He also assumes that if he tells the truth Sohrab would no longer fight him, nor would he yield to his earlier request. Hence, he decides to fight him anonymously. The basic idea behind Rustum's thought here is again from Sainte-Beuve: 'But the old chieftain, who does not wish to make this youngster too proud, replies with guile that it is not Rustum.'[60] But this is still one of the few moments in 'Sohrab and Rustum' where Arnold appears to have deliberately tried to fill a gap in the design of the original. Arnold, here, has given a human motive to Rostam's logic for hiding his identity, although no such explanation exists in Firdausi's tale. As said earlier, Rostam's behaviour is particularly irrational in this chapter of the *Shahnameh*, and no real explanation is offered as to why he acts as such. One explanation is that the tragic incident of paternal filicide has to happen, no matter how unrealistically thoughtless and irrational Rostam, the great hero of the book, may appear. There may be also another reason: Rostam's attempt to protect his fame. We read numerously in the original poem that Rostam is old and timeworn. Having 'been labeled "afflicted" by age', observes Fraser Clark, 'it is [therefore] not inconceivable that Rustam should lie in order to protect his own legend. For one so high on self-pride as Rustam, shame would be a natural reaction to the accusation that his physicality is failing, and hence he denies his own identity to protect its renown.'[61] There is an indication of Rostam's age and his diminishing physical abilities in Arnold's poem too: in Peran Wisa's introductory mention of Rustum, it is suggested that the old warrior's 'mighty strength' at last may '[Feel] the abhorred approaches of old age' (ll. 82–3). But this suggestion is not followed up: fame, not vanity, is the main reason for Rustum's hiding of his identity.

The final battle between the protagonists of these stories unfold differently in each version. In the original, Rostam and Sohrab fight each other in their third encounter. Rostam downs Sohrab, then stabs him, immediately, to prevent him from regaining position. But no such interaction occurs in Arnold's episode: Rustum and Sohrab plunge into combat where they make sure no truce will be reached. Rustum is the first to act; he hurls his spear; Sohrab follows course, throwing his. Rustum then seizes his club 'which none but he | Could wield' (ll. 408–9). Despite his strength and experience, Rustum, however, misses Sohrab and the club 'leap[s] from Rustum's hand': the great warrior 'follow[s] his own blow', loses his balance, and falls to his knees (ll. 419–21). But seeing Rustum at his mercy, Sohrab, instead of slaying him, courteously steps back and smiles, making one last attempt to reach peace:

> Thou strik'st too hard! that club of thine will float
> Upon the summer-floods, and not my bones.

But rise, and be not wroth! not wroth am I;
No, when I see thee, wrath forsakes my soul.
Thou say'st, thou art not Rustum; be it so!

                                        (ll. 427–34)

Part of Arnold's image at this point mirrors Sainte-Beuve's narrative: there is a short exchange before the two renew their confrontation on the second day. Firdausi's Sohrab pleads with Rostam to cease pursuing combat:

> My heart will communicate its love to you, and I will make tears of shame flow from your eyes. Since you are of a noble race, let me know your origin; do not hide your name from me, since you are going to fight me: are you not Rustum?[62]

But in Arnold's poem, Rustum, who has now fallen on the ground and is trembling with rage, refuses Sohrab's plea and draws his sword again. After delivering two effective passes, Sohrab shatters his sword on Rostam's shield and becomes unarmed and vulnerable. Here, Rustum has the opportunity to be as magnanimous towards his rival as he was towards him moments ago. But the Rustum of Arnold's account is akin to Firdausi's; pride and heroism are exceptionally important to him. So, he screams his own name and pierces Sohrab's side.

Rustum's shouting of his own name is another one of Arnold's interventions. To remain unknown is something on which Rustum, in the vein of his Persian counterpart, insists throughout the story, but there is no clear indication as to why he would shout his name at this critical point. Clearly, he does not do so to reveal his identity, and even if he means to, it goes entirely unnoticed by his rival. Sohrab remains ignorant of the identity of his impending murderer, even after the deadly strike:

And, with a fearless mien, Sohrab replied: –
'Unknown thou art; yet thy fierce vaunt is vain.'

                                        (ll. 540–1)

No justification for Rustum shouting his name as a 'battle-cry' is given in the poem. Rustum does not speak of it, nor does Sohrab ask why his subjugator does so. We may, however, explain Rustum's strange act by recalling Arnold's previous attempt to omit those elements of the original that he might have found to be odd and inexplicable, including Rustum's insistence on hiding his identity. Arnold, as we saw, removed this from his rendition by explaining Rustum's hiding of his name with a human motif. Arnold was perhaps unconvinced by Firdausi's fatalism (in the original account, Sohrab has to die, no matter what, even if that makes Rostam appear foolish). Similarly, Arnold might have thought that the defeat of the warrior who is less likely to be beaten in this battle needs to be justified with something believable. The older combatant in both of these narratives is after all repeatedly described as aged and exhausted, which means it is less likely for him to overpower his rival who is not only of his own tremendous lineage but also significantly younger. But the age dynamic in Arnold's account, as with Firdausi's, is used in favour of Rustum and against Sohrab, though something is different in Arnold's story. In the original, it is only in the second battle, when Sohrab has defeated Rostam and is ready to terminate him, that Rostam uses his dexterity to trick Sohrab into not killing him; Rostam tells Sohrab that by tradition he is only allowed to slay him if he has defeated him for a second time. There is no such exchange in Arnold's poem. True, Arnold's Rustum, like Firdausi's Rostam, is old and experienced; and Arnold's Sohrab, in the vein of Firdausi's Sohrab, is young and gullible, however vigorous and mighty he may be. But Sohrab's gullibility is highlighted in Arnold's poem more palpably and with a more consequential outcome. It is Sohrab's juvenile emotions that practically lead to his downfall in 'Sohrab and Rustum'. Upon hearing the name 'Rustum' from the man whom he thinks could be the father that he has come to seek, Sohrab becomes unnerved; he loses his defence, and then 'recoiled one step | And scanned with blinking eyes the advancing form | And then he stood bewildered; and he dropped | His covering shield, and the spear pierced his side' (ll. 517–20).

There is a remarkable resemblance between the dying words of the young warrior in both Sainte-Beuve and Firdausi. After his initial admission of defeat and downfall, the young man introduces himself as Rostam's son, and warns his murderer of the threat that will everlastingly follow him. The Sohrab of Firdausi:

> And you could be a fish within the sea,
> Or pitch black, lost in night's obscurity,
> Or be a star in heaven's endless space,
> Or vanish from the earth and leave no trace
> But still my father, when he knows I'm dead,
> Will bring down condign vengeance on your head.
> One from this noble band will take this sign

To Rostam's hands, tell him it was mine,
And say I sought him always, far and wide,
And that, at last, in seeking him, I died.

کنون گر تو در آب ماهی شوی

و گر چون شب اندر سیاهی شوی

وگر چون ستاره شوی بر سپهر

ببری ز روی زمین پاک مهر

بخواهد هم از تو پدر کین من

چو بیند که خاکست بالین من

ازین نامداران گردنکشان

کسی هم برد سوی رستم نشان

که سهراب کشتست و افگنده خوار

ترا خواست کردن همی خواستار

Sohrab in Arnold's poem delivers the same message in his final words:

And now thou boastest, and insult'st my fate.
But hear thou this, fierce man, tremble to hear:
The mighty Rustum shall avenge my death!
My father, whom I seek through all the world,
He shall avenge my death, and punish thee!

(ll. 551–5)

Both youngsters warn their antagonist, now their murderer, of the inescapability of his father's forthcoming revenge. No matter where the killer hides or what he does, the father, Rostam, will eventually find him and seek his son's vengeance. But they do not know that the mighty father and the heartless murderer are the same.

Sohrab in Arnold's narrative, as in Firdausi's, dies. But the narrative of the aftermath of his death introduces a unique image:

And the great Rustum drew his horseman's cloak
Down o'er his face, and sate by his dead son.
As those black granite pillars, once high-rear'd
By Jemshid in Persepolis, to bear
His house, now 'mid their broken flights of steps
Lie prone, enormous, down the mountain side –
So in the sand lay Rustum by his son.

(ll. 858–64)

Arnold here shifts geographic location. Persepolis is far from the Oxus, not to mention that Rostam's house is in Samangan (in the northern part of today's Afghanistan) and not in the north-east of the modern city of Shiraz, where Persepolis is located. Why does Arnold introduce this image? The aftermath of Sohrab's death is an unusual moment in 'Sohrab and Rustum' where Arnold seems to assume the role of a commentator rather than a narrator. Here, Arnold introduces a modern sentiment in his rendition of a classical tale. The death of Sohrab, this moment of immense sorrow, offers a fine opportunity to reflect on the state of modern Persia, to echo the narrative of Persia's decline. There is of, course, no such reflection in either Sainte-Beuve or Firdausi, though there is a germane sentiment in Burnes's *Travels*: on his way to the coast of 'Bushire', Burnes visits the 'tomb of Cyrus, and those imperishable remnants of antiquity, the ruins of Persepolis'.[63] This is a rare moment in the *Travels*, too, where Burnes shows disappointment with the state of modern Persia. Immediately after his description of the ruins of Persepolis, he refers to Morier and his *Hajjî Baba* (1824), indicating that Morier does not offer 'to present my views and picture of the inhabitants [of Persia], after the inimitable sketches that have appeared in Hajee Baba, which, with a due deduction for the thread of the tale, appeared to be both just and correct'.[64] Burnes's judgement on Morier's book says enough of his opinions on nineteenth-century Persia. To him, the Persians are a declining nation, a people whose 'empire' is in a 'weak state and tottering condition'; but their country, their 'empire' is still of some significance 'for its weight and influence in the scale of nations'.[65] Both Malcolm's *History* and Morier's *Hajjî Baba* contributed to the narrative of Persia's decline. Arnold had read the former, and it is likely that he knew the latter either at first hand or by repute. Let us also recall that Persepolis and the incident of its destruction were featured in Tennyson's 'Persia' (*Poems by Two Brothers*, 1827). Here, the self-inflicted loss caused by the death of Sohrab by Rustum's hand is used as a token to reflect and repeat the devastation that was inflicted on modern Persia by its chiefs and authorities. It is an acute instance in the poem where Arnold's imitation of Homer or Milton, in the form of the epic simile of the fallen columns of Persepolis, acquires a more modern, 'historical' perspective. Firdausi's own sense of Persia's past greatness is a major theme of the *Shahnameh*, as Arnold would have learned from Sainte-Beuve. But Firdausi did not, of course, treat this theme with the kind of melancholy that infuses Arnold's image, which belongs to an already established Romantic tradition of musings on ruins and the fall of empires. The image of

Rustum's sorrow at the death of Sohrab stands in Arnold's text as a 'universal' response to an action (the killing of a son by his father) which resonates across different cultures; at the same time it registers a specific historical consciousness which differentiates it from its 'original' source (the *Shahnameh* as mediated by Sainte-Beuve).[66] Such readings draw attention to the difficulty of aligning our own cultural 'situation' with that of an ancient 'other' culture, but also to the dynamic and productive process of cultural exchange.

Notes

1. Sainte-Beuve, 'Le Livre des Rois'. All further quotations from the text are identified by the first word in French.
2. Yarshater, 'The Development of Iranian Literatures', p. 13.
3. On the revival of the Persian language, see Lazard, 'The Rise of the New Persian Language'. With relation to epic poetry and Firdausi's role, see Lazard, 'The Rise of the New Persian Language', pp. 624–8; Arberry, 'Persian Literature', pp. 211–12.
4. Bosworth, 'The Tāhirids and Saffārids', p. 90.
5. Peacock, *Medieval Islamic Historiography*, p. 15.
6. There was opposition towards Persian during the Samanids; 'while the elite preferred Arabic and Islamic culture, Persian culture based on Iranian tradition appealed to the broader populace'; see Peacock, *Medieval Islamic Historiography*, pp. 35–6.
7. The Persian poet Rudaki, for instance, thrived under the patronage of the Samanids. For a detailed discussion of the state of Persian and Arabic poetry at the court of the Samanids, Peacock provides an insightful discussion of the circumstances that led to the rebirth of the Persian literature in 'Politics, religion and culture in the late Sāmānid state' in *Medieval Islamic Historiography*, pp. 15–49.
8. For more information on the Samanids, see Frye, 'The Sāmānids', pp. 136–62. On the development of epic in Persian literary traditions, see Clinton, 'Court Poetry at the Beginning of the Classical Period', pp. 75–96; Hanaway, 'Epic Poetry', pp. 96–109.
9. Dabiri, 'The Shahnama: Between the Samanids and the Ghaznavids', p. 23.
10. It is beyond the scope of this study to discuss why Firdausi lost Sultan Mahmoud's favour. Mahmoud's Turkish origins, his Sunni views, which would put him against Firdausi's (possible) Shiite sympathies, together with courtly conspiracy are amongst the reasons that Mahmoud might have had for dismissing Firdausi. For more on this see Browne, *Literary History*, vol. 2, pp. 134–9; Shahbazi, *Ferdowsi*, pp. 89–95; Dabiri, 'The Shahnama: Between the Samanids and the Ghaznavids', p. 24.

11. The origins of these legends have been examined in Shahbazi, *Ferdowsi*, pp. 1–8, Browne, *Literary History*, vol. 2, pp. 132–43, and Atkinson, *The Sháh námeh of the Persian poet Firdausí*, pp. x–xv.
12. Shahbazi, *Ferdowsi*, p. 38 and pp. 64–5.
13. See Banani, 'Ferdowsi and the Art of Tragic Epic', p. 116; Browne, *Literary History*, vol. 2, p. 132. On the *dehqans*, See Zarrinkub, 'The Arab Conquest of Iran and its Aftermath', pp. 43–5. For information on Firdausi's family background and the work of his precursors in preserving Persians traditions, see Shahbazi, *Ferdowsi*, pp. 21–38 and pp. 39–59.
14. Davis, 'The "Shahnameh" as World Literature', p. 26.
15. Davis, *Epic and Sedition*, p. xxiii.
16. The theme of 'Sohrab' has repeatedly found its way into literature. It has appeared in its oldest forms in the Indian *Mahabharata*, in Greek myth (Ulysses and Telegonus), in the Irish Cuchulainn (Cú Chulainn) Saga, in the German *Hildebrandslied* and elsewhere in popular literature. It also occurs in Ossian's poem, *Carthon*, and in Voltaire's *Henriade*, both of which Arnold may quite conceivably have read before his own poem was written.
17. For more on 'A Persian Passion Play', see Chapter 5, p. 196.
18. Malcolm, *History of Persia,* vol. 1, pp. 36–8.
19. The letter in French is in Lang, *Letters*, vol. 1, pp. 284–5.
20. See Yohannan, *Persian Poetry*, pp. 81–2 and p. 276.
21. For more on Sainte-Beuve and Arnold's relationship, see Whitridge, 'Matthew Arnold and Sainte-Beuve'; Super, 'Documents in the Matthew Arnold-Sainte-Beuve Relationship'.
22. For the letter, see Lang, *Letters*, vol. 1, pp. 284–5. There is a similar indication in Arnold's letter of 28 May 1872 to Cardinal Newman, in which he names four men, (Goethe, Wordsworth, Sainte-Beuve, and Newman himself), from whom, he claims, he not only received a strong impression but consciously learned 'habits, methods, [and] ruling ideas'; the letter is in Whitridge, *Unpublished Letters*, pp. 65–7.
23. Sainte-Beuve, 'Le Livre des Rois', p. 332.
24. Ibid. p. 332; French sentence begins 'Ce poëme, où il a appliqué son genie . . .'
25. Six volumes were published in Mohl's lifetime, and Barbier de Meynard completed the seventh after Mohl's death.
26. Sainte-Beuve, 'Le Livre des Rois', p. 342; French sentence beginning 'Le poëte a conçu le sentiment profound . . .'
27. Sainte-Beuve, 'Le Livre des Rois', p. 342.
28. Ibid. p. 68. I am indebted in this part to Amanat for his insightful analysis of the tale of 'Iraj'. For more information, see his 'Divided Patrimony', pp. 49–70.
29. Davis, 'In the Enemy's Camp: Homer's Helen and Ferdowsi's Hojir', p. 17.

30. Banani, 'Ferdowsi and the Art of Tragic Epic', p. 117.

31. In writing this section, I have relied on Banani, 'Ferdowsi and the Art of Tragic Epic', pp. 117–19; Gray, *Milton and the Victorians*, pp. 84–7; and Davis, 'In the Enemy's Camp: Homer's Helen and Ferdowsi's Hojir'.

32. Mohl, preface to volume 1 of *Le Livre des Rois, par Abou'lkasim Firdousi* (1876). Available at <http://remacle.org/bloodwolf/arabe/firdousi/rois4.htm> (last accessed 21 October 2019). The 1876 edition was a re-issue of the original edition of 1838. All quotations are taken from this text, identified by the first words (in French) in order to help readers locate the original; this quotation begins 'Je parle ici de la véritable poésie épique'.

33. Ibid. 'Il est certainement arrivé bien souvent'.

34. Ibid. in sentence beginning 'S'il est adopté par le peuple'.

35. Ibid. see paragraph beginning 'On pourrait s'étonner'.

36. This idea is latent in Mohl's preface, which traces the history of Persian epic after Firdausi in terms of progressive decline and deterioration; but Sainte-Beuve does not extend the argument to include the appropriation by other writers of Firdausi's themes.

37. Mohl expounds this theory in his preface.

38. Sainte-Beuve, 'Le Livre des Rois', p. 332; French sentence beginning 'Il s'agit d'un immense poëme . . .'

39. Sainte-Beuve, 'Le Livre des Rois', p. 341; French sentence beginning 'La véritable poésie épique . . .'

40. Sainte-Beuve, 'Le Livre des Rois', pp. 343–4; French sentence beginning 'Le plus célèbre épisode du poëme'. The *Henriade* is an epic poem in honour of Henry of Navarre, later King Henry IV of France, set during Henry's siege of Paris in 1589. As in the *Shahnameh*, a father and son find themselves on opposite sides of a conflict in which a throne is at stake, though Voltaire's poem concerns a civil war, not a struggle against a foreign invader. Book VIII contains an episode in which the old warrior d'Ailly, a partisan of Henry IV, unknowingly kills his own son: 'Enfin le vieux d'Ailly, par un coup malheureux, | Fait tomber à ses pieds ce guerrier généreux. | Ses yeux sont pour jamais fermés à la lumière, | Son casque auprès de lui roule sur la poussière. | D'Ailly voit son visage: ô désespoir! ô cris! | Il le voit, il l'embrasse: hélas! c'était son fils. | Le père infortuné, les yeux baignés de larmes, | Tournait contre son sein ses parricides armes; | On l'arrête; on s'oppose à sa juste fureur: | Il s'arrache en tremblant, de ce lieu plein d'horreur; | Il déteste à jamais sa coupable victoire . . .' [At last old d'Ailly, with an unlucky blow, makes this noble warrior fall at his feet. His eyes are shut out forever from the light, his helmet rolls beside him in the dust. D'Ally sees his face: O despair! O cries! He sees him, he embraces him: alas, it was his son. The unlucky father, his eyes bathed in tears, is about to turn his parricidal weapons against his own breast; he is stopped; his

just fury is opposed: trembling, he tears himself away from this place of horror; he detests ever after his guilty victory . . .] Sainte-Beuve's scorn for Voltaire's neoclassical diction and metre resembles that of English Romantics such as Keats for Pope, and stems from the same assumption that eighteenth-century verse had followed a false path of lifeless imitation.

41. Sainte-Beuve, 'What is a Classic?', p. 11.
42. Lang, *Letters*, vol. 1, pp. 284–5.
43. Super, 'Documents in the Matthew Arnold-Sainte-Beuve Relationship', p. 206.
44. The letter is in Whitridge, *Unpublished Letters*, pp. 23–6.
45. Whitridge, *Unpublished Letters*, p. 25.
46. For Sainte-Beuve's letter in French, see Whitridge, *Unpublished*, pp. 68–70.
47. The letter in French is available in Lang, pp. 292–4. Arnold's letter, as Super observes, is in response to a letter from Sainte-Beuve written around 15 September, which is probably the date of Sainte-Beuve's first letter to Arnold. See Super, 'Documents in the Matthew Arnold-Sainte-Beuve Relationship', p. 206.
48. Sainte-Beuve calls Mohl's method 'religiously faithful' ('la méthode fidèle et religieuse de traduction', Sainte-Beuve, 'Le Livre des Rois', pp. 341); Mohl himself says at the end of his preface that he has 'tried to translate in as literal a manner as possible, without doing violence to the rules of the French language [. . .] My intention has always been to prefer exact expression to stylistic elegance' (sentence beginning 'J'ai tâché de traduire').
49. Terhune and Terhune, *Letters*, vol. 2, p. 305.
50. See FitzGerald's letter of 5 June 1857 in Terhune and Terhune, *Letters*, vol. 2, p. 273.
51. Burnes, *Travels into Bokhara*. For more on the influence of Burnes on 'Sohrab and Rustum', see Walker, 'Burnes's Influence on Sohrab and Rustum: A Closer Look'; Morgan, 'With "Bokhara" Burnes'.
52. Sainte-Beuve, 'Le Livre de Rois', p. 344; French sentence beginning 'Un jour, il était allé seul à la chasse . . .'
53. Malcolm also introduces Sohrab as the champion of the Tartars (vol. 1, p. 40).
54. Davis, *Epic and Sedition*, p. 59.
55. Here, I am using Davis's rendering of the title of the story. For an English version of the episode, see his *Shahnameh*, pp. 174–87.
56. Sainte-Beuve, 'Le Livre de Rois', p. 348; French sentence beginning 'Le duel commence . . .'
57. Ibid. French sentence beginning 'O jeune homme si tendre!'
58. Ibid. French sentence beginning 'En entendant ces paroles. . .'
59. The English translations of 'Sohrab' are from Davis, *Shahnameh*, pp. 187–214. All Persian excerpts from the *Shahnameh* are from *Shahnameh*, ed. Jalal Khaleghi-Motlagh (Tehran: Afkar, 2006).

60. Sainte-Beuve, 'Le Livre de Rois', p. 348; French sentence beginning 'Mais le vieux chef . . .'
61. See Clark, 'From Epic to Romance', p. 66.
62. Sainte-Beuve, 'Le Livre des Rois', p. 349; French sentence beginning 'Mon coeur te communiquera son amour . . .'
63. Burnes, *Travels into Bokhara*, vol. 2, p. 139.
64. Ibid. p. 140.
65. Ibid. p. 140.
66. In his preface, Mohl draws attention to the resemblance between the story and various European versions, including the Irish legend of Cuchulain (see above). In this context, he cites Charlotte Brooke's *Reliques of Irish Poetry* (1788), a popular anthology of translations and adaptations reprinted in 1816; it is possible that Arnold had come across it.

Chapter 4

Rubáiyát of Omar Khayyám

Omar Khayyám is known in Persian literary history as the supreme exponent of the *rubáiy* (pl. *rubáiyát*), a short verse from consisting of a single stanza, rhyming *aaba*. The extent of Khayyám's fame, however, goes beyond the geographical or cultural boundaries of his place of origin. Thanks to Edward FitzGerald's translation, Khayyám is now celebrated globally, not just as one of Persia's classical poets, but as a learned philosopher who, in a collection of epigrammatic poems, has encapsulated some of the largest and most enduring preoccupations of humankind. Ironically, there is very little evidence to suggest that Khayyám ever wrote poetry or that he was a poet by profession, in the way that men like Firdausi, for instance, was. A large number of poems have nevertheless come to be associated with the name Khayyám. Some of these poems express religious doubts; others celebrate earthly pleasure, to be grasped before the advent of death and oblivion. This far-reaching scepticism that manifests in Khayyám's poetry (or in the poetry that has been ascribed to him) has distinguished him from the majority of Persia's classical poets; while the latter have typically shared common religious sentiments with their society, Khayyám seems to have subverted in his poetry the orthodox religious ideologies that the contemporary rulers, the Saljuqs, were upholding at the time in Persia. This introduces further doubts as to whether the historical Khayyám could have ever written the type of sacrilegious, disbelieving poetry that has commonly been attributed to him; since at various points in his life the astronomer and the mathematician Khayyám appears to have worked closely with the Turkish Saljuqs.

Khayyám lived when the Saljuqs (1040–1220) were spreading and consolidating their Islamic reign over the north west of Persia. He was born in 1048 in Nishapur, in Khurasan in the north-east of today's Iran, and the date of his death is believed to be 1131.[1] Contemporary glimpses of his life are, however, rare. We know that he spent his youth in Samarqand which was at the time part of the Greater Khurasan. His mathematical talent then gained him the patronage of local dignitaries, such as Abu Taher, the Chief Justice of Samarqand. Under the patronage of the latter, Khayyám completed *Resala fi sharh ma' askala men mosadarat ketab Oqlides* ('Treatise on Demonstration of Problems of Algebra and Balancing'), a landmark treatise on algebra still cited in mathematical histories. In 1074, Khayyám was summoned by Sultan Saljuq Jalal ul-Din Malik Shah, and his minister Nizam ul-Mulk, to help with the reform of the old solar calendar and the construction of an observatory.[2] But after Malik Shah's death in 1092, Khayyám appears to have not been able to find favour with his successors; so, he returned to Nishapur. In 1112 or 1113, in Balkh, as narrated in Nezami Aruzi Samarqandi's *Chahar Maqale* ('Four Discourses', c. 1055–6), Khayyám prophesied the location of his burial place.[3] Some time in the following two years, he was recorded to have met the renown Persian historian, Zahir ul-din Baihaqi, who would have been eight years of age at the time; Khayyám taught Baihaqi Arabic and geometry.[4] We also know that in the winter of 1114, in Marv, Khayyám, at the age of sixty-seven, was asked by a Saljuqi prince, probably Sultan Mohammad, to forecast a propitious time for hunting.[5]

There is no record of Khayyám in the last sixteen years of his life apart from a deathbed scene of doubtful authority. Khayyám is said to have been reading from Avicenna's *Ketab-e Shefa'* ('The Book of Healing', c. 1027) the chapter on metaphysics dealing with 'the One and the Many'. Putting the book aside, he then says his Evening Prayers, postulates, and utters: 'Oh God, be aware that I have known You as much as I could do; thus, pardon me, since, for me, knowing you is a pathway to you.'[6] Khayyám dies shortly afterwards. Another dubious, and perhaps the most renowned account of Khayyám's life is the story of the three schoolboys (which is also told in FitzGerald's preface to the *Rubáiyát*). The legend envisages Khayyám in his early youth where he is schoolmates with Nizam ul-Mulk, the future Saljuq statesman, and Hasan Sabah, the future heresiarch and founder of the 'Order of Assassins'. Here, the three make a pact that whichever of them attains worldly success would assist the others. Nizam ul-Mulk eventually becomes a vizier, and so Hasan Sabah demands political preferment and Khayyám asks for a modest allowance to pursue his studies. This, however, cannot be true: Nizam ul-Mulk was born almost thirty years before Khayyám. Yet the symbolic purport of the story is more significant than its literal truth. The Khayyám of the fable of the three schoolboys is a retiring, modest man, heedless of materiality and wealth, befitting the popular image of him as a poet-philosopher.

Curiously, Khayyám's fame during his lifetime was that of a mathematician, astronomer, and philosopher. As noted earlier, there is no contemporary record of him as a poet. The first reference to him as a poet comes from verses in Arabic in Katib Isfahani's *Kharidat ul-Qasr* ('*Virgin Pearl of the Palace*', 1176–7). Najm ul-Din Razi in his *Mirsad ul-Ebad* ('*Watch Towers of Devotees*', 1223) also attributes two Persian verses to Khayyám.[7] A reference work of 1249, *Tarikh ul-Hukama* ('*History of Philosophers*'), also cites him as a poet. But none of these texts mentions Khayyám as an author of the *rubáiyát*. The first such reference, citing a single *rubáiy*, appears in Ata ul-Mulk Juvaini's *Tarikhe Jahangosha* ('*History of the World Conqueror*', 1260).[8] Further attributions of the *rubáiyát* to Khayyám dates from anthologies compiled after the Mongol invasion of Persia in the fourteenth century.[9] A total of around eighty manuscripts are extant, dating from the fourteenth to the sixteenth centuries, and compiled by scribes in Persia and the Indian subcontinent. The verses attributed to Khayyám in these manuscripts frequently appear in other compilations as the work of other twelfth-century Persian poets and savants.[10] Scholars, therefore, have remained divided over how many of the hundreds of the *rubáiyát* attributed to Khayyám in later centuries are his. A conservative estimate would be about thirty, though there is no certainty even with that small number of poems.[11] But despite that, Khayyám's cultural significance as the foremost proponent of the *rubáiy* has remained unaffected by debates over attribution.[12]

The substance of Khayyám's writing has also been controversial, and given the uncertainty surrounding his life and poetic output, no single authoritative account of either the man or the poet has been possible. Scholars and biographers have normally coloured Khayyám in accordance to their own fancy: to some, he is a Sufi mystic whose poetry speaks of divine love; to others, he is a debauched reveller whose poetry encourages hedonism; but neither of these interpretations can be proved or disproved, and final ruling needs be left to the judgement of individual readers. However, there is also a third group: those who are concerned with the philosophy rather than the philosopher. To these people, the imaginary reconstruction of this literary figure on the basis of the attributed *rubáiyát* is less important than the significance of the collection of speculative reasoning on deep philosophical and theological questions, which is gathered in one place under the name of Omar Khayyám.

A further issue concerning Khayyám is the unconventionality of the poetry that we think he might have written. From a purely literary

perspective, Khayyám's place among both contemporary and classical poets is odd and incongruous: his poetry compares neither to
that of contemporary lyricists such as Manuchehri or Farrokhi, who
wrote mostly panegyrics; nor to that of the more prominent poets
such as Firdausi or Nizami.[13] Still, the *rubáiyát*, particularly those
whose authenticity is less doubted, bear the essence of the works of
the poets of Khurasan, though without the complexity and formal
rigidity of their style. Judged by the poems that can be more confidently ascribed to him, Khayyám writes in simple Persian, relatively
unaffected by linguistic borrowing. His diction is plain, unpreten-
tious, and epigrammatic. Ideas are often communicated in his poetry
in rapid sequence without the verbosity that is pervasive in classical
Persian poetry.

The poems that have been attribute to Khayyám, when studied
without any external (allegorical) presumptions, resonate with an
unprecedented sense of philosophical scepticism towards divinity.
Khayyám disapproves of fixed dogma; he rejects the legitimacy of
celestial phenomena that cannot be validated by reason and rational-
ity. One of the most recurrent themes in the *rubáiyát* is, for instance,
the disbelief in the independent existence of the soul, which is founded
in a materialist philosophy: all matter, including that which makes
up human beings, circulates and returns to nature after death. This
is Khayyám's vision of the human existence: humankind is a helpless
entity in the cycle of creation with no alternative than conforming to
the will of nature. But nature, as immense and insensitive as it may
be, is also embracing and all-encompassing in Khayyám's scheme of
things. The eschatological future that Khayyám contemplates in his
poems is not that of a paradise or hell but is of mixing with earth and
returning to the basic elements in the form of a wine jug or a flower.
There is nothing supernatural after this life in Khayyám's vision;
although, at the same time, Khayyám does not lament this unknown,
puzzling termination of human existence; there is no grievance for
death in the *rubáiyát*. On the contrary, many of Khayyám's bleak
thoughts concerning human death are delivered with sardonic enjoyment, though, this, too, arguably emanates from his vision of human
life which is unrelentingly materialist. Not only does Khayyám not
envision a sacred, otherworldly existence to human existence, but
he also sees this earthly life as too short and futile. To him, life is so
ephemeral that tomorrow is not even worthy of concern; the past is
a part of history and the future a doubtful dream. Hence, it is the
moment that should be treasured with joy. This understanding forms
an ideological core to Khayyám's poetry; the projection of life's

futility is mixed with pleasure in the *rubáiyát*. Khayyám draws in a single frame the dark 'reality' of life's impermanency alongside the encouragement for delight.

Khayyám in England

Up until the mid-nineteenth century, Khayyám was a minor figure in Persian poetry, far less read and studied in his own country than poets such as Firdausi, Sa'di or Hafiz, and virtually unknown in the West apart from a few citations in scholarly works or anthologies. Then, in 1856, a young scholar named Edward Byles Cowell discovered a fifteenth-century manuscript of Khayyám's poems in the Bodleian Library, Oxford. Cowell made a copy for his friend Edward FitzGerald, and subsequently gave him a copy of another manuscript, compiled in Calcutta in the sixteenth century. From these sources FitzGerald produced his translation, *Rubáiyát of Omar Khayyám, the Astronomer-Poet of Persia*, in 1859, which contained seventy-five quatrains, framed by a biographical and critical preface and by endnotes. The second edition of 1868 had 110 quatrains and a greatly expanded preface, the third edition of 1872 had 101 quatrains, as does the fourth of 1879; in this latter edition the major addition to the preface in 1868 had disappeared, so that the preface reverted more or less to its original form. The endnotes also underwent revision and expansion.[14]

In these successive editions, FitzGerald revised and expanded his poems, then thought better of some of his revisions, but continued to make changes and additions. These continuous revisions were partly caused by FitzGerald's anxiety over his understanding of Khayyám's historical context and partly by his discomfort over his knowledge of Persian. Learning a non-European language with an entirely different writing system would not have been an easy task for him at that age. FitzGerald started learning Persian in his mid-forties, not to mention that he could have not had any exposure to Persian as a living language prior to that. Also, judged by modern standards of Persian scholarship, the tools that Cowell had supplied him to study Persian were not wholly dependable. To learn the basic structure of the Persian language, FitzGerald had to rely on the classic foundation of Persian philology, Sir William Jones's *A Grammar of the Persian Language*.[15] His dictionary was Francis Johnson's *A Dictionary, Persian, Arabic, and English* published in London in 1852.[16] But then an unanticipated and rather unpleasant development made things even harder for FitzGerald; Cowell left England only two weeks after presenting FitzGerald with the copy he had made of the Ouseley MS.[17] FitzGerald was working on the text single-handedly for a period of several months until he was able to re-establish contact with Cowell by correspondence. Under such circumstances, it was not unusual for FitzGerald to doubt the veracity of his historical understanding of Khayyám, to question the accuracy of his knowledge of Persian.

But there was also another, and a more personal, reason behind FitzGerald's continuous revisions of the poems: his obsession with authenticity. More than anything else, FitzGerald, in his rendition of the *rubáiyát*, was driven by a desire for fidelity, which exceeded the surface layer; FitzGerald's *Rubáiyát* needed to encapsulate its counterpart not just in body but also in spirit. Of course, the aesthetic taste of nineteenth-century England expected to find an Oriental sentiment in a work of Oriental origin. But FitzGerald was untroubled by such external motives; the *Rubáiyát* was a self-funded enterprise, and FitzGerald was under no pressure to conform to a contemporary taste for which, in any case, he had little respect. Rather, his approach to the *rubáiyát* was discerned by the strong affinity he felt with the Persian language, the figure of Omar Khayyám as the author of the quatrains, and the cynical and sacrilegious philosophy that he thought they contained.

From an early stage, FitzGerald thus decided that a literal translation of the *rubáiyát* would not do them justice: 'Better a live sparrow than a stuffed Eagle', he wrote to Cowell in his letter of April 1859.[18] To enliven his 'sparrow', he then devised a method of translation which was free, yet suffused with the original, and in which the adaptation of Persian to English was counterpointed by the adaptation of English to Persian; although the process is not fully reciprocal: the *Rubáiyát* is, in the end, an English poem. Curiously, FitzGerald's new method of translation differed from that of his previous works, from Spanish (*Six Dramas of Calderón*, 1853) and Persian (*Salámán and Absál*, 1856). FitzGerald did not want his translation of *Calderón* to be 'irreconcilable with English Language and English Ways of Thinking'.[19] But with *Salámán and Absál*, he was unsure whether he should leave his translation to be 'Orientally obscure' or make it 'Europeanly clear'; though, at the end, he decided to 'lay the raw material as genuine as may be' so that the readers could 'work up to their own better Fancies'.[20] But with the *Rubáiyát*, he did not do any of these. Instead, he came up with a process which partly resembled both: he rendered the Persia poems in a familiar idiom so that their thematic core would not be lost in translation; but then he also imported many 'raw' and estranging 'foreign' elements to preserve their Oriental flavour. This hybrid nature of FitzGerald's translation has made the *Rubáiyát* a poem of peculiar construction: quintessentially English but also curiously Persian (Oriental). The English side of the poem has been studied profusely in the past.[21] Its Persian side has also received huge scholarly attention, most notably by men like Edward Heron-Allen and Arthur J. Arberry.[22] In this chapter, I, too, will focus on the Persian dimension of the poem, but I will go beyond examining the purely poetic components that FitzGerald might have borrowed from the manuscripts. Instead, I aim to explore the scattered, and often unseen, Persian constituents of the poem, to unveil and argue that the Persian-ness of the *Rubáiyát* comprises not just what is directly, and overtly, translated from the *rubáiyát*, but also a huge body of linguistic, literary, and cultural materials that are infused latently across the poem, things that FitzGerald had learned from Cowell or borrowed from a wide range of sources and manuscripts that he could have come across during his studies of Persian.

Persian Form

FitzGerald knew from the start that in order to retain something of the essence of original poems, he would need to find, or formulate, a poetic pattern that resembles its unusual *aaba* rhyme scheme. The *rubáiy* is considered to be one of the most distinctive verse forms in Persian poetic tradition. It is unique because it is short; it only contains two lines, or four if laid out as a quatrain. But it is also unique because it is complete in itself; in the traditional arrangement of a Persian *divan*, the *rubáiy* has no thematic connection with the preceding or the following quatrains; a Persian collection of the *rubáiyát* is arranged alphabetically by end-rhyme.[23] This thematic singularity, not to mention density, of the *rubáiy* has had its inevitable impact on its construction, making it a particularly awkward and unaccommodating poetic medium. Oddly enough, and despite its limitations in form as opposed to other forms of Persian verse, the *rubáiy* has been a rich instrument for the artistic expression of complex thoughts.[24] Yet, it is still not the pattern best suited for the delivery of extended narratives, because of its concision, singularity, and epigrammatic nature.[25] FitzGerald, however, thought otherwise. He transmuted a group of them which were not intended to represent a continuous story into an English narrative. In his own words, he 'ingeniously tessellated [Persian quatrains] into a sort of Epicurean Eclogue in a Persian Garden'.[26] Oddly enough, the text in which he showed his first understanding of the *rubáiy* was not in English. FitzGerald had previously put a number of quatrains into what he called 'monkish Latin', and in many of these the metre and rhyme were correctly imitated.[27] By contrast, his first attempt at metrical transformation of Persian quatrains into English was not close to the rhyming pattern of the *rubáiy*:

> I long for Wine! oh Sáki of my Soul,
> Prepare thy Song and fill the morning Bowl;
> For this first Summer Month that brings the Rose
> Takes many a Sultan with it as it goes.

The above stanza was included in FitzGerald's letter of 14 July 1857 to Cowell.[28] But this is not a *rubáiy*; it consists of two couplets with an *aabb* rhyme scheme rather than *aaba*. Only after this false start, and influenced perhaps by the Latin version he had abandoned, did FitzGerald decide to convert this formal aspect of the *rubáiy* into English, even though he knew that the result would be atypical in English poetry. FitzGerald's first translation later became quatrain VIII in the first edition of the *Rubáiyát*. The vocabulary of the third line of the original draft has remained almost unchanged here:

> And look – a thousand Blossoms with the Day
> Woke – and a thousand scatter'd into Clay:
>   And this first Summer Month that brings the Rose
> Shall take Jamshýd and Kaikobád away.

But other changes have been made: the third line is, for instance, visibly different from the other lines: it is indented and unrhymed. The indentation, technically known as 'eisthesis', is standard in the text of all editions, signalling that the line is almost invariably unrhymed. In this instance, 'away' deviates from 'Rose' but agrees with the ending sounds of 'Clay' and 'Day'. The digression is the consequence of FitzGerald's understanding of the significance of the third line, that its variance provides a breaking point in the *rubáiy*. FitzGerald knew well that in order to preserve the conceptual force of the *rubáiy*, which depends on the fusion of meaning and form, he would need to contrive the imbalance of the third line in his translation; hence, not only did he indent all of his third lines, he also left almost all of them unrhymed.[29] In the Persian *rubáiy*, the third line prepares the reader for the upcoming message of the fourth line, the message, which, in the words of the seventeenth-century Persian poet, Mirza Sa'eb Tabrizi (1592–1676), 'thrusts the finger nail into the heart'; something of the effect of this is perceptible in FitzGerald's *Rubáiyát*.[30]

Persian Sounds

FitzGerald was also interested in the sound of Persian, although his sense of 'sound' was probably purely imaginary (the closest that he would have come to experience Persian as a living language was perhaps through Cowell's words). Nevertheless, he thought Persian possessed an audible pleasantness, stating once that the word *afsoos* in Persian is a beautiful and suitable equivalent for the word 'alas' in English because they both sound similar.[31] He also liked the word *carevanserai* because he thought it had a pleasant rhythmic sound and a proportionate pitch for English speakers.[32] We see the repercussion of FitzGerald's fervour for the sound of Persian in his *Rubáiyát*; there are phonetic resemblances between his poems and the originals. We see an example of this in the final version of his first English translation, in quatrain VIII which has no equivalent in the manuscripts. The quatrain is composed of the first two lines of quatrain 497 in the Calcutta MS and the last two lines of quatrain 518 in the same manuscript. The following is an English transliteration of FitzGerald's concocted verse:

> *az amadan-i bahar. w-az raftan-i <u>dai</u>*
> *auraq-i wujud-i ma hami gardad <u>tai</u>*
>
> *k-afkand. ba-khak. sad hazar. Jam u <u>Kai</u>*
> *in amadan-i tir.-mah o raftan-i <u>dai</u>* [33]

If we compare the rhyming words of the above transliteration with its translation in the *Rubáiyát*, we can see how FitzGerald has effectively followed the sound correspondence of the *qafieh* (rhyming word): the articulation of Persian words '*dai*', *tai*' and '*Kai*' sounds very similar to 'Day', 'Clay' and 'away'.

Quatrain XXIII offers another example of FitzGerald's commitment to maintaining phonetic semblance in his poems. The quatrain, again, is the outcome of FitzGerald's editorial skill:

> Ah, make the most of what we yet may spend,
> Before we too into the Dust descend;
>   Dust into Dust, and under Dust, to lie,
> Sans Wine, sans Song, sans Singer, and – sans End!

In the fourth line, though, FitzGerald appears to have wanted to follow the sound pattern of the original. The Persian source for the line reads *bi munis o bi harif o bi hamdam o juft*: 'without companion and without match and without partner'. To communicate this, the Persian negating prefix *bi* has been repeated three times in the original. The reiteration of *bi*, meaning 'without' in Persian, adds an alliterative rhythm to the line. It also reinforces the bleakness of the verse's tone: death, from which no one returns, separates all from those they love, from their earthly belongings. FitzGerald follows a very similar pattern in his rendition of the line. He finds an equivalent for *bi* in English, the prefix 'sans', and repeats it four times in his verse.[34] It is curious that while FitzGerald's translation does not give a direct translation of its original, his choice of word creates phonetic and philosophical affinities with it, implementing and communicating a matching sentiment. The monosyllabic prefix 'sans' has a similar grammatical function to that of *bi*; its repetition, therefore, gives a corresponding undertone to the fourth line of his poem. The repetition also brings an alliterative rhythm to the line. But there is one difference here: FitzGerald repeats the prefix four times, once more than the original. The first three repetitions emulate the effect of *bi* in the original; 'Wine', 'Song', and 'Singer' are preceded with 'sans' to suggest that death separates everyone from their worldly delights. But in the fourth occurrence 'sans' loses its functionality, as everything material is already ended and nothing is left to be taken away. 'Sans End' does not denote the loss or absence of something, but is a negative formula for infinite duration. We could extend the series 'Wine', 'Song', 'Singer' indefinitely, but this series would still contain the element of human identity and attachment, and would still differ essentially from what lies on the other side of the dash.[35]

Persian Metaphors

FitzGerald's personal, intuitive response to the *rubáiyát* prompted him to learn more about the language, but it was learning directed to the specific end of understanding these particular poems. In other words, FitzGerald's yearning to read the poems in the manuscripts was enthused, at least partly, by his own personal needs, because the *rubáiyát* spoke to him in a personal way and provided a sort of healing for many of its perplexities. To gratify his want, he thus needed to improve his Persian, and the more he learned the more his interest grew. Curious and strenuous as he certainly was, FitzGerald ultimately became fairly competent in Persian, to the extent that he could read Hafiz, a task that required a good level of understanding of the language. The depth of FitzGerald's knowledge of Persian is evident in his treatment of the language in the *Rubáiyát*. To a reader who knows both Persian and English, FitzGerald's understanding of the nuances of Persian literature, language, and culture speaks of direct personal contact with the Persian social and verbal world, even though we know FitzGerald was reliant on Cowell's expertise; for much of the period in which he was composing his translation, he was a kind of distance learner with Cowell, in Calcutta, acting as his tutor. What is curious here is that FitzGerald's fervour in the pursuit of the shades of meaning in the *rubáiyát* did not preclude him from treating the texts as his own. On the contrary, his method of translation encouraged him to consider the Persian language a vital element required for the infusion of a Persian life into his translation, as a pulse that needed to be kept alive in his poem, though of course not in its original conception. Among the Persian components that FitzGerald incorporated in his poems, the most conspicuous and complicated ones are those of symbolic expression. The *Rubáiyát* adopts complex Persian metaphors to introduce similar connotations in English. A reader acquainted with these metaphors in Persian will find them active in FitzGerald's poem in a double sense: first, as part of a conceptual design, in which a foreign idiom matches an English spirit, and second as conscious embellishment, which marks the poem as an exotic artefact. As an example, take quatrains II and III:

> Dreaming when Dawn's Left hand was in the Sky[2]
> I heard a Voice within the Tavern cry,
>   'Awake, my Little ones, and fill the Cup
> Before Life's Liquor in its Cup be dry.'

> And, as the Cock crew, those who stood before
> The Tavern shouted – 'Open then the Door!
>   You know how little while we have to stay,
> And, once departed, may return no more.'

In endnote 2, FitzGerald glosses the phrase 'when Dawn's Left Hand was in the Sky' as 'The *"False Dawn;" Subhi Kházib*, a transient Light on the horizon about an Hour before the *Subhi Sâdhik*, or True Dawn; a well known Phenomenon in the East.' It is at this ambiguous time that 'the Voice within the Tavern' exhorts drinkers to resume drinking. In quatrain III, however, the time of early morning (in Persian, *sahar*) is indicated by a more familiar English idiom: 'And as the Cock crew . . .' No endnote is needed here because FitzGerald's readers would already know about this idiomatic indication. But FitzGerald's reference has a direct counterpart in Persian too: *khorooskhan* (or *khorooskhoon*) is a metaphoric denotation of the time of the sunrise in Persian. Although this belief is not very accurate and varies geographically, the rooster, in Persian cultural tradition, is believed to crow three times during the night: once at midnight, once an hour after midnight, and once before the time of *sahar*. The last was traditionally important in Muslim religious practice, since the rooster's crowing indicated both the time of the Morning Prayer and of the *sahari* (which is the food that Muslims consume before dawn during the fasting month of Ramadan). The *khoroos* and its crowing may have given way to other, more mechanical measurements of time, but the expression *khorooskhan* has remained an idiomatic expression that designates the very early morning time. How much of all this FitzGerald knew, we cannot tell; but we may at least say that his use of 'cock crow' is by no means incompatible with the way the metaphor is used in colloquial Persian. It would, in fact, be unfair to accuse him of imposing a Western (English) idea onto the original because his application of the image fits well with how it is conceived in Persian. Here, FitzGerald uses the expression to denote how closely the sequence of incidents in the opening parts of the poem happen one after another. The mention of the 'cock crow' also fits well with ideological design of FitzGerald's poem: there are numerous occasions in the *Rubáiyát* where a symbol or reference with strong religious implication is brought in to denote something irreligious. Here, the 'cock crow' invites 'those who stood before | The Tavern' not to say their prayer, which would be expected and pious, but to recommence drinking, which would be sinful in this imaginary Muslim Persian locality. I will come back to this connection later in the chapter.

Another example of Persian metaphorical expression comes in the renowned quatrain XI. FitzGerald's rendering here is not a word-for-word translation, but the quatrain perfectly conveys the sentiment of the original using the same metaphorical image:

> Here with a Loaf of Bread beneath the Bough,
> A Flask of Wine, a Book of Verse – and Thou
>   Beside me singing in the Wilderness –
> And Wilderness is Paradise enow.

The above stanza is an embodiment of the *carpe diem* philosophy of the *Rubáiyát*. FitzGerald opens his verse by naming similar simple elements to those of the original. Then, with the use of dash, he distinguishes the importance of the beloved's presence in this imaginary transformation of the 'Wilderness' to 'Paradise'. The verse follows its Persian counterpart by reaffirming that the company of the beloved, along with some other simple things, can bring heavenly pleasure to an isolated desert:

> I need a jug of wine and a book of poetry,
> Half a loaf for a bite to eat,
> Then you and I, seated in a deserted spot,
> Will have more wealth than a sultan's realm.[36]

تنگی می لعل خواهم و دیوانی

سد رمقی خواهد و نصف نانی

وانگه من و تو نشسته در ویرانی

خوش تر بود از مملکت سلطانی

This is *rubáiy* 149 in the Ouseley MS. The idea is that the satisfaction of the simplest appetites can turn *virani* (desolation) into a *mamlekate sultani* (Sultan's realm). In the second line, the speaker, in order to emphasise the plainness of his desires, uses the expression *nesfe-nani* (half a loaf). But this reference here is metaphorical. While a loaf of bread might still be considered literally as an adequately nutritive substance at that time, to be satisfied with a loaf of bread is a familiar Persian idiom for contentment with simple pleasure: the poet's modest diminishment of it in the verse elucidates the simplicity of his needs. *Nan* or bread has a long history in Persian culture. In literary art as well as the everyday speech of the people Persia, *nan* stands as the humblest and simplest nutritive substance. From a religious perspective, *nan* is also regarded as a blessing conferred by God. It could be interpreted symbolically as income or means of livelihood, as in the Christian phrase 'our daily bread' in the Lord's Prayer. FitzGerald's understanding of this Persian metaphor is even more tangible in the final revision of the verse in the third (1872) edition of the *Rubáiyát*:

> A Book of Verses underneath the Bough,
> A Jug of Wine, a Loaf of Bread – and Thou
>   Beside me singing in the Wilderness –
> Oh, Wilderness were Paradise enow!

FitzGerald moves 'a Book of Verses' to the first line, bringing into immediate juxtaposition the 'Jug of Wine' and the 'Loaf of Bread'. The conjunction of bread and wine is familiar in English, not least because of the Eucharist, and to a British reader who knew nothing of Persian it might seem that this is a witty reversal of a Christian motif. But in Persian the juxtaposition carries a different connotation. The *nan* is the narrator's selected food; wine is his chosen beverage (wine is repeatedly mentioned in the *rubáiyát*, yet there are far fewer references to bread). But these two are dissimilar substances, and their juxtaposition creates a dichotomy. Wine is the product of a complex process of manufacture, which includes fermentation; the unleavened *nan*, on the other hand, is the humblest form of food. Wine is forbidden pleasure; bread has religious sanction. It seems that the narrator is daring and epicurean in his choice of drink, humble and pious in his choice of food. This is what the speaker in the original *rubáiy* seeks to achieve by using the allegorical expression of 'half a loaf'. The *nan* denotes a type of food but is also a sign of contentment in life. The wine (and the beloved), on the other hand, denotes the poet's desire to enjoy this earthly life. Each expression inflects the other. In one sense, the pleasure of wine is assimilated to the modest contentment of half a *nan*. In another sense, the poet needs no more than half a *nan*, because he has wine and his beloved, and as long as those are present, even a wasteland can seem a heavenly place.

Persian Idioms

Despite the risk of making his translation dense and perhaps even unreadable, FitzGerald goes a step further, introducing Persian colloquial idioms into his composition. He does this partly out of a real relish for the language, whose praises fill his letters to Cowell. But the deployment of such idioms is also affected by his translation strategy. The *Rubáiyát* does not simply transmit its Persian idioms, but gives a modified representation of them, so that they remain conceptually close to their counterpart. In other words, FitzGerald takes Persian idiomatic expressions, distorts them, and then deploys them in his translation. Several quatrains in the *Rubáiyát* bear the marks of this process, for example quatrain XII:

> 'How Sweet is mortal Sovranty!' – think some:
> Others – 'How blest the Paradise to come!'
>   Ah, Take the Cash in hand and wave the Rest;
> Oh, the brave Music of a *distant* Drum!

It is difficult to give a judgement on FitzGerald's translation. The quatrain carries a similar message to that of the original but it is not a literal conversion. In the first two lines of the original *rubáiy*, which is 34 in Ouseley MS, the poet compares two analogous phenomena, analogous in the sense that they are both delightful:

> They say houris make the gardens of Paradise delicious
> I say that the juice of the vine is delicious
> Take the cash and reject the credit –
> The sound of a distant drum, brother, is sweet.[37]

گویند بهشت عدن با حور خوشست

من میگویم که اب انگور خوشست

این نقد بگیر و دست از این نسیه بدار

اواز دهل شنیدن از دور خوشست

The poet juxtaposes 'they say' alongside that of his own; what 'they say' to be pleasant is the erotic delight, set in the promised gardens of heaven. But what the poet deems pleasurable is the immediate earthly pleasure of drinking the 'juice of the vine'. To put differently, the poet ridicules what 'they say' as a basis for conduct because it is imaginary and unseen; instead, he insists on his own worldly assumptions because they are present and proven. To highlight the falseness of the promised 'gardens of Paradise', he then uses two Persian proverbs (*masal*) in the last two lines of the *rubáiy*. These set phrases are brought in to complete the meaning of the verse. The first one, 'take the cash and reject the credit', underscores the importance of treasuring the present moment. The expression originates from an outdated trading practice, whereby *nesye* (credit) would be of notable value, since commerce depended largely on reputation rather than mere cash; *nesye*, in other words, would have been a purchase with a promised or indefinitely postponed payment. It was usually bestowed upon a person who had existing credit with the owner, though trading with cash was still regarded as more reasonable, more satisfactory than the *nesye*. The idiom is easily adapted to a philosophical reflection: what is earthly pleasure is immediate and empirical. Future bliss depends on the uncertainty of a promise that may turn out to be false. The second proverb is similarly adapted to the poet's purpose Traditionally, playing the *dohoul* (kettledrum) was a common practice through which people would be notified about an event which was commonly of a festive nature. The loud music of the *dohoul* would generate a feeling of delight in a distant listener; but the very same sound would cause great irritation for one nearby. The idiom derives its moral point from this paradox.

Ideas that might seem cheering from afar can be disturbing or even futile in actuality.

The two idioms complement each other. They play with distance and closeness in an opposed way. Reach out for what lies to hand, says the first; beware the allure of what is distant, says the second, for on closer inspection it may show itself to be false and shallow. FitzGerald understood the meaning of the quatrain as well as the importance of the proverbs in completing its message. But in translating it, he diverges from it, which ironically is an indication of his understanding of it. While there are only two voices in the Persian ('they' and 'I'), there are three in his: those who think 'How Sweet is mortal Sovranty'; those who believe 'the Paradise to come' is 'blest'; and the narrator, who is presumably Omar, and who concludes the stanza with the proverbs. To convey the presence of these voices in his verse, he relies on dashes and inverted commas, distancing and isolating the phrases. These appear as inset panels in an internal monologue (or spoken aloud, if the line was written to be performed). The panels are bookended around 'think some: Others', which also separates the phrases, and weakens their arguments by isolating them as well as pitting them against each other (the two phrases exhibit opposing arguments). The power in the line, nonetheless, remains in the narrator's hand; he has the last word, which gives the impression that we are the audience and he is the judge. FitzGerald finishes the first proverb with the 'Rest' followed by a semicolon. The semicolon functions as an equaliser; the 'Rest', which ought to be set aside, is identical to the brave music of a drum. From there, the final textual mark of the line comes into play. The word '*distant*' is italicised because it has a major role in conferring the deceptiveness of paradise. The adjective *distant*, applied to the music of a drum, has an eye on the unreachable and unseen paradise, which is promised to be enjoyable; but it might turn out to be futile and shallow when it comes close. Also, the speaker in FitzGerald's line is making a decision by aligning the two notions, 'mortal Sovranty' and 'the Paradise to come'. After considering what both groups have to say, the speaker, who is Omar and sits in judgement in the verse, implicitly expounds his thought through the Persian idioms. For him, 'mortal Sovranty' is just as delusive a prospect as 'the Paradise to come'. Neither gives the pleasant and reassuring feeling of having 'Cash in hand'. Therefore, what has not been seen and is merely a matter of promise – the *nesye*-like heaven – should be disregarded.

The 'KÚZA-NÁMA' offers another example of how the *Rubáiyát* stays conceptually faithful to its Persian origin. FitzGerald, who was very much impressed with the personification of clay in the original, and its use as a living, speaking entity, gathered all the quatrains with a similar theme in one place under the title of 'KÚZA-NÁMA', and coined the story of the speaking pots in the first edition of the poem. He starts his anecdote by dividing a *rubáiy* into two quatrains, numbers LIX and LX:

> Listen again. One Evening at the Close
> Of Ramazán, ere the better Moon arose,
> In that old Potter's Shop I stood alone
> With the clay Population round in Rows.

> And strange to tell, among that Earthen Lot
> Some could articulate, while others not:
> And suddenly one more impatient cried –
> 'Who is the Potter, pray, and who the Pot?'

Although some elements and images, such as 'Ramazán', the rising of the better moon, or the 'one more impatient cried', are FitzGerald's additions, the definitional essence of the original has remain intact in the translation, particularly in the closing line of quatrain LX which is not translated directly but is still remarkably close to the original: *rubáiy* 103 in the Ouseley MS or 306 in the Calcutta MS (which does not follow the *aaaa* rhyming scheme of the *rubáiy*):

> I was in the potter's shop last night,
> And saw two thousand jugs some speaking, some dumb;
> Each was anxiously asking,
> 'Where is the potter, and the buyer, and seller of pots?'[38]

> رفتم به در کوزه گری گیرم دوش
> دیدم دو هزار کوزه گویا و خموش
> ناگه یکی کوزه بر اوارد خروش
> کو کوزه گر و کوزه خر و کوزه فروش

FitzGerald was not sure about the translation of the word *ku* (کو). He wrote to Cowell in May 1857 asking about this quatrain:

> I must transcribe my *Sketch* for the second of those Potter Tetrastichs, as I am not sure of the meaning of the last line [.] I have taken it to be – 'What? Does he who moulds the Pots *traffic* in them?' [. . .] But does it only mean – 'here are we Pots made – *by* whom, *for* whom, and for what end?' Which I suppose is right after all.[39]

However, as Daniel Karlin points out, FitzGerald 'knew perfectly well that *ku* means "where", since a pun on this word formed the climax of the stanza found by Binning at Persepolis and translated by FitzGerald in endnote 11':

> This Palace that its Top to Heaven threw,
> And Kings their forehead on its Threshold drew –
>   I saw a Ring-dove sitting there alone,
> And 'Coo, Coo, Coo,' she cried, and 'Coo, Coo, Coo.'[40]

The beauty of FitzGerald's translation lies in the fact that even though he could not have known the difference between *koja* ('where') and its abbreviated form *ku* in the Persian language, as well as the reasoning behind the use of *ku* instead of *koja* in the *rubáiy*, he preferred to use the word 'who' instead of 'where' as he thought it would better convey the concealed message of the original. *Dehkhoda* makes clear that even though *ku* and *koja* have similar meanings, they are grammatically different: the word *ku* can appear on its own; it does not need to precede a verb, whereas *koja* has to be followed by a verb for the completion of the meaning. In addition, unlike *koja*, *ku* should only be used in referring to the third person or object. Clearly, these grammatical differences make them quite dissimilar in their context of use: while *koja* can be used in any context, *ku* should only be used where one has already been unable to find or locate a sought-after object.[41] In other words, the word *ku* indicates the previous vain efforts in finding an object as well as expressing disappointment. With that token, the question of the 'KÚZA' is not a question of geographical location or individual position. It is a lamentation for the disappointment in finding no rationale behind the mysteries of creation. FitzGerald knew well that neither 'where' nor 'who' could accurately convey this photophysical idea, but he thought using 'who' would establish a better thematic association with the original. He recognised that the word 'who' would more lucidly demonstrate that the intention of the quatrains is not to question place, position, or circumstance but to demand an answer for the question of creation, a demand which originates chiefly from despondency and scepticism.

Islamic Allusions

As noted at the start, a large number of the *rubáiyát* in the manuscripts bear a strong sense of philosophical scepticism towards divinity, at least in the forms conveyed by religious dogma. Theological beliefs are not merely questioned in these poems but are strongly challenged. This ideological aspect of the poems, as FitzGerald understood it, mirrored his own religious perplexities. FitzGerald took the scepticism, or antagonism, shown towards orthodox religion in the *rubáiyát* as a consequence of their author's sense of nationalism. He believed Khayyám was a conserver of that 'older-Time' Persia who disapproved of, and rejected, an imported ideology, Islam, imposed by the Arab conquest and by subsequent dynasties, including the Saljuqs (1040–1220) under which the poet himself was born. To him, Omar was not only an agnostic but also a nationalist who had revolted against his country's 'false Religion, and false, or foolish, Devotion to it', a figure who expressed his contention through advocating hedonism and joviality.[42] But however true, such contentions had roots in FitzGerald's own Victorian attitudes too. FitzGerald's conception of Islamic culture was shaped by the prejudices of his period. He was simply not fond of Islam. Like many of his contemporaries, he thought of Islam as an importation that had ruined the glory of ancient Persia; FitzGerald speaks about this in his Preface, that Persia's native soul 'was quite broke by a foreign Creed as well as foreign Conquest'.[43] The repercussion of such disapproving outlooks is the resentment towards Islam that permeates the *Rubáiyát*; for example, FitzGerald's endnote on how the fasting month of Ramadan 'makes the Musulman unhealthy and unamiable'.[44] The irony here, though, is that despite its largely impious orientation, Islam and Islamic notions are still part of the fabric of the *Rubáiyát*; though not in an overt fashion as these might have been unknowingly and accidentally added to the poem as the result of FitzGerald's haphazard study of Persian.

It must be remembered that FitzGerald's encounter with Persian literature was not limited to Khayyám. He had made other ventures into Persian poetry, much of which is founded on Islamic teachings. In a period of four to five years, while he was learning Persian, FitzGerald read Firdausi, Attar, Rumi, Hafiz, and Jami.[45] Apart from Firdausi whose antiquarian writings are less influenced by Islam but are not necessarily anti-Islamic, the poetry of Hafiz, Attar, and Rumi is essentially built with Islamic thoughts. FitzGerald's choice of Jami's *Salámán and Absál* as his first translation of Persian, for instance, suggests that he could have not been unaware of the presence of Islam in Persian poetry. His interest in, and work on, Attar's *Mantiq ul-Tair* ('The Conference of the Birds') also alludes to the same fact, that he knew Islam looms large in

Persia's classical poetry.[46] It is, however, significant in this light to note that the Islamic manifestations in the *Rubáiyát* do not for the most part signify religious teachings, or conform to Qur'anic reasoning. They are embedded in the poems for aesthetic reasons: to render them more Oriental rather than Islamic, although this goes against the conventional practice that prevails amongst the Persian classics: Islamic notions circulate as a matter of course in Persian poetry, borrowed by one poet from another, sometimes with profound religious intention, sometimes as a matter of form. FitzGerald would have encountered examples of either practice: he was free, or felt himself free, to interpret the Islamic elements of Khayyám's poetry, which he could not help seeing entwined in the body of the text, as *not* necessarily reflecting the poet's subservience to actual Islamic doctrines.

Returning to the second quatrain in the *Rubáiyát*, let us now consider FitzGerald's reference to the concept of the 'False Dawn' as an illustration of the use of Islamic elements:

Dreaming when Dawn's Left Hand was in the Sky[2]
I heard a Voice within the Tavern cry,
    'Awake, my little ones, and fill the cup
Before Life's Liquor in its Cup be dry.'

As we saw earlier on, FitzGerald glosses the phrase 'when Dawn's Left Hand was in the Sky' as 'The "*False Dawn*;" *Subhi Kházib*, a transient Light on the horizon about an Hour before the *Subhi Sâdhik*, or True Dawn; a well known Phenomenon in the East.' But no reference to any of these phenomena exists in the original *rubáiy*, apart from the word *sahar*, which, in Persian, means the very early morning. Such digressions are, however, part of FitzGerald's translation strategy and the ideological scheme of his *Rubáiyát*. In rendering the *rubáiyát*, FitzGerald, in the vein of the poet of the originals, incorporates religious convictions to imply paradoxically irreligious connotations. An example of this occurs here in quatrain II. In early Islamic astronomy, the observation of daytime twilight, known as 'true dawn', indicated the start of *sahar*, the time to commence the Morning Prayer (which lasts till sunrise). Muslims view this period as holy, as a time for seeking repentance and supplication, a belief which is, in fact, supported by a verse in the Qur'an: 'And in the mornings they would ask for forgiveness'.[47] But FitzGerald turns this notion on its head. He transforms the idea of *sahar* in the original verse into something decadent, conducive to committing the 'sin' of wine drinking; the 'Voice within the Tavern' summons the drinkers to 'fill the cup' and drink at the time of the 'False Dawn'. To complete his narrative, and to underline the 'falseness' of his depicted dawn, he then introduces a second Islamic motif: he personifies the dawn by attributing a 'Left Hand' to it, which in Islam (as in other religions) is considered a symbol of transgression and guilt. In Chapter 56 of the Qur'an, for instance, sinners are described as the 'Companions of the Left (O Companions of the Left!) mid burning winds and boiling waters and the shadow of a smoking blaze neither cool, neither goodly; and before that they lived at ease and persisted in the Great Sin'.[48] It is unlikely that FitzGerald knew about the Qur'anic origin of the image of the 'left hand', but he certainly knew that the 'left hand' would complete his poetic picture: the false dawn of the drinkers needs a wicked image, and the left hand fits this description. It is, however, likely that he might have come upon the allusion in Persian poetry. There are, for examples, mentions of the 'True Dawn' and the 'False Dawn' in Hafiz's and Rumi's poetry, but it is difficult to ascertain how FitzGerald could have obtained his knowledge of Islamic astronomy, perhaps from his reading of Barthélmy d'Herbelot's *Bibliotheque orientale* (1697), which was one his principal sources for learning about Persian and Arabic history and culture, or perhaps from his conversations with Cowell.[49] But in any case, the allusion fits his depiction of Omar: the poem's subtitle, after all, names Omar Khayyám as 'The Astronomer-Poet of Persia'; there is also a mention of the role that Khayyám played in the reform of the calendar and his authorship of 'astronomical tables' in the Preface.[50]

Quatrain IV offers another example of Islamic allusions in the *Rubáiyát*:

> Now the New Year reviving old Desires,
> The thoughtful Soul to Solitude retires,
>   Where the WHITE HAND OF MOSES on the Bough
> Puts out, and Jesus from the Ground suspires.

There are two counterparts to this verse in the manuscripts, and FitzGerald's quatrain gives an accurate representation of both. One of them is *rubáiy* 80 in the Ouseley MS:

> This is the time when the world is adorned by the eastern breeze,
> and fountains are released from the eye of the clouds;
> blossoms (white) like Moses' hand show the palms from the branches,
> herbs (reviving) as Jesus' breath come forth from the earth.[51]

وقت است که از صبا جهان ارایند
وز چشم سحاب چشم ها بگشایند
موسی دستان ز شاخ کف بنمایند
عیسی نفسان ز خاک بیرون ایند

The other is quatrain 13 in the same manuscript:

Now that the world has the means of attaining happiness
Every man alive in heart has a yearning for the wilderness;
On every branch is the budding of a (cluster white as) Moses' hand,
In every moment is the sighing of a (breeze reviving as) Jesus' breath.[52]

اکنون که جهان را به خوشی دسترسی است
هر زنده دلی را سوی صحرا هوسی است
بر هر شاخی طلوع موسی دستی است
در هر نفسی خروش عیسی نفسی است

FitzGerald opens his quatrain by referring to an ancient but existing practice amongst the Iranians: the celebration of the *Norouz*.
New Year, or *Norouz* (new day), as it is known in Iran and around
the world, is a celebration of the spring equinox. FitzGerald shows
his awareness of the importance of the tradition, and perhaps he
thinks his readers might not know about it, in an elaborate endnote,
where he talks about the origin of the *Norouz* and the transforma-
tions that nature goes through at this time.[53] In his commendation
of the spring, he then follows what the poet of the original has done
in these poems: describing the beauty of the spring by using familiar
Persian idioms. But these idioms both have their roots in the Qur'an.
That means, the charm of the spring is described in these poems
through adopting Qur'anic paradigms. FitzGerald, in his rendition
of these poems, uses similar Islamic implications. The first allusion,
'the WHITE HAND OF MOSES', refers to a verse in the Qur'an which
narrates the miracle of the white hand of Moses: 'So he (Moses) cast
his staff, and behold, it was a serpent manifest. And he drew forth his
hand, and lo, it was white to the beholders.'[54] Similarly, *masiha nafas*
(Messiah-like breath) or *masiha dam* is an ancient Persian religious
motif, the origin of which goes back to the story of Jesus's miracle narrated in the Qur'an: 'and when I taught thee the Book, the Wisdom,
the Torah, the Gospel; and when thou createst out of clay, by My
leave, as the likeness of a bird, and thou breathest into it, and it is a
bird, by My leave; and thou healest the blind and the leper by My
leave, and thou bringest the dead forth by My leave'.[55] FitzGerald,

in his endnote, relates the first reference to the book of 'Exodus iv.
6; where Moses draws forth his Hand – not, according to the Persians,
"*leprous as Snow,*" – but *white* as our May-Blossom in Spring
perhaps!'[56] In reference to the second one: 'According to them [the
Persians] also the Healing Power of Jesus resided in his Breath.'[57] But
there is no mention of the Islamic origin of these sayings. FitzGerald perhaps was either unaware of their roots or wanted to point
his readers towards a familiar landscape: the Bible. The Qur'anic
references, nevertheless, inevitably introduce a new dimension to
his piece: even though he may have not noticed their origin, he is
still aware of the estranging (other) experience that the peculiarity of
these allusions would bring to his text.

Islamic influence manifests also in quatrains XXXI–XXXIII:

Up from Earth's Centre through the Seventh Gate
I rose, and on the Throne of Saturn sate,
    And many Knots unravel'd by the Road;
But not the Knot of Human Death and Fate.

There was a Door to which I found no Key:
There was a Veil past which I could not see:
    Some little Talk awhile of ME and THEE;
There seem'd – and then no more of THEE, and ME.

Then to the rolling Heav'n itself I cried,
Asking, 'What Lamp had Destiny to guide
    Her little Children stumbling in the Dark?'
And – 'A blind Understanding!' Heav'n replied.

These quatrains narrate the fictional story of Omar's ascent to the
'Seventh Gate' of heaven. But the narrative, despite its imaginary
nature, shares striking similarities with the account of the Islamic
prophet's Ascension. In Islamic tradition, *al-Mi'raj* is the story of
Prophet Mohammad's ascension to heaven and his return in a few
minutes to Mecca. There is a direct mention of Mohammad's celestial journey in the Qur'an, in Chapter 17, verse 1: 'Glory be to Him,
who carried His servant by night from the Holy Mosque to the further Mosque the precincts of which We have blessed, that We might
show him some of Our signs. He is the All-hearing, the All-seeing.'
Different parts of paradise and hell are believed to have been revealed
to the prophet during his celestial tour of the heavens. FitzGerald's
quatrain XXXI draws a similar image: many of Omar's puzzles are
resolved through observing the celestial signs ('And many Knots

unravel'd by the Road'); although his main perplexity, the 'Knot of Human Death and Fate', remains unresolved, as he is only allowed to visit certain parts of heaven; Omar is not permitted to see behind the curtain of fate and to become apprised of the mystery of creation: 'There was a Door to which I found no Key: | There was a Veil past which I could not see'. But, then, this leads us to another resemblance between these two narratives and their leading characters: according to Islamic traditions, Mohammad too was not allowed to see everything that the higher levels of heaven contained; God was also never revealed to him. But there is also a key difference between these two characters. Mohammad is a true believer and the prophet of a sacred religion. This means he would not need to be given such a celestial revelation to supplement his religious assurance, since as a prophet his belief would have been already perfected. Put differently, the prophet would never have been granted such a journey unless his faith had *already* reached to its highest level. By contrast, FitzGerald's Omar is a sceptic who needs to observe and experience phenomena to believe them. It is in fact because of his disbelief that he is given permission for a tour of 'the Seventh Gate'. He visits the sky to witness and to believe.

Whether the similarities and deviations between Omar and Mohammad are the result of an accidental infusion of knowledge of Islamic values in Persian literature, or whether FitzGerald was knowingly marshalling such references, we do not know. But what is clear is that the design of Omar's character at this part of FitzGerald's narrative is polemically against the Islamic prophet and what he embodies in Islamic belief. Omar is a symbol of cynicism and hedonism, Mohammad an embodiment of piety and faith. Mohammad returns to earth in utmost belief. But the outcome of Omar's journey is absolute disbelief. After discovering that he is not permitted to see every celestial sign, Omar, who is increasingly puzzled by his failure to find the 'truth', turns to the 'rolling Heav'n' (a metaphor for the creator in English and Persian) and asks for a guiding 'Lamp' to lead himself out of this scepticism. But the 'Lamp' that the 'rolling Heav'n' provides does not lessen his puzzlement; on the contrary, it amplifies his doubt and disbelief. The sign that 'Heav'n' offers to Omar is not a guiding 'Lamp' but a pathway returning to darkness. The disappointing response of the 'rolling Heav'n' leaves Omar with no alternative than his earlier companion: 'Then to this Earthen Bowl did I adjourn' (XXXIV).

FitzGerald was an unusual poet amongst the Victorians. Most of those who adapted Oriental themes did not know the languages from which they were telling their stories. FitzGerald, by contrast, learned Persian: the distinctiveness of the *Rubáiyát*, in fact, comes in part from FitzGerald diligent use of a dictionary. Unlike many of his contemporaries, and thanks to his friendship with Cowell, he possessed at least an outline of Persian history and culture, however imperfect. Nevertheless, his versions of what he understood as Omar Khayyám are not quite translations, neither are they quite original poems: yet they are an extraordinary fusion of two cultures and two sensibilities. There is a unified fluency in the *Rubáiyát* that constantly speaks to the reader of the foreignness of its origin; although there are few actual Persian words, FitzGerald has fittingly and seamlessly incorporated Persian phrases, metaphors, and idioms in his translation that mark the cultural distinctiveness of Persia. The *Rubáiyát* is filled with many Persian borrowings that recreate the 'touch' of an original piece of writing. But not every reader of the text can appreciate this technical aspect of the poem, since that requires a good understanding of Persian as well as English; yet the cumulative effect of FitzGerald's hybrid method makes itself felt even without such technical knowledge.

Notes

1. For a detailed discussion of Khayyám's date of birth and death, see Boyle, 'Omar Khayyam: Astronomer, Mathematician and Poet', pp. 30–2. An abridged version of Boyle's essay is also available as a chapter in *The Cambridge History of Iran* (vol. 4) under the title of ''Umar Khayyam: Astronomer, Mathematician and Poet'.
2. Boyle, 'Omar Khayyam', p. 34; Avery, 'Introduction', p. 32.
3. Boyle, 'Omar Khayyam', p. 35; Avery, 'Introduction', pp. 27–8.
4. Boyle, 'Omar Khayyam', p. 35.
5. Boyle, 'Omar Khayyam', pp. 35–6; Avery, 'Introduction', p. 27.
6. See Boyle, 'Omar Khayyam', p. 36; Avery, 'Introduction', pp. 33–4. For more on Khayyám's life, Avery, 'Introduction', pp. 15–18 and pp. 25–34; Amin Razavi, *Wine of Wisdom*, pp. 18–31; Elwell-Sutton, 'Omar Khayyám'; Minorsky, 'Omar Khaiyām', p. 985 (a translation of Minorsky's essay by Khoramshahi is also available in *May o Mina*). And in Persian, see Dashti, *Dami ba Khayyám* ('A Moment with Khayyám'); Forouzanfar, 'Ghadimitarin Etela' az Zendegi-e Khayyám' ('The Oldest Data on Khayyám's Life'); Minorsky, 'Omar Khaiyām'; Foroughi, 'Introduction'. Dashti's book is also available in English as *In Search of Omar Khayyám*, translated by Elwell-Sutton.
7. Morton, 'Some 'Umarian Quatrains from the Lifetime of 'Umar Khayyām', p. 55.

8. Avery, 'Introduction', p. 34.
9. For example, twenty-one in *Nuzhat ul-Majales* ('Delight of Assemblies', 1330–1), and thirteen in *Munis ul-Ahrar fi Daqayeq ul-Ash'ar* ('The Noble Men's Companion to Verses' Subtitles', 1340–1). See Avery, 'Introduction', p. 38.
10. For my exploration of the textual history of the *rubáiyát*, I am indebted to Avery's 'Introduction', pp. 34–42.
11. For a discussion of Khayyám's non-literary writings, see Amin Razavi, *Wine of Wisdom*, pp. 31–9 and pp. 188–203.
12. For more on the question of the authorship of the *rubáiyát*, see Arberry, *Omar Khayyám*; Morton, 'Some 'Umarian Quatrains from the Lifetime of 'Umar Khayyām'; Minorsky, 'Omar K̲h̲aiyām', pp. 986–8 (Minorsky's entry is available in Persian); Arberry, 'Omar Khayyam and FitzGerald'. And in Persian; Dashti, *Dami ba Khayyám*, pp. 17–30; Homai', 'Moghaddamey'e bar *Tarabkhane*' ('An Introduction to *Tabarkhane*'); Qani, 'Tahghighat Darbareye Khayyám' ('Investigations about Khayyám'); Hedayat, 'Khayyám-e Philsooph' ('Khayyám the Philosopher'); Foroughi, 'Introduction'; Khorramshahi, 'Foreword'.
13. Dashti, *Dami ba Khayyám*, pp. 177–8
14. The four editions appear in sequence in Decker, *Edward FitzGerald*. The revisions are tracked in Karlin's *Rubáiyát*, which takes 1859 as its copy-text.
15. Terhune, in his notes on FitzGerald's letter of 7 October 1853, indicates that it was the second edition (1775) of Jones's *Grammar* that FitzGerald used in his learning of Persian; 'EFG's annotated copy of the second edition is now in Cambridge University Library.' See Terhune and Terhune, *Letters*, vol. 2, p. 111; Gail, *Persia and the Victorians*, p. 33.
16. See Arberry, *The Romance*, p. 14.
17. The Oxford MS is known as the 'Ouseley MS', since it was found in the collection of Oriental manuscripts belonging to the diplomat and traveller Sir William Ouseley, purchased by the Bodleian in 1843.
18. Terhune and Terhune, *Letters*, vol. 2, p. 335.
19. In a letter of 19 December 1878 to James Russell Lowell, FitzGerald speaks of his translation strategy in rendering the Spanish dramas. See Terhune and Terhune, *Letters*, vol. 4, p. 167.
20. See FitzGerald's letter to Cowell of May 1855 (Terhune and Terhune, *Letters*, vol. 2, p. 164): 'I am more and more convinced of the Necessity of keeping as much as possible to the Oriental *Forms*, and carefully avoiding any that bring one back to Europe and the 19th Century. It is better to be Orientally obscure than Europeanly clear.'
21. For the poem's indebtedness to English literature, see, for instance, Karlin, *Rubáiyát* (pp. xliii–xlv) and Decker, 'Edward FitzGerald and Other Men's Flowers'.
22. Heron-Allen, *Rubáiyát*; Arberry, *The Romance*; Davis, *Rubáiyát*.

23. *Divan*, also transliterated as *deevan*, is a word in Persian for a collection of poetry.
24. It should be noted that these limits are also opportunities, as they are for short forms in other cultures; for example, the Japanese haiku.
25. For more information on the origin and nature of *rubáiy*, see Elwell-Sutton, '"The Rubā'ī" in Early Persian Literature'.
26. FitzGerald's letter to Cowell of 2 November 1858 (Terhune and Terhune, *Letters*, vol. 2, p. 323).
27. FitzGerald told Cowell of his attempt to translate Khayyám into Latin in a letter of June 1857: 'you will think me a perfectly Aristophanic Old Man when I tell you how many of Omar I could not help running into such bad Latin' (Terhune and Terhune, *Letters*, vol. 2, p. 273). The MS of FitzGerald's Latin translations is in the library of Trinity College, Cambridge. They were first published as an appendix to the Golden Cockerel edition of the *Rubáiyát* by Sir Edward Denison Ross (who acknowledged help from Sir Steven Gaselee) in 1938. See Terhune, *The Life of Edward FitzGerald*, p. 205. They are also reprinted in Arberry, *The Romance*, pp. 58–64, and in Decker, *Edward FitzGerald*, pp. 233–8.
28. Terhune and Terhune, *Letters*, vol. 2, p. 289.
29. Quatrains X, XXVI, XXXII, and XLIX have *aaaa* rhyme scheme, though quatrain X follows the *aaaa* rhyming pattern of its Persian original. The counterparts to the other three quatrains have the rhyming pattern of a *rubáiy*.
30. Mirza Sa'eb's words are quoted in Avery and Heath-Stubbs, *The Ruba'iyat*, p. 11.
31. See FitzGerald's letter to Cowell of 10 January 1856 (Terhune and Terhune, *Letters*, vol. 2, pp. 193–4) as an example of his interest in the 'musical' pleasantness of Persian.
32. See Peter Avery's paper, 'FitzGerald and Hakim Omar Khayyám', delivered at the FitzGerald Centennial Conference at Cambridge in 1959, and translated into Persian by Houshang Pirnazar, in Dehbashi (ed.), *May o Mina*, pp. 758–76.
33. The transliterations are from Arberry, *The Romance*, p. 198.
34. The vocabulary of this line bears Shakespearean associations. See Karlin, *Rubáiyát*, p. 154.
35. There are only a small number of quatrains in the *Rubáiyát* that bear strong phonetic resemblance with their originals. FitzGerald's fidelity to the sound system of the *rubáiyát* perhaps deteriorated in later stages of his work.
36. Quatrain 98 in Avery and Heath-Stubbs, *The Ruba'iyat*, p. 71. The Persian verse is not a *rubáiy*, as it rhymes *aaaa* instead of *aaba*.
37. Quatrain 90 in Avery and Heath-Stubbs, *The Ruba'iyat*, p. 69.
38. Quatrain 73 in Avery and Heath-Stubbs, *The Ruba'iyat*, p. 64.
39. Terhune and Terhune, *Letters*, vol. 2, p. 275.

40. See Karlin, *Rubáiyát*, pp. 86–7. It should be noted that the word 'Coo' in the above verse is not necessarily an interrogative term. It can also be the Persian onomatopoeia for the bird's sound. The sound of the *morgh* (bird), which is translated as the 'Ring-dove' in the quatrain, in Persian poetry often represents the religious reverence and homage to the deity. The quatrain expresses a Sufi belief: all the creatures in the universe are praising their creator in their own way. It is also possible that *ku* is meant to remind the reader of the Sufis' chant *hu(wa),* which means 'He' in Arabic but is a reference to God in this context; *ku* and *hu* sound noticeably similar in Persian.
41. Dekhoda, *Dehkhoda,* vol. 12, p. 18657.
42. *Rubáiyát,* p. 13.
43. Ibid. p. 11.
44. Ibid. p. 59.
45. The rapid growth of FitzGerald's understanding of Persian is evidenced in his letters to Cowell. For more detail on his study of Persian poetry, see 'Introduction' in Arberry, *The Romance,* pp. 41–99; Terhune, *The Life of Edward FitzGerald,* pp. 170–8; Ferrier, 'Edward Fitzgerald, a Reader "Of Taste", and 'Umar Khayyām 1809–1883', pp. 174–9.
46. FitzGerald worked sporadically for almost two decades on a translation of *Mantiq ul-Tair,* though he never managed to publish the fruits of his labours. His translation, 'Bird-Parliament', upon Cowell's approval, was published posthumously in 1889 in William Aldis Wright's *Letters and Literary Remains,* vol. 7, pp. 255–312. The work presented 'a "Bird's Eye" View of the Bird Poem in some sixteen hundred lines'. FitzGerald's letter to Cowell of 2 November 1858 in Terhune and Terhune, *Letters,* vol. 2, p. 322.
47. Chapter 51, verse 18.
48. Verses 45–52.
49. See, for example, part 78 in the *Daftar Panjom* (the fifth book) of Moulavi's *Masanvi Ma'navi.*
50. FitzGerald, *Rubáiyát,* p. 7.
51. Arberry, *The Romance,* p. 109.
52. Ibid. pp. 194–5.
53. Binning's book was one source from which FitzGerald learned about *Norouz.* See Karlin, *Rubáiyát,* pp. 148–9.
54. Chapter 26, verse 32.
55. Chapter 35, verse 110.
56. FitzGerald, *Rubáiyát,* p. 55.
57. Ibid.

Chapter 5

Ferishtah's Fancies

Ferishtah's Fancies was a work of Robert Browning's old age, the first of the three volumes he published after he turned seventy, before his death in 1889. All these volumes, but especially the first two, *Ferishtah's Fancies* (1884) and *Parleyings with Certain People of Importance in Their Day* (1887), were reflective works, in which Browning revisited the major themes and imaginative locations of his life and work. But they were also characteristically restless works, formally complex and innovative, and polemical in spirit. They contained some of Browning's least engaging writing: dense, prickly, mannered, full of a kind of late-Browning poetic lingo which is not quite demotic and not quite high art. Oddly enough, *Ferishtah's Fancies* was a success when it was first published; it was the only volume Browning ever published to be reprinted twice in a year. But this success did not last beyond the First World War, and in modern critical terms it is probably the most neglected of all his work. There are good reasons for this. When you know that Henry Jones based most of his 1912 book, *Browning as a Religious and Philosophical Teacher* on *Ferishtah's Fancies*, you can guess what is coming. To Jones, what was earnest, profound, and consoling about Browning's ideas was exactly what the next generation rejected with a kind of nausea. Since these ideas no longer came clothed in the verse that had enraptured the Pre-Raphaelites, the verse of *Men and Women* (1855), *Dramatis Personae* (1864), and even *The Ring and the Book* (1868–9), it failed utterly to make its way into the twentieth century, and has lain buried.

As a poetic entity, *Ferishtah's Fancies* might not have the artistic value of an unread masterpiece like *Sordello* (1840), or an odd, difficult, dangerous poem like *Fifine at the Fair* (1872). But it is still a fascinating poem, full of thought, as opposed to thoughts, permeated with complex theological teachings and shaped by Browning's passionate undimmed creative intelligence. This imaginative creativity is spread across the poem but is least tangible when it comes to the

Persian fabric of the poem. This is mostly because Browning himself never claimed this facet of his poem to be integral or authentic – which was rather unconventional at the time, as most of his contemporaries would state the opposite, however Oriental their work was. But on 19 October 1884, only a month before the poem's release, Browning wrote to his friend, G. B. Smith: 'Do not suppose there is more than a thin disguise of a few Persian names and allusions.'[1] Browning was telling the truth, though only in part: there is more to the Persian framework of *Ferishtah's Fancies*. But Browning's unassuming attitude led many to take the Persian fabric of his poem to be threadbare. Most critics took him at his word and either ignored the Persian dimension altogether or treated it as a purely conventional backdrop, which does not deserve a separate study. Even critical scholarship on the influence of Persia and Persian poetry on English literature overlooked the Persian design of *Ferishtah's Fancies*.[2] However, the presence of Persia in *Ferishtah' s Fancies* is far more paramount and complex than has been acknowledged by critics or confessed by Browning.[3] It is especially of significance when it is studied in relation to Browning's attitude towards Edward FitzGerald and his *Rubáiyát of Omar Khayyám* (1859), as it reveals itself to conceal another less demonstrative layer of Persian understanding, embedded in the poem by an unintended infusion of knowledge about Persian culture picked up from many sources, among them, of course, FitzGerald's own poem, to whose hero Ferishtah, the leading character of Browning's poem, is, in fact, polemically opposed. To explore the motives behind Browning's adaptation of the Persian theme and the way the less perceptible layer of Persian-ness manifests itself in the poem is my primary purpose in this chapter. But in doing so, I will break down the poem into its constitutive elements, in ways that were not required for FitzGerald's poem, or Arnold's, in part because *Ferishtah's Fancies* is little-known, and has received minimal critical attention, and in part because the very process of close reading is what uncovers its buried, unregarded Persian dimension.

Ferishtah's Fancies: An Overview

Ferishtah's Fancies is a collection of twelve narrative poems, or 'fancies', about the life and teachings of an imaginary Persian sage, Ferishtah, a 'dervish'. It consists of conversations between Ferishtah and his students and is framed by an authorial 'Prologue' and

'Epilogue'. The setting of the poem is medieval Persia, after the Islamic conquest but well before the modern period. Each of the narrative poems is followed by a lyric, printed in smaller type after the closing line yet not given a separate title, and not separately listed in the 'Table of Contents'. The structural composition of the volume makes it hard to assign these lyrics either to the main character, Ferishtah, or to Browning as author. The 'fancies' fall into two uneven categories. The first two poems, 'The Eagle' and 'The Melon-Seller', are set in Ferishtah's youth or early manhood, before he becomes a 'dervish'. The other ten are narratives of occasions on which Ferishtah, now an established teacher, answers a question or solves a problem on theology and moral philosophy posed by one of his pupils. An unnamed narrator sets up the scene for each poem and sets up the dialogue between Ferishtah and his interlocutor, in which the sage always has the last word. This is, however, not quite true when we look at the volume as a whole, because in each poem, after Ferishtah finishes speaking, a different voice comes into play, the voice of the lyrics, which neither belongs to the main poem nor is fully separate from it. I will look at the physical layout, and the vocal structure, of the poems in more detail later in the chapter, but it is worth noting here that Browning appears to have designed the interaction between these two voices to make visible and audible a clash between two kinds of authority in his own poetics, a divide which goes back to his earliest writings and which is truly representative of him in a way the one-dimensional theology of his Ferishtah could never be. Besides the main text, the volume has two epigraphs, one from an entry on Shakespeare in a long-outdated eighteenth-century historical dictionary, and one from *King Lear*. The *King Lear* epigraph is from Act III, scene vi, when the mad king addresses Edgar as Poor Tom: 'You, sir, I entertain for one of my hundred, only I do not like the fashion of your garments. You will say they are Persian; but let them be changed'. The latter quotation operates as an obscure literary joke directed at the process of cultural translation, or the travesty of such a process, that has led Browning to take up an Oriental garb in order to perform on the London literary stage of 1884.

Despite its curiously exotic title, *Ferishtah's Fancies* is not a translation of any kind. Nowhere in the poem does the narrative conform to the Western typology of Persian verse; *Ferishtah's Fancies* is not a transfiguration of a form of Persian poetry. The 'fancies' are all written in English blank verse and the intercalated lyrics that appear at the end of each are in various rhyming and metrical patterns.

Ferishtah's Fancies also does not attempt to imitate Oriental qualities of mystical obscurity, sagacity, or sensuousness; Browning did not want to put on a persona of a Persian poet, nor did he want his poem to appear or sound distinctively Persian – in the way that a poem like the *Rubáiyát* does, for instance. There are, of course, various Persian names and allusions in the poem; but while their inclusion has added an Oriental sentiment to the poem, it has not altered the thematic consistency of Browning's poetry. The tone and the poetic expression in *Ferishtah's Fancies* are noticeably similar to those of Browning's former writings.[4]

Ferishtah's Fancies: Sources

Browning had an interest in the Orient. This is evident in his various uses of Semitic themes in previous works, such as, 'Holy-Cross Day' (*Men and Women*), 'Rabbi Ben Ezra' (*Dramatis Personae*), and 'Jochanan Hakkadosh' (*Jocoseria*, 1883). There are Oriental allusions and images scattered, sometimes rather insignificantly, in his other works too; for example, the underground chamber in the castle of Goito in *Sordello* is covered in occult inscriptions in Arabic. Yet we know little about the extent of Browning's knowledge of Oriental (Arabic and Persian) languages and literatures. With Arabic, we know that he was in touch with Charles J. Lyall, a distinguished Orientalist, since 1878. Lyall's first letter to him concerned Browning's accidental use of the *tawil*, a compound metre in Arabic poetry, in 'Abt Vogler' (*Dramatis Personae*).[5] On 3 June 1878, Lyall sent Browning 'some translations of old Arabic poetry', which was his work on the *Mo'allaqat*.[6] A year later, on 10 June 1879, he wrote a following letter to Browning, thanking him for his 'kind acknowledgment' of his 'translations of ancient Arab verse'.[7] Browning made use of Lyall's scholarship too: once in his Arabic-inspired poem 'Muléykeh' (*Dramatic Idylls, Second Series*, 1880), and later in *Ferishtah's Fancies*. After receiving Lyall's letter of 13 December 1884, in which he had suggested six corrections 'chiefly in Persian names', Browning made a number of changes to the third edition of *Ferishtah's Fancies*.[8]

With Persian, however, Browning had little engagement prior to *Ferishtah's Fancies*. He had little, if any, knowledge of the Persian language, and his exposure to Persian literature was limited to only a few sources in English, one of which he had read in his early manhood. As he explained to his friend and future biographer, Alexandra

Orr, the story of 'The Eagle', the second poem in *Ferishtah's Fancies*, 'is from Pilpay's Fables: I read it when a boy and lately put it into verse: then it occurred to me to make the Dervish one Ferishtah and the poem, the beginning of a series'.[9] The incident of the eagle is indeed taken directly from Chapter II, Fable III of *Kalila and Dimna or The Fables of Bidpai*, which was translated by Rev. Wyndham Knatchbull in 1819.[10] There are similarities between Bidpai and Ferishtah. In the opening chapter, for instance, Bidpai is described as 'a man of so distinguished a reputation for wisdom, that his opinion was asked in all matters of great difficulty'.[11] Bidpai is also a sage who teaches through parables; while giving lessons to his disciples in the same chapter, he, for example, relays a story of a lark that seeks other animals' aid to take vengeance against an elephant that has destroyed its brood. Browning's Ferishtah does this too, in the sense that his didactic parables are akin to Bidpai's animal fables. Both of these forms of storytelling are integral, and ever-present, in Persian literary-cultural tradition – something that Browning might have had in mind while writing *Ferishtah's Fancies*. The source text of the book of *Bidpai*, *Kalila va Demneh*, is, in fact, an iconic example of the Oriental mode of storytelling; the book is a collection of fables in which animals are given human qualities. These stories are told for instructive purposes, for the delivery of moral lessons, as with the parables of the Qur'an. From a Persian perspective, the Qur'an is indeed an epitome of the parabolic mode of teaching; the Islamic scripture contains various tales of edifying nature, and Ferishtah seems to be following the same practice in his teaching of ethics and faith; although the Bible, and particularly the Gospels, many of whose teachings are conveyed through the same technique, is more likely to have been a model for him. To an English reader, Ferishtah is, in fact, more reminiscent of Jesus than an Oriental sage. Jesus, as recorded, for instance, in the book of Matthew, Mark, or Luke in the New Testament, speaks in parables, and he does so to make his message more intelligible for his disciples, particularly for those who are unlikely to grasp scriptural thoughts without applying earthly measures: 'Therefore speak I to them in parables: because seeing they see not; and hearing they hear not, neither do they understand' (Matthew 13: 13). The parables of Ferishtah similarly have both didactive and spiritual application; they are told for the sake of clarity in comprehending theological edicts.

Prior to *Ferishtah's Fancies*, Browning, however, did not seem to have been fond of the parable form. There are instances in his earlier works in which the use of parables is disparaged and

derided. We see this, for example, in Pompilia's confrontation
with the Archbishop in Book VII ('Pompilia') of *The Ring and The
Book*. While on her deathbed, Pompilia, the heroine and victim of
the poem, talks about her abusive relationship with her husband,
Count Guido Franceschini. She recalls the night when, in order
to escape sleeping with her aged husband, she had to take refuge
in the Archbishop's lodging (Pompilia, only twelve years of age,
had married a malignant aristocrat who was much older than her).
But Pompilia had already seen the Archbishop on this subject, and
his advice had been for her to submit: 'Since your husband bids, I
Swallow the burning coal he proffers you!' (ll. 729–30). But this
time the Archbishop decides to advise Pompilia with a parable:
'the honeyed cake' instead of the 'rod'; Pompilia is too young to
be punished. To add more religious sanctity to his aphorism, the
Archbishop then compares himself to Jesus, reciting a line from
Matthew (13: 34): 'Without a parable spake He not to them'
(l. 821). But here Browning is not giving the Archbishop credit;
rather, he is actually making fun of him. The Archbishop is a
debased Jesus. He is deficient and uncaring. Neither he, nor his
parable, are helpful. The latter, in particular, offers no consolation
to Pompilia; on the contrary, it only reveals how incompetent and
uncaring the Archbishop is:

"There was a ripe round long black toothsome fruit,
"Even a flower-fig, the prime boast of May:
"And, to the tree, said . . . either the spirit o' the fig,
"Or, if we bring in men, the gardener,
"Archbishop of the orchard – had I time
"To try o' the two which fits in best: indeed
"It might be the Creator's self, but then
"The tree should bear an apple, I suppose, –
"Well, anyhow, one with authority said
"'Ripe fig, burst skin, regale the fig-pecker –
"'The bird whereof thou art a perquisite!'
"'Nay', with a flounce, replied the restif fig,
"'I much prefer to keep my pulp myself:
"'He may go breakfastless and dinnerless,
"'Supperless of one crimson seed, for me!'
"So, back she flopped into her bunch of leaves.
"He flew off, left her, – did the natural lord, –
"And lo, three hundred thousand bees and wasps
"Found her out, feasted on her to the shuck:
"Such gain the fig's that gave its bird no bite!

"The moral, – fools elude their proper lot,
"Tempt other fools, get ruined all alike.
"Therefore go home, embrace your husband quick!

$$(ll.\ 822–44)^{12}$$

The Archbishop stumbles at the beginning of the parable. He is uncertain about its content: whether the speaker is 'the spirit o' the fig' or 'the gardener', he does not know – perhaps because he is making up the 'parable' on the spot? He also seems to have forgotten, or not to have given enough thought to, the parable before relating it: 'had I time | "To try o' the two which fits in best'. He doubts whether the fruit is a fig or an apple. But the Archbishop's incompetence lies not only in his (in)ability to relay the parable, but also in his choice of the parable. In the Archbishop's narrative, Pompilia is likened to a 'toothsome fruit', a ripened 'fig' that is figuratively ready for sex. But the fig, like Pompilia who is refusing her husband's wish, rejects the fig-pecker's demand and is thus devoured by 'three hundred thousand bees and wasps'. The appalling nature of the imagery, being consumed by a horde of pests, is meant to convey the moral of the story: the ramification of Pompilia rejecting her husband's sexual desires would make a fig-like woman out of her, a strumpet who would attract other men and eventually be ruined by their sexual hunger. However, the Archbishop's anecdotal response is neither convincing, nor comforting; it is thoughtless and cold-hearted: the alternative that he draws is more degrading and disgusting for Pompilia than sleeping with the Count. It is of little wonder then why Pompilia's view of him, previously referred to as God's representative ('he stands for God' (ll. 726 and 748)), changes after this: 'So home I did go; so, the worst befell: |So, I had proof the Archbishop was just man, | And hardly that, and certainly no more' (ll. 847–9).

In this light, what are we to make of Browning's use of parables in *Ferishtah's Fancies*? In 'Pompilia', the parable method is brought in to debase the speaker, especially if we consider the Archbishop's boastful, but ironic, comparison of himself with Jesus, whereas in *Ferishtah's Fancies* the parables are told to highlight Ferishtah's aptitude and wisdom, likening him to spiritual teachers like Jesus. But what is it about Ferishtah that makes him so dear to Browning and so different to the Archbishop? The answer lies, in part, in a familiar Orientalist paradox, in this case related to Browning's ideas about religion. The corruption of the Catholic Church, and indeed of conventional Christianity as a whole, is one of the great themes of *The Ring and the Book*. And although that poem is set at the end of the seventeenth century, it is clear that Browning has his own Victorian age equally in mind. The Oriental figure of Ferishtah, on the other hand, is free from the stigma of superficial or hollow Christianity. This means he is able to stand for real Christian ideas and values more convincingly than an actual Christian sage. Had he been a Christian hermit, Ferishtah, too, would not have been as well adapted to Browning's purpose.

Returning to the discussion of the sources of *Ferishtah's Fancies*, it needs be noted that Browning had other, and more recent, encounters with Persian too. While learning German, he, for instance, had studied Goethe's *West-östlicher Divan* (1819).[13] He had also read Helen Zimmern's verse translation of Firdausi, *The Epic of Kings, Stories Retold from Firdausi* which was published only two years before *Ferishtah's Fancies*. Zimmern was a friend of Browning; she pays tribute to him in the first edition of her translation.[14] The partnership appears to have worked both ways though: the spelling of some of the foreign names in *Ferishtah's Fancies*, such as 'Mihrab', which is the name of the son of Zahhak (the Serpent) in the *Shahnameh*, are from Zimmern.

Yet there remains another source, the *Rubáiyát of Omar Khayyám*. We have no biographical evidence to suggest that Browning might have consulted the *Rubáiyát* for writing *Ferishtah's Fancies*. There is also no mention of FitzGerald's poem in relation to *Ferishtah's Fancies* in any of Browning's letters available to us. We do, however, know that Browning was mindful of FitzGerald and his work; he owned a copy of the third edition (1872) in his personal library. There are also several names and references in *Ferishtah's Fancies* that parallel some of FitzGerald's in the *Rubáiyát*: for example, 'Parwin' in 'A Bean-Stripe: also, Apple-Eating', and 'Mushtari', repeated three times in 'Cherries' and once in 'A Pillar at Sebzevar', were most likely borrowed from Quatrain LIV (Quatrain LXXV in the 1872 edition) of the *Rubáiyát*. The word 'Rhuibayat' was even mentioned in the MS, 1. 133 of 'Mihrab Shah'; although this was later changed to 'poetry'.[15] The impact of the *Rubáiyát* on *Ferishtah's Fancies*, however, goes beyond these outward, textual influences. On the surface, FitzGerald's poem does indeed seem like another source with Persian origin from which Browning has borrowed a number of foreign elements to ornament and Orientalise his work. But in truth FitzGerald and the *Rubáiyát* have had a far greater influence on the conception of Browning's poem than these. Strangely, this is an influence stirred not by Browning's praise and admiration for FitzGerald or his work, but by the dislike and aversion apparent between the two men. But before discussing the impact of this correlation on the composition of *Ferishtah's Fancies*, let us first look more closely at the construction of Browning's poem.

Ferishtah's Fancies: Structure

The popularity of *Ferishtah's Fancies* was largely due to Browning's reputation as a sage. Browning was in his early seventies when *Ferishtah's Fancies* appeared in print. After a career of fifty years, he had an established reputation as one of the leading literary figures of the century. A clear indication of this rising fame, particularly in the final quarter of the nineteenth century, was the establishment of several Browning societies in Britain and America.[16] Interestingly, though, Browning's route to fame was different to that of people like Tennyson, Arnold, or his own wife, Elizabeth Barrett. None of Browning's early and mid-century writings was a success. The publication of *Sordello* in 1840, in fact, blighted Browning's reputation, and subsequent collections such as *Dramatic Lyrics* (1842), *Dramatic Romances and Lyrics* (1845) and *Men and Women* (1855) were all critical and popular failures. But the appearance of *Dramatis Personae* in 1864 began a change: over the next five years, Browning gradually recovered his lost reputation, and the publication of *The Ring and the Book* (1868–9) became a watershed in his poetical career, bringing him unprecedented fame. After this, it was no longer possible to simply disregard Browning. Critics, and the reading public, started to recognise him as a major poet, with some venturing to reassess the earlier works in the light of his growing stature; although even with his late-life success, Browning never became a truly popular poet in his lifetime.

There was, however, something unique about Browning and his poetry. By the time *Ferishtah's Fancies* was published, the Victorians had grown accustomed to Browning's unorthodox poetics, to the complexity of his language, to the unconventionality of his style, and to the eccentricity of the themes that he would often explore in his poetry. These elements became significantly more apparent, more dominant, in his later poetry, particularly in the poetry he wrote in the last decade of his life. By the 1880s, and after the publication of *Jocoseria*, this enigmatic style became a source of his appeal: 'One of the reasons of Mr. Browning's popularity', wrote an anonymous commentator in *The Saturday Review* (6 December 1884), 'is the activity of mind which he stimulates by insisting on laborious efforts to appreciate his imaginative wisdom.'[17] *Ferishtah's Fancies* is a perfect example of this kind of poetry: it is perplexing, impenetrable, unfamiliar. Its design is, for example, curiously dialogic. Apart from the 'prologue' and the 'epilogue', which have very little to do with the dramatic character of Ferishtah, the poem is built upon the exchange of arguments and counter-arguments between Ferishtah and one or other of his pupils. The language of the poem is also particularly intricate, the locus of meaning ever more vexing for the reader. The poems also are all syntactically correct, coherent, and highly punctuated, yet the content of these ordering structures works against such rationalities. Browning's dense, elliptical syntax, as well as his persistent use of extended metaphor, richly ornamented with detail and digression, forms intricate patterns that purposefully work to occlude meaning.

This complexity of design is visible in the larger structure of the poem. *Ferishtah's Fancies* can be divided into a frame, consisting of the 'prologue' and the 'epilogue', and a core containing the twelve 'fancies'. What differentiates the two framing poems from those they contain is their lack of a thematic uniformity, voice, and the type of design that exists in the 'fancies'. There is, for example, no dialogical arrangement or multiplicity of speakers in the 'prologue' and the 'epilogue'. The narrative is relayed by one voice which does not emerge anywhere else in the poem. But there appear to be slight similarities between the voice behind the 'epilogue' and the one that utters the interspersed lyrics: both, for example, show signs of doubt in their discourse (a point to which I will return). There is also no layering of disguise or Oriental sentiment in the 'prologue' and the 'epilogue'. Both of these poems have a personal, confessional note to them; the 'fancies', however, are third-person narratives containing dramatic dialogue in the voices of different speakers. With the exception of the first two poems, 'The Eagle' and 'The Melon-Seller', the third-person speaker in the poem does little more than briefly set the scene for each particular dialogue. Although the narrator is demonstrably on Ferishtah's side, his presence in the poems is fairly unobtrusive.

The Framing Poems

The 'prologue' and the 'epilogue' are themselves thematically dissimilar. While the content of the 'prologue' is pertinent to the 'fancies', with the narrator symbolically, and comically, describing his poetics, the 'epilogue' digresses from the central idea in the 'fancies'. The narrator in the 'epilogue' shifts, noticeably, from the teachings of Ferishtah apparent in the poems. By this point in the book, Ferishtah has repeatedly – confidently, even – proclaimed devotion and trust in God to be the solution for man's earthly troubles. Yet the speaker in the 'epilogue', who seems to be Browning abandoning the guise of the Persian sage, in order to return to a voice that more closely resembles himself, expresses consternation about this hopeful philosophy of life, worries that his positive view of the universe might be mistaken:

> Only, at heart's utmost joy and triumph, terror
>   Sudden turns the blood to ice: a chill wind disencharms
> All the late enchantment! What if all be error –
>   If the halo irised round my head were, Love, thine arms?
>
> (ll. 25–8)[18]

A dim sentiment of this incongruous, and rather unexpected, expression of doubt is recognisable in the lyrics at the end of, for instance, 'The Melon-Seller': 'What if words were but mistake, and looks – too sudden, say!' (l. 44); or, in the lyric in 'A Pillar at Sebzevah':

> Ask not one least word of praise!
>   Words declare your eyes are bright?
> What then meant that summer day's
> Silence spent in one long gaze?
>   Was my silence wrong or right?
>
> (ll. 152–6)

The 'prologue', on the other hand, has less conceptual divergence from the 'fancies', though it, too, does not follow their thematic or structural patterns. The 'prologue' has the poet self-mockingly comparing the recipe for preparing ortolans to the structure of the 'fancies'. The eating of the ortolans involves three parts:

> First comes plain bread, crisp, brown, a toasted square:
>   Then, a strong sage-leaf:
> (So we find books with flowers dried here and there
>   Lest leaf engage leaf.)
> First, food – then, piquancy – and last of all
>   Follows the thirdling:
> Through wholesome hard, sharp soft, your tooth must bite
>   Ere reach the birdling.
>
> (ll. 13–20)

Whether Browning himself had ever tried ortolan or not remains unknown, but he soon reveals how the analogy works with the ingredients of the 'fancies':

> So with your meal, my poem: masticate
>   Sense, sight and song there!
>
> (ll. 29–30)

The three parts of the ortolan dish: a toasted square of bread, a sage leaf, and a bird correspond to the three structural parts of the 'fancies': 'sense', 'sight', and 'song'. As Daniel Karlin notes, 'the "sense" is the "plain bread", the "sight" is the "strong sage-leaf", and the "song" is the "birdling," which is apt of course because the ortolan is a singing-bird as well as a delicacy'.[19] With that same token, the 'sense' can be taken as the main story in each 'fancy', the 'sight' as the moral element that runs through the narrative (the 'sage leaf' can be taken here as Ferishtah's lessons); and, finally, the song, as the name suggests, is the lyric that ends each poem. Such explanation may help us discern what Browning might have had in mind in using the analogy. In one sense, the ortolan metaphor can be taken as a kind of vindication against any impending criticism. Browning knew about the overwhelmingly didactic tone of his poem, that it could be, to use his own metaphor, indigestible to some readers. Hence, he used the analogy to convey, implicitly and rather strangely, that while his poem might seem hard and rather inedible on the outside, it is meaty, that is, uplifting and enriching, at the centre. In another sense, the food recipe can be taken as Browning's instruction on how the poem should be treated. Like the ortolan, *Ferishtah's Fancies* is delectable when it is taken as a whole with all its balancing ingredients, or, in Clyde de L. Ryals's language, with 'the three together being a mixture more succulent than any one alone'.[20]

The 'Fancies'

These each consist of two parts: the main poem, which involves a central, ongoing debate in the form of a dialogue, and a brief lyrical reiteration of the poem's discussion that comes at the end. Some critics see the lyrical interludes as love lyrics, as Browning's yearning for his lost wife. Thomas Blackburn, for instance, attests to this: the lyrics, he says, 'although of little value in themselves, do show up by their uncertainty and blurred sentiment both the

virtues of Browning's finest love poetry and predicament in later
age – a predicament which is anticipated by *Any Wife to Any Husband*'.[21] This is true but to deem the lyrics insignificant because
they appear trifling next to the 'fancies' is erroneous and unfair. The
lyrics are curtailed restatements of the poem's meditations; they
alternate with the parables and the philosophy voiced in them.
In 'Mihrab Shah', for instance, the central dispute revolves around
the following question, asked at the beginning by one of the
pupils:

> Wherefore should any evil hap to man –
> From ache of flesh to agony of soul –
> Since God's All-mercy mates All-potency?
> Nay, why permits He evil to Himself –
> Man's sin, accounted such? Suppose a world
> Purged of all pain, with fit inhabitant –
> Man pure of evil in thought, word and deed –
> Were it not well? Then, wherefore otherwise?
>
> (ll. 11–18)

Ferishtah's rationale in justifying God's wisdom in permitting evil
on earth and allowing fleshly pain is that there would be no 'bond
'twixt man and man' (l. 45) without them; it is the 'sad accidents'
(l. 35) and 'humanity's mischance' (l. 36) that awake compassion in
humankind. But to deliver his point, he needs a concrete example,
so he tells a secret about the Shah, whom the pupil does not seem to
admire. The student responds to Ferishtah's question: 'Our Shah – I
How stands he in thy favour?' (ll. 46–7) with a shrug, related by
Ferishtah: 'Why that shrug? I Is not he lord and ruler?' (ll. 47–8).
Ferishtah himself does not think highly of the Shah either: later in the
poem, he states that Mihrab Shah has no individual qualities, that it
is his kingship or, so to speak, his accident of birth, that has endowed
him with his gracious, charitable qualities. None of Mihrab Shah's
merits, he admits to his students, bring respect for him: '"So be it,
then! He wakes no love in thee I For any one of divers attributes"'
(ll. 85–6). There is, however, a reason behind Ferishtah's mention
of the Shah: to prove that one's pain can cause others' compassion,
Ferishtah unveils that the much-despised Shah has an 'internal ulcer'
and the student's reaction verifies his point: on hearing this, the pupil
worriedly asks if the 'leech I Of fame in Tebriz' (ll. 91–2) can come
to the Shah's rescue; or if Ferishtah himself can 'counsel in the
case?' (l. 92). Ferishtah, however, remains ostensibly indifferent to

the pupil's concern: the odious Shah is better left to suffer and die. Agitated and saddened by witnessing Ferishtah's uncaring attitude, the student then objects:

'Attributes?
Faugh! – nay, Ferishtah, – 't is an ulcer, think!
Attributes, quotha? Here's poor flesh and blood,
Like thine and mine and every man's, a prey
To hell-fire! Hast thou lost thy wits for once?'

(ll. 97–101)

Ferishtah uses the student's reaction to teach him how the plea of suffering conjures sympathy. Pain teaches us to pity and care. If pain were to be taken out of the bounds of human suffering, there would be no love, no sympathy, no friendship.

As we see, the idea of fleshly pain and the limits of human physical existence is central to the ideological design of 'Mihrab Shah', and so the lyric that follows the 'fancy' focuses on a similar theme, though in an entirely different fashion. The lyric begins with what appears to be a man's response to a woman's (earlier) complaint of her physical weakness:

So, the head aches and the limbs are faint!
Flesh is a burthen – even to you!

(ll. 137–8)

One distinct quality of the lyrics is their personal sentiment. Compared to the 'fancies', their tone is less complicated, far from Ferishtah as a sage or Browning as a philosopher. The lyrics are also detached from the medieval Persian backdrop of the 'fancies'; there is no Ferishtah in them, nor is there a narration of Oriental anecdotes. Given this, it is easier to see a reflection of Browning's self in them (as well as the reason why the reader may take the speaker of the lyrics to be a man). Here, the reader is also irresistibly drawn to think of the woman as Elizabeth Barrett Browning; the speaker's image of the woman in this conversation resembles the familiar image of E. B. Browning as an ethereal, physically weak but luminously intelligent and spiritual individual. The lyric, however, becomes even more personal in the following lines, particularly after the speaker's attempt in cheering the ailing woman: 'Can I force a smile with a fancy quaint?' (l. 139). The man's retort to the woman's earlier confession is an admission of his own flaw, which matches the woman's weakness.

The latter has a weak body and strong soul, whereas the man has a 'Body so strong and will so weak!' (l. 142). Regardless of the possible biographical reading of these lines, the relationship between the man and woman here is a metaphor for a perfect union of body and soul. What the man desires is owned by the woman; what the woman lacks is held by the man:

> My dim to-morrow – your plain to-day,
>   Yours the achievement, mine the aim?
>   (ll. 147–8)

The perfect unification of soul and body is what the speaker seeks, though he also seems to know that such flawless amalgamation is unattainable on earth:

> So were it rightly, so shall it be!
>   Only, while earth we pace together
> For the purpose apportioned you and me,
>   Closer we tread for a common tether.
>
> You shall sigh 'Wait for his sluggish soul!
>   Shame he should lag, not lamed as I!'
> May not I smile 'Ungained her goal:
>   Body may reach her – by-and-by?'
>   (ll. 149–56)

One may read these lines as a manifestation of Browning's personal life; the lyric has a tone of lamentation to it, with the description of the woman, as ailing and fragile, evoking the image of E. B. Browning. Of course, Browning's longing for his lost wife might have prompted his writing of these lines, but such a biographical reading is only part of a larger conception of the poem. The message of the lyric is universal: it is not just an individual's lamentation for a lost love, nor is it merely a person's yearning for a more robust body or a stronger sense of purpose. The poem's plea has a wider audience, with the human relationship being the central focus of attention. In earthly relationships, each partner's shortcomings need to be rectified by the attributes of the other. But, in the afterlife, what is disproportionate on either side will be made whole. A romantic communion on earth, in other words, is prone to human flaws because humankind is by nature incomplete; the perfect union thus has to be sought beyond earthly conditions. Yet the absences in earthly relationships can still be mitigated by the qualities each partner brings.

Ferishtah's Fancies: A Thin Layer of Persian Disguise

Let us now look at the Persian disguise of Browning's poem, beginning with Edward FitzGerald and his book. Browning seems to have never liked the *Rubáiyát*. He first shows his dislike, only a few years after the poem's release, in one of his most popular works, 'Rabbi Ben Ezra' (1864), which, in Maisie Ward's language, was his 'reply of hope to FitzGerald's hedonistic but despairing Omar Khayyam'.[22] Ironically, in 'Rabbi Ben Ezra', Browning speaks to FitzGerald in his own language. He adopts the metaphor of the 'Potter': 'Ay, note that Potter's wheel, | That metaphor!' (ll. 151–2) – which FitzGerald himself had borrowed from the Persian *rubáiyát* in the manuscripts – and looks at the 'KÚZA-NÁMA' section of the *Rubáiyát* with a completely opposing perspective:

> Fool! All that is, at all,
> Lasts ever, past recall;
> Earth changes, but thy soul and God stand sure:
> What entered into thee,
> *That* was, is, and shall be:
> Time's wheel runs back or stops: Potter and clay endure.
>
> (ll. 158–63)

Here, Browning is contesting the principles that were put forward by FitzGerald. To him, the *carpe diem* philosophy of Omar ('Since life fleets, all is change; the Past gone, seize to-day!' (l. 156)) is not really the solution to religious perplexity; nor is the drinking of wine. True, physical existence is ephemeral, but the soul remains. God is also undisputedly infinite: '*That* was, is, and shall be' (l. 162). For Browning, however, this was not an adequate response to Omar's Epicureanism; hence, he returned to the *Rubáiyát* almost twenty years later, though this time he seems to have had more reasons for revisiting this familiar territory.

Browning wrote *Ferishtah's Fancies* in a period of six months through the autumn and winter of 1883–4, around three or four months after FitzGerald's death on 13 June 1883. *Ferishtah's Fancies* came out on 21 November 1884.[23] By this time, the *Rubáiyát* was at the peak of its popularity in Britain and America. It was more popular than any poem that Browning had ever written, and Browning knew this. It is thus possible that the celebrity of the *Rubáiyát* and the aftershock of FitzGerald's death prompted Browning to adopt FitzGerald's favourite theme in one of his poems. This assumption becomes more plausible if we consider Browning's knowledge of Tennyson's love for FitzGerald, his own peculiar relationship with Tennyson, and his unfavourable opinion of FitzGerald. Browning admired Tennyson but he had complex, ambivalent feelings for him. Tennyson was always a step ahead of him. It was Tennyson who became the Poet Laureate in 1850. It was his poems that were being published in large print runs, whereas Browning's writings had a smaller circulation. This is, of course, not to suggest that Browning was averse to Tennyson; on the contrary, he truly respected him. But there was a disparity here: Browning's adoration of Tennyson was incongruous with his ill-disposed attitudes towards FitzGerald, to whom, as Karlin notes, Tennyson was close, 'closer than Browning would ever be'.[24]

Browning's discovery of FitzGerald's callous comment about Elizabeth Barrett Browning's death, which William A. Wright had (thoughtlessly) included in *Letters and Literary Remains of Edward FitzGerald* (1889), and his furious response, 'To Edward FitzGerald', published in the *Athenaeum* on 13 July 1889, is evidently not a reason behind the Persian design of *Ferishtah's Fancies*. But the language of Browning's fierce sonnet and, specifically, his use of 'Fitz' in referring to FitzGerald, are evidence that Browning was aware of Tennyson's love for FitzGerald. 'Fitz' was the abbreviation that was often used by FitzGerald's close friends. It was used as a term of endearment in the opening line of Tennyson's 'To E. Fitzgerald', published in *Tiresias, and Other Poems* (1885):

Old Fitz, who from your suburb grange,
Where once I tarried for a while,
Glance at the wheeling orb of change,
And greet it with a kindly smile . . .

(ll. 1–4)

Browning borrowed the abbreviation and used it in his poetic response to FitzGerald's remark: he learns 'That you, Fitzgerald, whom by ear and eye | She never knew, "thanked God my wife was dead." | Aye, dead! And were yourself alive, good Fitz, | How to return you thanks would task my wits'.[25]

To have a Persian sage as the leading character of the poem proves further that the formulation of *Ferishtah's Fancies* was influenced by Browning's unfriendly attitude towards FitzGerald and his book. 'There was no such person as Ferishtah', Browning wrote in his letter (of October 1884) to G. B. Smith.[26] He was telling the truth: Ferishtah was his creation, but the name was not. 'Ferishtah' was Browning's transliteration of the Persian word *fereshteh*, meaning angel, or to be more precise, a spiritual being believed to act as an attendant of God on earth. Where could Browning have learned about the word *Ferishtah*? There is no clear answer to this. But whatever source he might have had, there is evidently a purpose behind his choice of the name; the definition of the word *fereshteh* in Persian fits perfectly well with what Browning wanted the protagonist of his poem to embody. Ferishtah is designed to polemically oppose FitzGerald's Omar. He represents certain kinds of orthodoxies that are in absolute conflict with Omar's philosophy; he is a '*fereshteh*', a profound Muslim, a spiritual teacher, who fundamentally believes in the nature and existence of God, whereas Omar is an opposing figure: a drunkard 'sinner' who questions the existence of God while he carries the reputation of being a Muslim.

The more we explore Browning's characterisation of Ferishtah, the more we realise how Ferishtah has been purposefully put together to rival FitzGerald's Omar. Yet what makes Browning's imaginative characterisation of Ferishtah fascinating is that in his fictional construction of a Persian anti-Omar sage, he seems to have enriched the Persian fabric of the poem. Whether this was a conscious act, or was done fortuitously by Browning's scattered knowledge of Oriental and, in this case, Persian sources, is hard to tell. But there is certainly more to Browning's seeming adoption of a Persian costume than meets the eye. *Ferishtah's Fancies* has an occluded engagement with Persia. Yet, unlike the two previous case-studies in this book, its engagement with Persia is with its religious culture, and not the prominent figures of Persia's poetic tradition. We see evidence of this, for example, in the poem's historical context, which is fictive but taken to be real in the poem's world. The overall setting in *Ferishtah's Fancies* is a medieval Persian world, resembling the conventional image of the Orient in which there is an old, unpopular shah like Mihrab Shah, a prime minister, a vizier, who has fallen from favour like the wretched vendor in 'The Melon-Seller', or a renowned 'leech' who knows a cure for every pain in 'The Family'. There is, however, more to the poem's setting. Persia is typically a Muslim country. Ferishtah is a spiritual teacher of Islam, and his disciples are adherents of Islam. But the understanding that the poem offers in constructing this image of a Muslim country implies that Persia is not just an Islamic country but it is a Shiite state. For instance, the third poem in the volume is titled 'Shah Abbas', which is the name of one of the most prominent kings of the Safavids, the dynasty that actually made Shiism the official religion of Persia in the sixteenth century (the name of another Safavid ruler, Tahmasp, Shah Abbas's predecessor, is also mentioned in the poem, although this one comes in an unconnected context and not as a Persian shah). It is also in this poem that Ferishtah delivers his first lesson as a 'full dervish' and the lesson happens to be on Ali ibn Abi-Talib, cousin and son-in-law of prophet Mohammad, known by Shiite Muslims as the rightful inheritor of the prophet: 'Said someone, as Ferishtah paused abrupt | Reading a certain passage from the roll | Wherein is treated of Lord Ali's Life . . .' (ll. 4–6). There is indeed a curious correlation between the supposed Safavid setting of the poem and Ferishtah's lesson on Ali. The central governmental policy of the Safavids was based on Ali's imamate, a combination of authority and spiritual sovereignty. The Safavid rulers did not see themselves as mere rulers; they thought of themselves as divine descendants of the twelve Imams (religious leaders) in Shiism.[27]

Other references to Shiism appear in 'Shah Abbas', too; for example, in the absurd hypothetical case that Ferishtah draws while contending that love should come prior to knowledge as the foundation of faith. It is known, or believed, in the poem that Shah Abbas died of fright at seeing a spider in his drink. Suppose, Ferishtah argues, that one of his pupils, the interlocutor of the poem, 'Yakub, son of Yusuf, son of Zal' (l. 47), has been fined twelve dinars for the 'inadvertency' of his distant ancestor:

I advertise thee that our liege, the Shah
Happily regnant, hath become assured,
By opportune discovery, that thy sires,
Son by the father upwards, track their line
To – whom but that same bearer of the cup
Whose inadvertency was chargeable
With what therefrom ensued, disgust and death
To Abbas Shah, the over-nice of soul?
Whence he appoints thee, – such his clemency, –
Not death, thy due, but just a double tax
To pay, on thy particular bed of reeds
Which flower into the brush that makes a broom
Fit to sweep ceilings clear of vermin. Sure,
Thou dost believe the story nor dispute
That punishment should signalize its truth?
Down therefore with some twelve dinars!

(ll. 48–63)

Not every reader of the text can tell why the Shah, in Ferishtah's fanciful account, would exact the sum of twelve dinars as the penalty for Yakub. But now that we know of the poem's Shiite backdrop, we may be able to ascertain a logic for the Shah's decision. As in other Abrahamic religions, certain numbers are held to possess special significance and veneration in Islam. Holy numbers that are derived from Shiite traditions have a particular significance for Shiite Muslims. For example, the Shiite inhabitants of today's Iran have great respect for the number fourteen (the number of fourteen infallibles in Shiism) or the number five which stands as the token of the *panj tane ale 'aba* (five bodies of the cloak family) or in Arabic *Ahl ul-Kisa* (people of the cloak), referring to the Prophet Mohammad, his daughter, Fatimah, his son in law, Ali, and two of their children, Hasan and Hosein. The Shah's exaction of twelve dinars may, therefore, have as one reason the religious sanctity of the number twelve in Shiite Islam, relate to the fundamental tenets of the *Ithna 'Ashari* ('Twelver') school of Shiism – which, again, the Safavids established in the sixteenth century in Persia. The name 'Twelver' is derived from the adherents' belief in twelve divinely Imams (ordained leaders), Ali and his descendants who are believed to be spiritual and political successors to the prophet, Mohammad. The sum of money that the 'sinner' is obliged to pay here matches the number of Shiite Imams, so he would remember the holiness of his Shiite state and assume that the sum is not paid to the Shah or his royal throne; but, rather, it is an homage paid to the Imams he praises. Browning's deployment of the number twelve in the poem is thus fitting in this context; twelve is also the number of the 'fancies', which may reveal something of the significance of the number in Browning's frame of cultural reference. But how and from where Browning could have obtained such a knowledge, we do not know. As a Christian poet, he would have, however, been familiar with number symbolism. There is, for instance, a mystical symbolism in 'Part IV. Night' in *Pippa Passes; A Drama* (1841), when Pippa sings: 'But I had so near made out the sun – , | Could count your stars, the Seven and One!' (ll. 218–19). As John Woolford and Daniel Karlin explain, 'the Seven and One' may be a reference to the 'constellation of the Pleiades or Seven Sisters, and one of the other major stars, perhaps Aldebaran or Fomalhaut'. But it may also allude to the '"seven stars" held in the right hand of Christ, *Revelation* i 16, and to Christ himself as the "bight and morning star", *Revelation* xxii 16'.[28] Another example of Christian numerology in Browning's poetry appears in 'Soliloquy of the Spanish Cloister' (*Dramatic Lyrics*, 1842):

> When he finishes refection,
>   Knife and fork across he lays
> Never, to my recollection,
>   As do I, in Jesu's praise.
> I, the Trinity illustrate,
>   Drinking watered orange-pulp;
> In three sips the Arian frustrate;
>   While he drains his at one gulp.
>   (ll. 33–40)

This is, however, a satire on the speaker's religious formalism. The bitter and twisted monk who speaks the poem envies 'Brother Lawrence'. To him, Lawrence's manners, expressive of his generosity and free-heartedness, are intolerable. Lawrence eats and drinks with gusto, indifferent to the obsessions of religious ritual; by contrast, the speaker's self-praise for matching his gestures to religious doctrines ('I the Trinity illustrate') actually reveals his narrow, sterile nature.[29] Again, we may ask what distinguishes Ferishtah from this figure of envy and malice. As it happens, we learn from several poems in the volume, notably 'The Eagle' and 'Two Camels' (both of which I will discuss later in the chapter), that Ferishtah rather resembles Brother Lawrence in his enjoyment of physical appetite and refusal to countenance a false asceticism. If he has an interest in religious symbolism, it is not because he mistakes the symbol for reality – or, in Browning's language, 'fancy' for 'fact'.

The poem 'Shah Abbas' reveals more of the latent presence of Persia in *Ferishtah's Fancies*. The poem is Ferishtah's vindication of the truthfulness of the account of Ali's life. Here, Ferishtah uses three anecdotes to argue that a fervent desire to believe, a desire that directly influences one's own life, has more value than an intellectual acceptance of belief, a state of mind in which belief becomes merely notional and does not affect one's actual behaviour. As in other poems in the book, the central argument is initiated by a disciple. As 'Ferishtah pause[s] abrupt' (l. 4), the pupil asks:

> Master, explain this incongruity!
> When I dared question 'It is beautiful,
> But is it true?' – thy answer was 'In truth
> Lives beauty.' I persisting – 'Beauty – yes,

In thy mind and in my mind, every mind
That apprehends: but outside – so to speak –
Did beauty live in deed as well as word,
Was this life lived, was this death died – not dreamed?'

(ll. 7–14)

The student is inadvertently voicing Keats's words in 'Ode on a Grecian Urn' (1820) to challenge the premise of Ferishtah's argument in defence of the credibility of the account of Ali's life. Two points are, however, unclear at this point: the name or the nature of the 'roll', from which Ferishtah is reading to his students, and the reason behind Ferishtah's pause. While the former remains unspecified, the latter becomes clear further in the poem: the interlocutor reveals that Ferishtah was 'disabled by emotion at a tale' (l. 75), and the 'tale' that he refers to is what Ferishtah was reading from: the narrative of Ali's death. Ferishtah weeps when he reaches the part in the 'roll' that relates the assassination of Ali. But how do we know this, since the cause of Ferishtah's tears can be any other part of the 'roll'? The student's opening question makes this clear, as he refers specifically to Ali's legendary death: 'Was this life lived, was this death died – not dreamed?' (l. 14).

Ferishtah's emotional reaction to Ali's death is recognisably Persian, but it may not be visible to a reader who knows little about Shiite religious culture. It is typical of Shiite preachers to burst into tears while relating the narrative of their Imams' deaths. Ali's death, and that of his younger son, Hosein, is the most valued martyrdom in the Shiite tradition. Ali is the central pillar in Shiism. Shiite, in fact, means to follow and reverence Ali and his descendants. But how did Browning come across Ali? As Allan Dooley and David Ewbank explain, Browning 'would have remembered that Ali is affectionately praised by Carlyle in the second lecture of *On Heroes and Hero-Worship and the Heroic in History*, which he had heard delivered in 1840'.[30] Carlyle describes Ali as

A noble-minded creature, as he shews himself, now and always afterwards; full of affection, of fiery daring. Something chivalrous in him; brave as a lion; yet with a grace, a truth and affection worthy of Christian knighthood. He died by assassination in the mosque at Baghdad; a death occasioned by his generous fairness, confidence in the fairness of others: he said, if the wound proved not unto death, they must pardon the Assassin, but if it did, then they must slay him straightaway, that so they two in the same hour might appear before God, and see which side of that quarrel was the just one![31]

Carlyle's words might well have encouraged Browning to choose Ali as the cornerstone of 'Shah Abbas'. But there may have been another source for the inclusion of Ali and Shiism in the poem: Matthew Arnold's 'A Persian Passion Play', first published in the *Cornhill Magazine* in 1871, and later included in the third edition of *Essays in Criticism* in 1875. Arnold's essay concerns the Shiite Muslim commemoration of the supreme martyrdom of their Imam Hosein (Ali's son) through a form of drama known as *ta'ziye* in Persia. Arnold was led to this topic by *Les religions et les philosophies dans l'Asie Central* (1866) by Joseph-Arthur de Gobineau, a French diplomat posted to Tehran from 1854 to 1864, first as secretary to the embassy, then from 1861 as minister.

The 'Persian Passion Play' gives a fairly detailed account of the historical events that led to the battle of Karbala in 680 CE. It contains a readable history of the early days of Islam. In his treatment of the topic, Arnold makes Shiism appear more attractive to Western sensibilities than its Sunni counterpart. In keeping with traditional literary treatments of *ta'ziye*, he offers a moving account of the tragic tale of the 'Marriage of Kassem' and his subsequent martyrdom. Arnold opens his narrative with Ali, before going on to relate the tragedy of Karbala and the death of 'Hussein' (Arnold's spelling), which, as Arnold himself describes, 'will awaken the sympathy of the coldest reader' (270). Arnold's tone is solemn and compassionate; it is elevating and moving, as though a grieving Shiite believer has authored it. He describes Ali as 'the Lion of God', Mohammad's 'brother, delegate, and vicar'. Ali is 'one of Mahomet's best and most successful captains' (264). The image that Arnold draws of Ali is that of a self-effacing, humble champion who righteously endures a great deal of agony after the death of the prophet:

> At his death (the year 632 of our era) Ali was passed over, and the first caliph, or *vicar* and *lieutenant* of Mahomet in the government of the state, was Abu-Bekr; only the spiritual inheritance of Mahomet, the dignity of Imam, or Primate, devolved by right on Ali and his children. Ali, lion of God as in war he was, held aloof from politics and political intrigue, loved retirement and prayer, was the most pious and disinterested of men.[32]

Browning knew Arnold well. They were well acquainted with each other for many years and were in regular contact after Browning's return to England in 1861, following the death of Elizabeth Barrett

Browning in Florence. They sent each other copies of their writings, poems, and queries. There are a number of instances in Arnold's essay, including the narrative of Ali's assassination and the tearful reaction of the Persians upon seeing the re-enactment of the murder of their Imams in the *ta'ziye*, that suggest Browning might have taken some of his descriptions from Arnold's essay.

The student's opening question in 'Shah Abbas' shows more of the inconspicuous Persian understanding that the poem retains. The question is multipart. The first part recalls an earlier enquiry: 'it is beautiful | But is it true?', to which Ferishtah had responded: 'In truth | Lives beauty'. The student describes his first question as a daring one. But this time, before asking another audacious question, he first acknowledges his master's rationale, admitting to his own trust in the account of Ali's life to avoid any accusation of infidelity: '"Beauty – yes, | In thy mind and in my mind, every mind | That apprehends'. The second part is the kernel of the enquiry: '"but outside – so to speak – | Did beauty live in deed as well as word, | Was this life lived, was this death died – not dreamed?"' The pupil is evidently unconvinced by his master's response to his earlier question; he is eager to know whether this beauty, which he suspects to be the outcome of religious partiality, can denote historical veracity. But what is striking, and relevant to our discussion here, is the understanding with which this exchange has been constructed. The student knows about the bold nature of his query; he knows asking as question as such can cast doubt on the strength of his belief in the eyes of others. So, this time, instead of expressing his apprehension verbally, he shows it with his pauses, indicated in the poem by the dashes.

The daring nature of the pupil's question becomes more notable, and more relevant to our purpose, if we consider the nature of Ferishtah's role in the poem. Ferishtah is devised to represent a Muslim-Shiite preacher. But he is also a dervish master, who, besides being a Shiite Muslim, is very likely to be a Sufi. Although the term 'dervish' is never clearly defined in the poem, there is enough evidence to suggest that Browning might have modelled Ferishtah on a Sufi dervish. *Dehkhoda* defines dervish as someone who solicits alms for a living. It was used in referenced to beggars who would often sing in the streets.[33] But in Persian, the word 'dervish' is usually used to refer to Muslim mystics. Persian poetry, too, uses the word in a similar context; there are numerous examples of it in classical Persian poetry in the work of Sa'di and Hafiz. But there is an explanation for this semantic correlation: in Sufism, the spiritual purification that ends in the enlightenment of heart (known as *safa*) is believed to be attainable through renunciation of earthly pleasure.[34] To be a Sufi, it is necessary to take a vow of poverty and endure extreme destitution until (to use Browning's phrase) 'dervishhood' is reached. The Sufis are required to be selflessly committed to the service of others and to show no concern for the possession of wealth.[35] But this vow of poverty, the worldly deprivation that Sufis are required to take, inevitably affects the most external aspects of their economic and social life and, therefore, makes them indistinguishable from beggars and mendicants. As a result of these external resemblances, the term 'dervish' has come to stand as a synonym for the Sufi in Persian language and literature. Even though it is unlikely for Browning to have known about the word's origin, his fitting deployment of it in the poem suggests that he is likely to have learned about its contextual use from one of his sources.

There is also textual evidence in the poem to display Ferishtah's adherence to Sufism. In 'The Eagle' Ferishtah appears to be an ascetic in the Sufi sense. This is a conspicuous incident in the poem from which Ferishtah's journey to 'dervishood', both literally and metaphorically, begins. Ferishtah is 'yet un-dervished' (l. 1) at this point in the grand narrative of the poem, and so he shows signs of immaturity with a hasty judgement, an occurrence which happens rarely in the poem (only once after this in 'The Melon-Seller'). Witnessing a raven's nest on a bough in which 'youngling [ravens] gaped with callow beak | Widened by want' (ll. 8–10) while their mother is lying dead beneath the tree, Ferishtah wonders: '"A piteous chance! | "How shall they 'scape destruction?"' (ll. 10–11) Here, the narrator describes Ferishtah's question as a misstep and tells the reader of its immaturity. After Ferishtah shows his sympathetic bafflement, which seems to undermine God's wisdom, the speaker refers to him as a sage ('sighed the sage', l. 11); but then it appears that the narrator himself is being injudicious and hasty in calling Ferishtah a sage, as he immediately corrects himself in the following line: '– Or sage about to be, though simple still' (l. 12). Ferishtah subsequently witnesses an eagle, unexpectedly, feeding the starving ravens. Saddened at his hasty judgement, he realises that his earlier verdict was mistaken:

'Ah, foolish, faithless me!' the observer smiled,
'Who toil and moil to eke out life, when lo
Providence cares for every hungry mouth!'

(ll. 17–19)

To expiate his sin, he then endures intense self-denial, resembling the phase of renunciation that Sufis undergo in their quest for the 'annihilation' of selfhood. The ultimate goal for Sufis is union with God, and this depends on the Sufis' utter separation from all else and resolute devotion to God. This uncompromising dedication to God involves detachment from the world, abstraction from material things and flesh (*tajrid*), and, ultimately, annihilation of the self (*fana*).[36] Ferishtah seeks isolation in the 'Woods' (l. 35) and abstains from food and drink. He starves himself until he loses consciousness:

> To profit by which lesson, home went he,
> And certain days sat musing, – neither meat
> Nor drink would purchase by his handiwork.
> Then, – for his head swam and his limbs grew faint, –
> Sleep overtook the unwise one, whom in dream
> God thus admonished: "Hast thou marked my deed?"
>
> (ll. 20–5)

While unconscious, he goes through the revelation of witnessing a divine omnipotence in his dream that admonishes him for his earlier misjudgement: '"Hast thou marked my deed?"' But Ferishtah has made another misjudgement: the 'unwise one' draws the wrong inference from witnessing the interaction between the eagle and the ravens. He identifies himself with the 'the helpless weakling' (ravens) instead of the eagle, 'the helpful strength | that captures prey and saves the perishing' (ll. 28–9). But the divine being that appears in Ferishtah's trance disapproves of his judgement. It rebukes him for isolating and starving himself and orders him not to waste his life in self-denial, but instead to 'feed' himself so he would be in a condition to help others: 'work, eat, then feed who lack!' (l. 30).

Despite this preliminary experience that leads to a celestial revelation, Ferishtah does not repent or fast any more, nor does he speak of the incident to any of his disciples. Quite the opposite: he completely abandons his former approach and follows his God's commandment. In fact, he does it so fervently that one of his disciples, in 'Two Camels', accuses him of self-indulgence:

> While thyself, I note,
> Eatest thy ration with an appetite,
> Nor fallest foul of whoso licks his lips
> And sighs – 'Well-saffroned was that barley soup!'
> Can wisdom co-exist with – gorge-and-swill,
> I say not, – simply sensual preference

For this or that fantastic meat and drink?
Moreover, wind blows sharper than its wont
This morning, and thou hast already donned
Thy sheepskin over-garment: sure the sage
Is busied with conceits that soar above
A petty change of season and its chance
Of causing ordinary flesh to sneeze?

(ll. 8–20)

The pupil believes that to indulge in worldly pleasure cannot coexist with wisdom, and he uses Ferishtah's care of his self to make his critical point. But Ferishtah thinks otherwise because he was ordered otherwise. His anecdotal response, the story of the two camels, symbolically echoes what he was told in 'The Eagle': the camel that feasted had 'praise and patting and a brand | Of good-and-faithful-servant fixed on flank' (ll. 57–8), and the 'carcass' of the other one, who preferred fasting to feasting, fed the vultures (l. 53).[37] Thus, to work and to feed others, one needs to eat. But Ferishtah's vindication of the pleasures of life as a gift of God is at odds with his persona as a 'dervish' Shiite Muslim. In William C. DeVane's words, the attribution of such notion to Ferishtah is 'much more suited to a Protestant occidental poet than to an oriental sage'.[38] There is, however, an explanation for Browning's inconsistent characterisation of Ferishtah: to fully conform to Western typology of Oriental models is not part of the design of *Ferishtah's Fancies*. That means the construction of Ferishtah, and that of almost every other Persian element in the poem, is partly imitative and partly innovative. Browning seems to have adhered to certain conventions, but he has also followed his own ideas.

Regardless of the issue of authenticity, the representation of Ferishtah as a Sufi is the result of Browning's resentment towards FitzGerald and his book. Since he had the third edition of the *Rubáiyát* in his library, he might have been familiar with FitzGerald's lengthy defence of Omar Khayyám against the imputation that he was a Sufi mystic, a defence which, though toned down from the polemical fire of the second edition (1868), was still strongly articulated. For FitzGerald, Khayyám was exactly what he professed himself to be: a sceptic and a pleasure-seeker. Browning's response was to create a Sufi sage who is not life-denying, as though to say to FitzGerald: 'You see? It is possible to love life, to enjoy the pleasures of the body, while holding opinions diametrically opposed to those of your Omar.' Ferishtah's philosophy, for all its complex reasoning, is grounded in common life, and his parables are homely and concrete. He may not drink or make love, but he tolerates those who do. As a teacher who holds court, in his own way, 'underneath the Bough', he is the antidote to Omar, though there has been no great rush, among modern readers, at least, to take their medicine.[39]

Notes

1. Dooley and Ewbank, *The Complete Works*, vol. 15, p. 295.
2. In *Persian Literary Influence* (p. xii), Javadi, for instance, says the poem 'does not display a great Persian influence'.
3. Browning's disavowal of the significance of the Persian dimension of the poem recalls a similar disclaimer made over twenty years earlier about *Sordello*. When the poem was reissued in 1863, in his dedication to his friend, the French critic Joseph Milsand, he stated, with reference to the notorious first edition of 1840, that 'the historical decoration was purposely of no more importance than a background requires; and my stress lay on the incidents in the development of a soul: little else is worth study'. This was not the whole truth, by any means, and a similar case can be made that the Persian decoration of *Ferishtah's Fancies* is being similarly downplayed. See Woolford and Karlin, *The Poems of Browning*, vol. 1, p. 361.
4. An undated leaf in Browning's handwriting, now held in the Armstrong Browning Library, is headed as 'Seriora—being divers fancies of the Dervish Ferishtah'. Browning, at some point, must have considered naming the volume as such, which would have had more affinities with the name of his preceding volume, *Jocoseria*. The meaning of 'Seriora' in Latin as 'the more serious things', however, would have implied a digression from the witty and light-hearted type of poetry that Browning had written in *Jocoseria*. Browning Database, ABL, 84:221. See Dooley and Ewbank, *The Complete Works*, p. 292.
5. *Tawil* is a verse form in Arabic poetry. Part of Browning and Lyall's correspondence is in the library of Somerville College, Oxford.
6. The letter is in Armstrong, *Intimate Glimpses*, p. 78. The *Mo'allaqat* or *Al-Mo'allaqat* ('The Hanged Poems') is a collection of seven ancient Arabic odes. Sir William Jones's *Moallakát, or Seven Arabian Poems* (1782) is believed to be the first English rendition of these poems. But Lyall has translated the poem, too. His first translation appeared in the Journal of Asiatic Society of Bengal in 1877. Almost eight years later, he released a more complete translation of the poems in *Mo'allaqat* in *Translations of Ancient Arabian Poetry* (1885).
7. Armstrong, *Intimate Glimpses*, p. 81.
8. Ibid. pp. 100–1.

9. From one of the marginal notes which Browning wrote in Mrs Orr's copy of the first edition, and which she later used as the basis of her account of the poem in her *Handbook to Robert Browning's Works* (1885, several times revised and reprinted). The letter is in Dooley and Ewbank, *The Complete Works*, p. 286.
10. DeVane, *A Browning Handbook*, p. 476. Almost two years before, Silvestre de Sacy had published a collection of the Arabic manuscripts of the book. E. B. Eastwick's translation of *Anvar Sohaili* ('the Lights of Canopus'), a collection of fables by Hosein Va'ez in the style of *Fables of Bidpai* and *Kalila and Dimnah* was also available in Britain in 1854. For more information on the origin and the history of the translation of *Kalīlah va Demneh*, see de Blois, *Burzōy's Voygae to India and the Origin of the Book of Kalīlah wa Dimnah*, pp. 1–18.
11. Knatchbull, *Kalila and Dimna or The Fables of Bidpai*, p. 6.
12. All the excerpts from *The Ring and The Book* are from Hawlin and Burnett, *The Poetical Works of Robert Browning*, vol. 8.
13. Ryals, *Browning's Later Poetry*, p. 190.
14. Dooley and Ewbank, *The Complete Works*, pp. 285–6.
15. Ibid. p. 287.
16. Fredrick Furnivall and Emily Hickey founded the first, and most prominent, Browning Society in London in 1881.
17. Anonymous review, 'As Wilful as Ever', reprinted in Litzinger and Smallty, *Browning: The Critical Heritage*, pp. 489–90.
18. All the excerpts from *Ferishtah's Fancies* are from the first edition of the poem (London: Smith Elder, 1884), in its second imprint, misleadingly called second edition on the title page. DeVane in *A Browning Handbook* (p. 478) comments that the tone here is 'creditable both to Browning's poetry and to his integrity'.
19. Karlin, 'Did he Eat Ortolans?', pp. 149–50.
20. Ryals, *Browning's Later Poetry*, p. 192.
21. Blackburn, *Robert Browning: A Study of his Poetry*, p. 71.
22. Ward, *Robert Browning and His world*, p. 17.
23. Marketing reasons had forced Browning's publishers, particularly those in America, to delay the book's release; 'the publication of my Poem might possibly be postponed for some three or four weeks, in consequence of an arrangement with America', wrote Browning to G. B. Smith on 19 October 1884. The main reason for the deferment was that *Jocoseria* had come out only a year before and a hasty announcement of *Ferishtah's Fancies* might have jeopardised its sale. See Dooley and Ewbank, *The Complete Works*, p. 291.
24. Karlin, 'One Word More', pp. 3–5. For more on FitzGerald's friendship with Tennyson, see Martin, *With Friends Possessed*, pp. 62–82; Barton, 'The Correspondence of Edward FitzGerald and Alfred Tennyson', Douglas-Fairhurst, 'Young Tennyson and "Old Fitz"'.
25. We see an example of Browning's admiration for Tennyson in the letters that he wrote to the Tennysons after the publication of his response

to FitzGerald. Fearing that Tennyson might take offence, Browning, on 21 July 1889, wrote a long, self-exculpating letter to Emily Tennyson, and another letter to Tennyson himself, almost two weeks after, on 5 August 1889, congratulating him on his eightieth birthday. See Browning's first letter in Collins, *Baylor Browning Interests*, pp. 48–50, and the second one in Hood, *Letters of Robert Browning*, p. 315.

26. Dooley and Ewbank, *The Complete Works*, p. 295.
27. For more information on the Safavids, their origins, and the introduction of Shiism in Persia, see Newman, *Safavid Iran*; Abisaab, *Converting Persia*; Momen, *An Introduction to Shi'a Islam*; Morgan, 'Rethinking Safavid Shī'sm'; Roemer, 'The Safavid Period'.
28. Woolford and Karlin, *The Poems of Browning*, vol. 2, p. 99.
29. Ibid. pp. 168–9.
30. Dooley and Ewbank, *The Complete Works*, p. 297.
31. Carlyle, *On Heroes, Hero-Worship, & the Heroic in History*, p. 51.
32. Arnold, 'A Persian Passion Play', p. 265.
33. *Dehkhoda*, vol. 7, pp. 10696–9.
34. Here, I am referring to Sufism in a more general sense, something that E. G. Browne in 'The Sufi Mysticism: Iran, Arabia and Central Asia' defines as the 'system of pantheistic, idealistic, and theosophical mysticism known amongst Muhammadans as *tasawwuf* and in Europe as Sufism'. Despite my rather simple interpretation of Sufism, I acknowledge that Sufism is a complex network of theological and mystical paths, and that to be fully understood, it requires an elaborate analysis and precise viewpoints. But considering Sufism is not my main focus in this chapter; I have tried to provide relevant information without going into much detail. For more information on Sufism, see Zarrinkoob, 'Persian Sufism in Its Historical Perspective'. Browne's quotation is from Archer, *The Sufi Mystery*, p. 192.
35. Nasr, 'The Rise and Development of Persian Sufism', pp. 1–18.
36. Mason, 'Hallāj and the Baghdad School of Sufism', p. 69. For more on annihilation in Sufism, see Lewisohn, 'In Quest of Annihilation: Imaginalization and Mystical Death in the Tamhīdat of ʿAyn Al-Qudāt Hamadhānī'.
37. Ferishtah is (incongruously) quoting the Bible here: 'His lord said unto him, Well done, thou good and faithful servant: thou hast been faithful over a few things, I will make thee ruler over many things: enter thou into the joy of thy lord' (Matthew 25: 21).
38. DeVane, *A Browning Handbook*, p. 485.
39. Ferishtah teaches ''neath a rock | Or else a palm, by pleasant Nishapur' ('Shah Abbas', ll. 2–3). For his poetry, see 'Plot-Culture' (ll. 1–3).

The Persian Presence in Victorian Poetry

This book has aimed to reveal something of the richness and variety in the treatment of Persia in Victorian poetry. The images and associations that Persia evoked in the cultural imaginary of nineteenth-century Britain certainly do not lend themselves to easy classification. To the Victorians, Persia was at once the enemy of the Greeks, the saviour of the Jews, the realm of legendary kings such as Cyrus, the throne of feeble monarchs like Ahasuerus, the battleground of extraordinary young men like Sohrab, the rose garden of wine-drinking lyricists such as Omar Khayyám, and the land of mystic dervishes like Ferishtah. But while the Victorians layered a multitude of meanings on Persia, they were reluctant to perceive it in its contemporary state. It was as though they had decided not to engage with the actual Persia, that they had conspired to portray Persia only in the context of the past – a past, moreover, in which history played a less important part than myth. Looking back at the numerous examples in Chapter 2, and at the case-studies of Arnold, FitzGerald, and Browning, we see that the Persia in all of these works figures as fictional, fabled, ancient, and far from its modern state. Even poems which purport to reflect contemporary Persia, such as Thomas Moore's 'Letter VI, from Abdallah, in London, to Mohassan, in Ispahan', which was included in *Intercepted Letters; or, the Twopenny Post-Bag* (1813), often turn out to be fanciful or deliberately distorted, since Persia in such poems is a means, not an end in itself.

It may be argued, though, that the disconnection between historical reality and poetic representation is not exclusive to Persia and its image in English poetry of the nineteenth century, that there is an inherent discord between socio-historical actualities and poetics in the period, as F. R. Leavis claimed: 'Nineteenth-century poetry, we realize, was characteristically preoccupied with the creation of a dream-world.'[1] Yet even if this judgement were accepted as

generally valid, it would apply with special force to the representation of Persia, in which the divide between 'fancy' and 'fact' (to
borrow Browning's terms) is both comprehensive and consistently
maintained by writers who differ from each other in almost every
other respect. The phenomenon is all the more striking when we
consider that it was taking place in a period during which Britain's
direct contact with Persia was historically at its highest.

One way of explaining this divide is to explore the literary traditions through which Persia was kept alive in Britain and the ways in
which these literary traditions were impacted by cultural preconcep-
tions and religious predispositions. For centuries, Persia was known
as a land of ancient tales and legends. The name 'Persia', whether
it was transmitted through the narratives of the Bible or the literature of ancient Greece, evoked the images of the glorious days of an
ancient non-Islamic empire; even the early-modern travel narratives
on Safavid Persia echoed some of these ancient perceptions. But only
an afterglow of a once burning light was discovered in nineteenth-
century Persia; modern Persia was far from what the British had
conceived it to be, or perhaps would have liked it to be. The Persia
of the Qajars was an Islamic realm, marked by social conservatism
and religious superstition, and ruled by despotic and ruthless elites.
Moreover, unlike India, Persia was not directly ruled by Britain;
so, while access to the real Persia was difficult and, seemingly, of
lesser strategic importance, access to the Persia of myth and romance
was all too easy. As such, those who came to report on nineteenth-
century Persia assessed and interpreted what they encountered in the
context of their old perceptions of the country. The influence that
Islam held over modern Persians also appeared particularly discon-
certing to men such as Malcolm or Morier whose early nineteenth-
century writings on Persia came to shape the British perception of
the country in the following decades (there is an ironic analogy here
with the way in which Romantic Hellenists sometimes viewed the
modern Greeks as unworthy of the lineage that connected them with
the Athens of Pericles).

In imaginative literature, the effect of such modern discoveries
was to prompt a retreat from reality and to portray Persia in the
light of an imagined past, as in Alfred Tennyson's 'Persia', where
the retelling of the defeat of the Persians by Alexander emphasises
the pervasive contemporary notion of Persia as a fallen nation, for
which the Arabs' imposition of Islam was largely blamed; or in the
Rubáiyát, where FitzGerald describes 'Omar' to be of 'that older
Time and stouter Temper, before the native Soul of Persia was quite

broke by a foreign Creed as well as foreign Conquest'.[2] Persia in Victorian poetry thus remained within the Orientalist paradigm of exotic 'otherness', but it wore its Oriental costume with a difference: the image of Persia in nineteenth-century English poetry was shaped not just by modern colonial ideology but also by ancient, primitive attitudes represented in the sacred texts of classical and biblical literature. Such attitudes were hard enough to shift in the political or economic domain; in literature generally, but especially in poetry, they were even more tenacious. If anything binds together the disparate texts that manifest the Persian presence in nineteenth-century English poetry, it is this attachment to a fantasised space, encapsulated in Edward FitzGerald's description of the *Rubáiyát* as 'an Eclogue in a Persian Garden'.[3] Such a vision was indeed the result of an ideological approach to Persia, one with little or no regard for historical truths and contemporary actualities; but we lose perhaps more than we gain if we simply dismiss this form of cultural engagement as shallow exoticism. FitzGerald, for example, may have interpreted the poetry of Khayyám as a kind of wish-fulfilment, but he also thought of himself as paying homage to, or even as helping to restore, a profound cultural-historical authenticity to his subject. The Persian presence in Victorian poetry was evidently not without myths and misperceptions, but from these misperceptions arose images that have their own distinctive value and deserve to be considered, at least, on their own terms.

Notes

1. Leavis, *New Bearings in English Poetry*, p. 10.
2. FitzGerald, *Rubáiyát*, p. 11.
3. FitzGerald's letter to Cowell of 2 November 1858. See Terhune and Terhune, *Letters*, vol. 2, p. 322.

Bibliography

Abisaab, R. J., *Converting Persia: Religion and Power in the Safavid Empire* (London: I. B. Tauris, 2004).

Aeschylus, *Persians*, ed. and trans. Edith Hall (Warminster: Aris & Phillips, 1996).

Allen, Grant, '*The Lower Slopes: Reminiscences of Excursions Round the Base of Helicon, Undertaken for the Most Part in Early Manhood* (London: Elkin Mathews & John Lane, 1894).

Amanat, Abbas, 'Divided patrimony, tree of royal power and fruit of vengeance: Political paradigms and Iranian self-image in the story of Faridun in the *Shahnama*', in Charles Melville (ed.), *Shahnama Studies I* (Cambridge: The Centre of Middle Eastern and Islamic Studies, 2006), pp. 49–70.

Amin Razavi, Mehdi, *Wine of Wisdom: The Life, Poetry and Philosophy of Omar Khayyam* (Oxford: Oneworld, 2005).

Amini, Iradj, 'Napoleon and Persia', *British Institute of Persian Studies*, 37 (1999), 109–22.

Andrea, Bernadette, 'Lady Sherley: The First Persian in England?', *The Muslim World*, 95 (2005), 279–95.

Anonymous review, 'As Wilful as Ever', *The Saturday Review*, 58 (1884), 727–8, in Boyd Litzinger and Donald Smallty (eds), *Browning: The Critical Heritage* (London: Routledge, 1970), pp. 489–90.

Arberry, A. J., *Omar Khayyám: A New Version based upon Recent Discoveries* (London: Murray, 1952).

Arberry, A. J. 'Persian Literature', in A. J. Arberry (ed.), *The Legacy of Persia* (Oxford: Clarendon Press, 1953), pp. 199–230.

Arberry, A. J. (trans.), *The Koran Interpreted* (London: Gorge Allen & Unwin, 1955).

Arberry, A. J., 'Omar Khayyam and FitzGerald', *Asian Review*, 55 (1959), 121–39.

Arberry, A. J., *The Romance of The Rubaiyat* (London: George Allen & Unwin, 1959).

Armstrong, A. Joseph (ed.), *Intimate Glimpses from Browning's Letter File* (Waco, TX: Baylor University, 1934).

Arnold, 'A Persian Passion Play', *Essays in Criticism* (London: Macmillan, 1875), pp. 259–308.

Atkinson, James, *The Shāh nāmeh of the Persian poet Firdausí; translated and abridged in prose and verse, with notes and illustrations* (London: Oriental Translation Fund, 1832).

Atkinson, A. James, 'Editor's Preface', in James A. Atkinson (ed.), *The Shāh Námeh of the Persian Poet Firdausí* (London: Fredrick Warne, 1886), pp. vii–viii.

Avery, Peter, 'Introduction', in Peter Avery and John Heath-Stubbs (trans.), *The Ruba'iyat of Omar Khayyam* (London: Penguin Books, 2004), pp. 9–44.

Avery, Peter and John Heath-Stubbs (trans.), *The Ruba'iyat of Omar Khayyam* (London: Penguin Books, 2004).

Avery, Peter, 'FitzGerald and Hakim Omar Khayyám', trans. Houshang Pirnazar, in Ali Dehbashi (ed.), *May o Mina: On the Life of Hakim Omar Khayyám Naishaburi* (Tehran: Sokhan Publication, 2005), pp. 758–76.

Awad, Abdul Aziz M., 'The Gulf in the Seventeenth Century', *British Society for Middle Eastern Studies. Bulletin*, 12 (1985), 123–34.

Baghal-Kar, Vali Erfanian T., 'Images of Persia in British literature from the Renaissance through the Nineteenth Century' (unpublished doctoral thesis, Bowling Green, OH: Bowling Green State University, 1981).

Banani, Amin, 'Ferdowsi and the Art of Tragic Epic', in Ehsan Yarshater (ed.), *Persian Literature* (New York: The Persian Heritage Foundation, 1988), pp. 109–20.

Barton, Anna Jane, 'Letters, Scraps of Manuscript, and Printed Poems: The Correspondence of Edward FitzGerald and Alfred Tennyson', *Victorian Poetry*, 46 (2008), 19–35.

Benes, Tuska, 'Comparative Linguistics as Ethnology: In Search of Indo-Germans in Central Asia, 1770–1830', *Comparative Studies of South Asia, Africa and the Middle East*, 24 (2004), 117–32.

Binning, Robert, *A Journal of Two Years' Travel in Persia, Ceylon, etc.* (London: Allen, 1857).

Blackburn, Thomas, *Robert Browning: A Study of his Poetry* (London: Eyre & Spottiswoode, 1967).

Bongie, Chris, *Exotic Memories: Literature, Colonialism, and the Fin De Siècle* (Stanford: Stanford University Press, 1991).

Bosworth, C. E., 'The Tāhirids and Saffārids', in Peter Jackson and Laurence Lockhart (eds), *The Cambridge History of Iran*, 7 vols (Cambridge: Cambridge University Press, 1986), vol. 4, pp. 90–136.

Boyle, J. A., 'Omar Khayyam: Astronomer, Mathematician and Poet', *Bulletin of the John Rylands Library*, 52 (1969), 30–45.

Boyle, J. A., ''Umar Khayyam: Astronomer, Mathematician and Poet', in R. N. Frye (ed.), *The Cambridge History of Iran*, 7 vols (Cambridge: Cambridge University Press, 1975), vol. 4, pp. 658–64.

Brancaforte, E. C., *Visions of Persia: Mapping the Travels of Adam Olearius* (Cambridge, MA: Harvard University Press, 2003).

Brantlinger, Patrick, *Rule of Darkness: British Literature and Imperialism, 1830–1914* (London: Cornell University Press, 1988).

Broadhead, H. D., *The Persae of Aeschylus* (London: Cambridge University Press, 1960).

Browne, E. G., *A Year Amongst the Persians* (London: Adam and Charles Black, 1893).

Browne, E. G., *A Literary History of Persia, from Firdawsí to Sa'dí* (Cambridge: Cambridge University Press, 1906).

Browne, E. G., 'The Sufi Mysticism: Iran, Arabia and Central Asia', in Nathaniel P. Archer (ed.), *The Sufi Mystery* (London: Octagon, 1980), pp. 192–221.

Browning, Robert, *Ferishtah's Fancies* (London: Smith Elder, 1884).

Burn, A. R., *Persia and the Greeks: The Defence of the West* (London: Edward Arnold, 1962).

Burn, A. R., 'Persia and the Greeks', in I. Gershevitch (ed.), *The Cambridge History of Iran*, 7 vols (Cambridge: Cambridge University Press, 1985), vol. 2, pp. 292–391.

Burnes, Alexander, *Travels into Bokhara; being the account of a journey from India to Cabool, Tartary, and Persia*, 3 vols (London: J. Murray, 1834).

Burton, Jonathan, 'The Shah's Two Ambassadors: *The Travels of the Three English Brothers* and the Global Early Modern', in Brinda Charry and Gitanjali Shahani (eds), *Emissaries in Early Modern Literature and Culture: Mediation, Transmission, Traffic, 1550–1700* (Aldershot: Ashgate, 2009), pp. 23–40.

Cadell, Jessie E., 'The True Omar Khayyam', *Fraser's Magazine*, 19 (1879), 650–9.

Cannon, Garland, *The Life and Mind of Oriental Jones* (Cambridge: Cambridge University Press, 1990).

Cannon, G. H., 'Sir William Jones's Persian Linguistics', *Oriental Society*, 78 (1958), 262–73.

Cannon, G. H., *Oriental Jones: A Biography of Sir William Jones: 1746–1794* (New York: Asia Publishing House, 1964).

Cannon, G. H., 'Sir William Jones and the New Pluralism over Languages and Cultures', *Yearbook of English Studies*, 28 (1998), 128–43.

Carlyle, Thomas, *On Heroes, Hero-Worship, & the Heroic in History* (Los Angeles: University of California Press, 1993).

Casellas, Jesús López-Peláez, 'The Travailes of the Three English Brothers and the Textual Construction of Early Modern Identities', *Interlitteraria*, 21 (2016), 253–74.

Chew, Samuel C., *The Crescent and the Rose: Islam and England during the Renaissance* (New York: Oxford University Press, 1937).

Clark, Fraser, 'From Epic to Romance, via Filicide? Rustam's Character Formation', *Iranian Studies*, 43 (2010), 53–70.

Clayden, Arthur, *The Revolt of the Field: A Sketch of the Rise and Progress of the Movement among the Agricultural Labourers. Known as the "National Agricultural Labourers Union"* (London: Hodder and Stoughton, 1874).

Clifford, J. 'On Orientalism', in J. Clifford (ed.), *The Predicament of Culture* (Cambridge, MA: Harvard University Press, 1988), pp. 255–76.

Clinton, Jerome W., 'Court Poetry at the Beginning of the Classical Period', in Ehsan Yarshater (ed.), *Persian Literature* (New York: The Persian Heritage Foundation, 1988), pp. 75–96.

Collins, Thomas J. (ed.), *Baylor Browning Interests – The Brownings to the Tennysons.* No. 22 (Waco, TX: Baylor University, 1971).

Cook, J. M., *The Persian Empire* (London: J. M. Dent, 1983).

Cowell, Edward B., 'Persian Poetry', *The Westminster and Foreign Quarterly Review*, 47 (1847), 273–308.

Crump, R. W. and Betty S. Flowers (eds), *Christina Rossetti: The Complete Poems* (London: Penguin Books, 2001).

Curzon, George N., *Persia and the Persian Question*, 2 vols (London: Green, 1892).

Dabashi, Hamid, *Persophilia: Persian Culture on the Global Scene* (Cambridge, MA: Harvard University Press, 2015).

Dabiri, Ghazzal, 'The Shahnama: Between the Samanids and the Ghaznavids', *Iranian Studies*, 43 (2010), 13–28.

Darwin, Erasmus, *The Botanic Garden, A Poem, In Two Parts* (London: J. Johnson, 1799).

Dashti, Ali, *In Search of Omar Khayyám*, trans. L. P. Elwell-Sutton (London: Columbia University Press, 1971).

Dashti, Ali, *Dami ba Khayyám* (Tehran: Asatir Publication, 1985 (in Persian)).

Davis, Dick (ed.), *Rubáiyát of Omar Khayyám* (London: Penguin Books, 1989).

Davis, Dick, *Epic and Sedition: The Case of Ferdowsi's Shahnameh* (Fayetteville: Arkansas University Press, 1992).

Davis, Dick, 'In the Enemy's Camp: Homer's Helen and Ferdowsi's Hojir', *Iranian Studies*, 25 (1992), 17–26.

Davis, Dick, 'Persian', in Peter France and Kenneth Haynes (eds), *The Oxford History of Literary Translation in English* (Oxford: Oxford University Press, 2006), pp. 332–40.

Davis, Dick, *Shahnameh: the Persian Book of Kings* (London: Penguin Books, 2007).

Davis, Dick, 'The "Shahnameh" as World Literature', in *Epic of the Persian Kings: The Art of Ferdowsi's Shahnameh* (London: I. B. Tauris, 2010), pp. 23–30.

Davis, Dick, *Faces of Love: Hafez and the Poets of Shiraz* (New York: Penguin, 2013).

Davis, H. W. C., 'The Great Game in Asia (1800–1844)', in *The Raleigh Lecture on History* (London: British Academy, 1927).

Day, John, George Wilkins and William Rowley, *The Travels of the Three English Brothers*, in Anthony Parr (ed.), *Three Renaissance Travel Plays* (Manchester: Manchester University Press, 1995), pp. 55–134.

De Blois, Francois, *Burzōy's Voyage to India and the Origin of the Book of Kalīlah wa Dimnah* (London: Royal Asiatic Society, 1990).

Decker, Christopher (ed.), *Edward FitzGerald, Rubáiyát of Omar Khayyám: A Critical Edition* (London: University of Virginia Press, 1997).

Decker, Christopher, 'Edward FitzGerald and Other Men's Flowers: Allusion in the *Rubáiyát of Omar Khayyám*', *The Literary Imagination*, 6 (2004), 213–39.

Dehkhoda, Aliakbar, *Dehkhoda Dictionary*, ed. Mohammad Mo'in and Ja'far Shahidi (Tehran: Tehran University Press, 1998).

DeVane, William Clyde, *A Browning Handbook* (New York: Appleton-Century-Crofts, 1955).

Dew, Nicholas, *Orientalism in Louis XIV's France* (Oxford: Oxford University Press, 2009).

Dooley, Allan and David Ewbank (eds), *The Complete Works of Robert Browning*, vol. 25 (Athens: Ohio University Press, 2007).

Douglas-Fairhurst, Robert, 'Young Tennyson and "Old Fitz"', *Tennyson Research Bulletin*, 8 (2006), 69–84.

Due, Bodil, in *The Cyropaedia: Xenophon's Aims and Methods* (Esbjerg: Aarhus University Press, 1989).

Dutt, Toru, *A Sheaf Gleaned in French Fields* (London: C. Kegan Paul, 1880).

Elwell-Sutton, L. P., '"The Rubā'ī" in Early Persian Literature', in R. N. Frye (ed.), *The Cambridge History of Iran*, 7 vols (Cambridge: Cambridge University Press, 1975), vol. 4, pp. 633–57.

Elwell-Sutton, L. P., 'Omar Khayyám', in Ehsan Yarshater (ed.), *Persian Literature* (New York: The Persian Heritage Foundation, 1988), pp. 147–61.

Emerson, J, 'Adam Olearius and the Literature of the Schleswig-Holstein Missions to Russia and Iran', in Jean Calmard (ed.), *Études Safavides* (Tehran: Institut Français de Recherche en Iran, 1993), pp. 31–56.

Ernst, Carl W., 'On Losing One's Head: Hallājian Motifs and Authorial Identity in Poems Ascribed to Attār', in Leonard Lewisohn and Christopher Shackle (eds), *Attār and the Persian Sufi Tradition: The Art of Spiritual Flight* (London: I. B. Tauris, 2006), 330–43.

Este'lami, Mohammad, 'Narratology and Realities in the Study of Attar', in Leonard Lewisohn and Christopher Shackle (eds), *Attār and the Persian Sufi Tradition: The Art of Spiritual Flight* (London: I. B. Tauris, 2006), pp. 57–74.

Fehling, D., *Herodotus and his Sources; Citation, Invention and Narrative Art* (Leeds: Francis Cairns, 1989).

Ferrier, R. W., 'The European Diplomacy of Shah Abbas I and the First Persian Embassy to England', *Persia, Journal of the British Institute of Persian Studies*, 11 (1973), 75–92.

Ferrier, R. W., 'Edward Fitzgerald, a Reader "Of Taste", and 'Umar Khayyām 1809–1883', *Iran*, 24 (1986), 161–87.

Firdausi, Abul-Qasim, *Shahnameh*, ed. Djalal Khaleghi-Motlagh (Tehran: Afkar, 2006).

FitzGerald, Edward, *Rubáiyát of Omar Khayyám, the Astronomer-Poet of Persia. Translated into English Verse* (London: Bernard Quaritch, 1859).

FitzGerald, Edward, *Rubáiyát of Omar Khayyám, the Astronomer-Poet of Persia. Rendered into English Verse* (London: Bernard Quatrich, 1872).

Flower, Michael, 'Herodotus and Persia', in Carolyn Dewald and John Marincola (eds), *The Cambridge Companion to Herodotus* (Cambridge: Cambridge University Press, 2006), pp. 274–89.

Foran, John, 'The Making of an External Arena: Iran's Place in the World-System, 1500–1722', *Review (Fernand Braudel Center)*, 12 (1989), 71–119.

Foroughi, Mohammad Ali, 'Introduction', in Baha ul-Din Khorramshahi (ed.), *Rubáiyát of Omar Khayyám* (Tehran: Nahid Publishing House, 2005), pp. 51–94 (in Persian).

Forouzanfar, Badiozzaman, 'Ghadimitarin Etela' az Zendegi-e Khayyám', in *May o Mina: On the Life of Hakim Omar Khayyám Naishaburi* (Tehran: Sokhan Publication, 2005), pp. 20–43.

Franklin, Michael J., *Orientalist Jones: Sir William Jones, Poet, Lawyer, And Linguist, 1746–1794* (Oxford: Oxford University Press, 2009).

Frye, N. R., 'The Sāmānids', in R. N. Frye (ed.), *The Cambridge History of Iran*, 7 vols (Cambridge: Cambridge University Press, 1975), vol. 4, pp. 136–62.

Gail, Marzieh, *Persia and the Victorians* (London: George Allen and Unwin, 1951).

Gera, Deborah Levine, *Xenophon's Cyropaedia: Style, Genre and Literary Technique* (Oxford: Clarendon Press, 1993).

Ghani, Cyrus, *Shakespeare Persia, and the East* (Washington, DC: Mage Publishers, 2007).

Good, Peter, 'The East India Company's *Farmān*, 1622–1747', *Iranian Studies*, 52 (2019), 181–97.

Grabar, Terry H., 'Fact and Fiction: Morier's Hajji Baba', *Texas Studies in Literature and Language*, 3 (1969), 1223–36.

Gray, Erik, *Milton and the Victorians* (London: Cornell University Press, 2009).

Grogan, Jane, *The Persian Empire in English Renaissance Writing, 1549–1622* (London: Palgrave Macmillan, 2014).

Grundy, G. B., *The Great Persian War* (London: John Murray, 1901).

Gwyn, D., 'Richard Eden: cosmographer and alchemist', *Sixteenth-Century Journal*, 15 (1984), 13–34.

Hall, Edith, *Aeschylus, Persians* (Warminster: Aris & Phillips, 1996).

Hanaway, William L., 'Epic Poetry', in Ehsan Yarshater (ed.), *Persian Literature* (New York: The Persian Heritage Foundation, 1988), pp. 96–109.

Harrison, Thomas, *The Emptiness of Asia: Aeschylus' 'Persians' and the History of the Fifth Century* (London: Duckworth, 2000).

Harrison, Thomas (ed.), *Greeks and Barbarians* (New York: Routledge, 2001).

Hawlin, Stefan and Tim Burnett (eds), *The Poetical Works of Robert Browning*, vol. 8 (Oxford: Clarendon Press, 2001).

Hawlin, Stefan and Tim Burnett (eds), *The Poetical Works of Robert Browning*, vol. 9 (Oxford: Clarendon Press, 2004).

Hedayat, Sadegh, 'Khayyám-e Philsooph', in Ali Dehbashi (ed.), *May o Mina: On the Life of Hakim Omar Khayyám Naishaburi* (Tehran: Sokhan Publication, 2005), pp. 605–19 (in Persian).

Herbert, Thomas, *Some Yeares Travels into Divers Parts of Asia and Afrique* (London: Richard Bishop, 1677).

Herodotus, *The Histories*, trans. Aubrey de Sélincourt (London: Penguin, 2003).

Heron-Allen, Edward, *The Rubáiyát of Omar Khayyám: A Facsimile of the MS in the Bodleian Library* (London: H. S. Nicholas, 1898).

Higgins, Ian M., *Writing East: The "Travels" of Sir John Mandeville* (Philadelphia: University of Pennsylvania Press, 1997).

Homai', Jalal ul-Din, 'Moghaddamey'e bar *Tarabkhane*', in Ali Dehbashi (ed.), *May o Mina: On the Life of Hakim Omar Khayyám Naishaburi* (Tehran: Sokhan Publication, 2005), pp. 180–243.

Hood, Thurman L. (ed.), *Letters of Robert Browning Collected by Thomas J. Wise* (London: John Murray, 1933).

Houston, Chloë, '"Thou glorious kingdome, thou chiefe of Empires": Persia in Early Seventeenth-Century Travel Literature', *Studies in Travel Writing*, 13 (2009), 141–52.

Houston, Chloë, 'Turning Persia: The Prospect of Conversion in Safavid Persia', in Lieke Stelling, Harald Hendrix, and Todd Richardson (eds), *The Turn of the Soul: Representations of Religious Conversion in Early Modern Art and Literature* (Leiden: Brill, 2011), pp. 85–108.

Ingram, David, *The Beginning of the Great Game in Asia, 1828–1834* (Oxford: Oxford University Press, 1979).

Ingram, David, 'Great Britain's Great Game: An Introduction', *The International History Review*, 2 (1980), 160–71.

Ingram, David, 'Approaches to the Great Game in Asia', *Middle Eastern Studies*, 18 (1982), 449–57.

Ingram, David, *In Defence of British India: Great Britain in the Middle East, 1775–1842* (New York: Routledge, 2013).

Ingram, Edward 'An Aspiring Buffer State: Anglo-Persian Relations in the Third Coalition, 1804–1807, *The Historical Journal*, 16 (1973), 509–33.

Irwin, Robert, *The Arabian Nights: A Companion* (London: Penguin, 1994).

Irwin, Robert, *For Lust of Knowing: The Orientalists and their Enemies* (London: Penguin Books, 2006).

Jahanpour, Farhang, 'Western Encounters with Persian Sufi Literature', in Leonard Lewisohn and David Morgan (eds), *The Heritage of Sufism*, 3 vols (Oxford: Oneworld, 1999), vol. 3, pp. 28–63.

Javadi, Hasan, *Persian Literary Influence on English Literature: with Special Reference to the Nineteenth Century* (Costa Mesa, CA: Mazda Publishers, 2005).

Jeffery, Francis, *General Politics: Essay on the Practice of the British Government, distinguished from the abstract Theory on which it is supposed to be founded'*, in *Edinburgh Review*, 3 vols (London: Longman, 1846), vol. 3, pp. 145–80.

Jones, Harford, *The Dynasty of the Qajars* (London: John Bohn, 1833).

Jones, William, 'An Essay on the Poetry of the Eastern Nations', in John Shore Teignmouth (ed.), *The Works of Sir William Jones*, 13 vols (Cambridge: Cambridge University Press, 2013), vol. 10, pp. 329–60.

Jones, William, *A Grammar of the Persian Language*, in John Shore Teignmouth (ed.), *The Works of Sir William Jones*, 13 vols (Cambridge: Cambridge University Press, 2013), vol. 5, pp. 163–446.

Jones, William, *Poems, Consisting Chiefly of Translation from the Asiatic Languages*, in John Shore Teignmouth (ed.), *The Works of Sir William Jones*, 13 vols (Cambridge: Cambridge University Press, 2013), vol. 10, pp. 195–400.

Jones, William, 'Preface' to *The History of the Life of Nadir Shah*, in John Shore Teignmouth (ed.), *The Works of Sir William Jones*, 13 vols (Cambridge: Cambridge University Press, 2013), vol. 12, pp. 313–54.

Jones, William, 'The Tenth Anniversary Discourse, on Asiatic History, Civil and Natural, delivered 28th February, 1793', in John Shore Teignmouth (ed.), *The Works of Sir William Jones*, 13 vols (Cambridge: Cambridge University Press, 2013) vol. 3, pp. 205–28.

Karlin, Daniel, 'Did he Eat Ortolans? Browning, Food and Italy', in John Woolford (ed.), *Robert Browning in Contexts* (Winfield, KS: Wedgestone Press, 1998), pp. 148–60.

Karlin, Daniel (ed.), *Edward FitzGerald Rubáiyát of Omar Khayyám* (Oxford: Oxford University Press, 2009).

Karlin, Daniel, 'One Word More', *Times Literary Supplement*, November 2013, 3–5.

Katouzian, Homa, *The Persians: Ancient, Mediaeval and Modern Iran* (London: Yale University Press, 2010).

Kaye, J. W., *The Life and Correspondence of Major-General Sir John Malcolm*, 2 vols (London: Smith, 1856).

Khorramshahi, Baha ul-Din, 'Foreword', in Baha ul-Din Khorramshahi (ed.), *Rubáiyát of Omar Khayyám* (Tehran: Nahid Publishing House, 2005), pp. 7–23 (in Persian).

Kitching, C. J., 'Alchemy in the reign of Edward VI: an episode in the careers of Richard Whalley and Richard Eden', *BIHR*, 44 (1971), 308–15.

Knatchbull, Wyndham, *Kalila and Dimna or The Fables of Bidpai* (Oxford: W. Baxter, 1819).

Kollmann, Nancy S., 'Tracking the Travels of Adam Olearius', in Maria Di Salvo, Daniel H. Kaiser, Valerie A. Kivelson, *Word and Image in Russian History: Essays in Honor of Gary Marker* (Boston, MA: Academic Studies Press, 2015).

Lambton, A. K. S., *Qajar Persia: Eleven Studies* (London: I. B. Tauris, 1987).

Lambton, A. K. S., 'Major-General Sir John Malcolm (1769–1833) and "The History of Persia"', *Iran*, 33 (1995), 97–109.

Lang, Cecil Y. (ed.), *The Letters of Matthew Arnold*, 3 vols (London: The University Press of Virginia, 1996).

Lateiner, Donald, *The Historical Method of Herodotus* (Toronto: University of Toronto Press, 1989).

Lazard, G., 'The Rise of the New Persian Language', in R. N. Frye (ed.), *The Cambridge History of Iran*, 7 vols (Cambridge: Cambridge University Press, 1975), vol. 4, pp. 595–633.

Leavis, F. R., *New Bearings in English Poetry* (London: Chatto & Windus, 1932).

Lewisohn, Leonard, 'In Quest of Annihilation: Imaginalization and Mystical Death in the Tamhīdat of 'Ayn Al-Qudāt Hamadhānī', in Leonard Lewisohn and David Morgan (eds), *The Heritage of Sufism*, 3 vols (Oxford: Oneworld, 1999), vol. 1, pp. 285–336.

Lewisohn, Leonard and Christopher Shackle, 'Introduction', in Leonard Lewisohn and Christopher Shackle (eds), *Attār and the Persian Sufi Tradition: The Art of Spiritual Flight* (London: I. B. Tauris, 2006), pp. xvii–xxvii

Litzinger, Boyd and Donald Smallty (eds), *Browning: The Critical Heritage* (London: Routledge, 1970), pp. 489–90.

Lockhart, Laurence, *Nadir Shah, Shah of Persia, 1688–1747* (London: Luzac, 1938).

Lockhart, Laurence, 'Persia as Seen by the West', in A. J. Arberry (ed.), *The Legacy of Persia* (Oxford: Clarendon Press, 1953), pp. 318–58.

Lockhart, Laurence, 'European Contact with Persia 1350–1736', in Peter Jackson and Laurence Lockhart (eds), *The Cambridge History of Iran*, 7 vols (Cambridge: Cambridge University Press, 1986), vol. 6, pp. 373–412.

Malcolm, John, *History of Persia, from the most early period to the present time*, 2 vols (London: John Murray, 1815).

Martin, Robert Bernard, *With Friends Possessed* (London: Faber, 1985).

Mason, Herbert, 'Hallāj and the Baghdad School of Sufism', in Leonard Lewisohn and David Morgan (eds), *The Heritage of Sufism*, 3 vols (Oxford: Oneworld, 1999), vol. 1, pp. 66–82.

Matthee, Rudi, 'The Safavids under Western Eyes: Seventeenth-Century European Travelers to Iran', *Journal of Early Modern History*, 13 (2009), 137–71.

Minorsky, Vladimir F., 'Omar Khaiyām', in *The Encyclopaedia of Islam* (London: Brill, 1936), pp. 985–9.

Minorsky, Vladimir F., 'Omar Khayyám', trans. Baha ul-Din Khorram-shahi, in Ali Dehbashi (ed.), *May o Mina: On the Life of Hakim Omar Khayyám Naishaburi* (Tehran: Sokhan Publication, 2005), pp. 443–54 (in Persian).

Mitchell, Colin P., *The Practice of Politics in Safavid Iran: Power, Religion and Rhetoric* (London: I. B. Tauris, 2009).

Mohl, Julius von, *Le Livre des Rois, par Abou'lkasim Firdousi*, vol. 1 (Paris: Imprimerie Nationale, 1876).

Momen, Moojan, *An Introduction to Shi'a Islam* (New Haven, CT: Yale University Press, 1985).

Morgan, David, *Medieval Persia 1040–1797* (New York: Longman, 1990).

Morgan, David, 'Rethinking Safavid Shī'sm', in Leonard Lewisohn and David Morgan (eds), *The Heritage of Sufism*, 3 vols (Oxford: Oneworld, 1999), vol. 3, pp. 12–28.

Morgan, Llewelyn, 'With "Bokhara" Burnes', *Times Literary Supplement*, November 2012, 14–15.

Morier, James, *A Journey through Persia, Armenia and Asia Minor to Constantinople* (London: Longman, 1812).

Morier, James, *A Second Journey Through Persia to Constantinople* (London: Longman, 1818).

Morier, James, *The Adventures of Hajjî Baba of Ispahan* (London: John Murray, 1824).

Morier, James, *The Adventures of Hajjî Baba of Ispahan in England* (London: John Murray, 1828).

Morier, James, *The Adventures of Hajjî Baba of Ispahan* (London: Macmillan, 1895).

Morier, James, *The Adventures of Hajjî Baba of Ispahan: illustrated by H. R. Millar, with an introduction by Charles E. Beckett* (London: Gresham, 1899).

Morton, A. H., 'Some 'Umarian Quatrains from the Lifetime of 'Umar Khayyām', in A. A. Seyed-Gohrab (ed.), *The Great Umar Khayyām: A Global Reception of the Rubáiyát* (Leiden: Leiden University Press, 2012), pp. 55–67.

Mukherjee, S. N., *Sir William Jones: A Study in Eighteenth-Century British Attitudes to India* (Cambridge: Cambridge University Press, 1986).

Murray, S. O., 'Corporealizing Medieval Persian and Turkish Tropes', in S. Murray and W. Roscoe (eds), *Islamic Homosexualities: Culture,*

History, and Literature (New York: New York University Press, 1997), pp. 132–41.

Nanquette, Laetitia, *Orientalism Versus Occidentalism: Literary and Cultural Imaging Between France and Iran Since the Islamic Revolution* (New York: I. B. Tauris, 2013).

Nasr, Hosein, 'The Rise and Development of Persian Sufism', in Leonard Lewisohn and David Morgan (eds), *The Heritage of Sufism*, 3 vols (Oxford: Oneworld, 1999), vol. 1, pp. 1–18.

Newman, Andrew J., *Safavid Iran: Rebirth of Persian Empire* (London: I. B. Tauris, 2006).

Nixon, Anthony, *The Three English Brothers* (London: John Hodgets, 1607).

Norton, Charles Eliot, 'Review of *Rubáiyát* (2nd edn) and of *Les quatrains de khèyam*', *North American Review*, 109 (1869), 565–84.

Parker, J. *Books to Build an Empire: a bibliographical history of English overseas interests to 1620* (Amsterdam: N. Israel, 1965).

Parr, Anthony (ed.), *Three Renaissance Travel Plays* (Manchester: Manchester University Press, 1995).

Parr, Anthony, 'Foreign Relations in Jacobean England: The Sherley brothers and the "voyage of Persia"', in Jean-Pierre Maquerlot and Michèle Willems, *Travel and Drama in Shakespeare's Time* (Cambridge: Cambridge University Press, 1996).

Peacock, A. C. S., *Medieval Islamic Historiography and Political Legitimacy* (London: Routledge, 2007).

Pennington, L. E. (ed.), *The Purchas Handbook: Studies of the Life, Times and Writings of Samuel Purchas* (London: Hakluyt Society, 1997).

Penzer, N. M., 'Preface' in *Travels in Persia 1673–1677* (London: Argonaut, 1927), pp. 13–20.

Perry, John. R., 'Persian in the Safavid Period: Sketch for an *Etat de Langue*', in Charles Melville (ed.), *Safavid Persia* (London: I. B. Tauris, 1996), pp. 269–85.

Poe, Marshall T., *'A People Born to Slavery': Russia in Early Modern European Ethnography, 1476–1748* (Ithaca: Cornell University Press, 2000).

Pope, Alexander, 'Epistle to Dr. Arbuthnot', in Pat Rogers (ed.), *Alexander Pope: The Major Works* (Oxford: Oxford University Press, 1993), pp. 336–49.

Provan, Iain, 'The Historical Books of the Testament', in John Barton (ed.), *The Cambridge Companion to Biblical Interpretation* (Cambridge: Cambridge University Press, 2002), pp. 198–212.

Publicover, Laurence, 'Strangers at home: the Sherley brothers and Dramatic Romance', *Renaissance Studies*, 24 (2010), 694–709.

Qani, Qasem, 'Tahghighat Darbareye Khayyám', in Ali Dehbashi (ed.), *May o Mina: On the Life of Hakim Omar Khayyám Naishaburi* (Tehran: Sokhan Publication, 2005), pp. 272–308 (in Persian).

Quinn, D. B. (ed.), *The Hakluyt* Handbook, 2 vols (London: Hakluyt Society, 1974).

Robinson, Benedict, *Islam and Early Modern Literature: The Politics of Romance from Spenser to Milton* (Basingstoke: Palgrave MacMillan, 2007).

Roemer, H. R., 'The Safavid Period', in J. A. Boyle (ed.), in *The Cambridge History of Iran*, 7 vols (Cambridge: Cambridge University Press, 1968), vol. 5, pp. 189–350.

Roemer, H. R., 'The Safavid Period', in Peter Jackson and Laurence Lockhart (eds), *The Cambridge History of Iran*, 7 vols (Cambridge: Cambridge University Press, 1986), vol. 6, pp. 189–373.

Ross, Christopher, 'Lord Curzon and E. G. Browne Confront the "Persian Question"', *The Historical Journal*, 52 (2009), 358–411.

Ross, E. Denison, *Sir Anthony Sherley and His Persian Adventure* (London: Butler & Tanner, 1933).

Ross, E. Denison (ed.), *Sir Anthony Sherley and his Persian Adventure, Including Some Contemporary Narratives Relating Thereto* (London: Routledge, 1933).

Ryals, Clyde de L., *Browning's Later Poetry 1871–1889* (London: Cornell University Press, 1975).

Said, Edward, *Orientalism* (London: Penguin Books, 2003).

Sainte-Beuve, Charles Augustin, 'Le Livre des Rois, par le poëte persan Firdousi, publié et traduit par M. Jules Mohl', *Causeries du Lundi*, 1 (1850), 332–50.

Sainte-Beuve, Charles Augustin, 'What is a Classic?', in Elizabeth Lee (trans.), *Essays by Sainte-Beuve* (London: Walter Scott, 1890), pp. 1–12.

Salisbury, Lord, Speech to The Primrose League, 4 May 1898, reprinted in *The New York Times*, 18 May 1898.

Savory, Roger M., 'The Sherley Myth', *Iran*, 5 (1967), 73–81.

Savory, Roger M., 'British and French Diplomacy in Persia, 1800–1810', *Iran*, 10 (1972), 31–44.

Shackle, Christopher, 'Representations of 'Attar', in Leonard Lewisohn and Christopher Shackle (eds), *Attār and the Persian Sufi Tradition: The Art of Spiritual Flight* (London: I. B. Tauris, 2006), pp. 165–93.

Shahbazi, Shapur, *Ferdowsi: A Critical Biography* (Cambridge, MA: Harvard University Press, 1991)

Shakespeare, William, *Twelfth Night*, in Stephen Greenblatt (ed.), *The Norton Shakespeare* (New York: Norton, 1997), pp. 1751–816.

Sidney, Philip, 'The Defence of Poesy', in Katherine Duncan-Jones (ed.), *Sir Philip Sidney: The Major Works* (New York: Oxford University Press, 2002), pp. 212–51.

Southgate, M., 'Men, Women, and Boys: Love and Sex in the Works of Sa'di', *Iranian Studies*, 17 (1984), 413–52.

Spencer, Edmund, *The Faerie Queene*, ed. Thomas P. Roche, Jr (Harmondsworth: Penguin Books, 1978).

Steensgaard, Niels, *The Asian Trade Revolution of the Seventeenth Century* (Chicago: Chicago University Press, 1974).

Stevens, Roger, 'Robert Sherley: The Unanswered Questions', *Iran*, 17 (1979), 115–25.

Stietencron, Heinrich von, *Hindu Myth, Hindu History, Religion, Art, and Politics* (Delhi: Permanent Black, 2005).

Stodart, Robert, *Journal; being the account of a sea voyage from 1626 to 1629 to the East Indies, Persia, etc* (London: Luzac, 1935).

Super, R. H., 'Documents in the Matthew Arnold Sainte Beuve Relation ship', *Modern Philology*, 60 (1963), 206–10.

Sykes, Percy M., *A History of Persia*, 2 vols (London: Macmillan, 2004).

Terhune, Alfred McKinley, *The Life of Edward FitzGerald* (London: Oxford University Press, 1974).

Terhune, Alfred McKinley and Annabelle Burdick Terhune (eds), *The Letters of Edward FitzGerald*, 4 vols (Princeton: Princeton University Press, 1980).

Thomas, Rosalind, 'The intellectual Milieu of Herodotus', in Carolyn Dewald and John Marincola (eds), *The Cambridge Companion to Herodotus* (Cambridge: Cambridge University Press, 2006), pp. 60–75.

Tucker, Gene M., 'Esther', in Bruce M. Metzger and Michael D Coogan (eds), *The Oxford Companion to the Bible* (New York: Oxford University Press, 1993), pp. 198–201.

Vlassopoulos, Kostas, *Greeks and Barbarians* (Cambridge: Cambridge University Press, 2013).

Walker, Warren S., 'Burnes's Influence on Sohrab and Rustum: A Closer Look', *Victorian Poetry*, 8 (1970), 151–6.

Ward, Maisie, *Robert Browning and His world: Two Robert Brownings? [1861–1889]* (London: Cassel, 1969).

Watson, Foster, 'Scholars and Scholarship, 1600–1660', in *The Cambridge History of English Literature* (New York: Cambridge University Press, 1910), vol. 7, p. 345.

Watson, Foster, 'Oriental Education in Great Britain', in *The Encyclopedia and Dictionary of Education* (London: I. Pitman, 1922), vol. 3, pp. 1232–6.

Whitridge, Arnold (ed.), *Unpublished Letters of Matthew Arnold* (New York: Yale University Press, 1923).

Whitridge, Arnold, 'Matthew Arnold and Sainte-Beuve', *MLA*, 52 (1938), 303–13.

Wilberforce-Clarke, H. (trans.), *The Dīvān-i-Hāfiz* (Bethesda, MD: Iranbooks, 1998).

Woolford, John and Daniel Karlin (eds), *The Poems of Browning*, 2 vols (London: Longman, 1991).

Wright, Dennis, *The English Amongst the Persians* (London: Heinemann, 1977).

Wright, Dennis, *The Persians Amongst the English* (London: I. B. Tauris, 1985).

Wright, William Aldis (ed.), *Letters and Literary Remains of Edward FitzGerald*, 7 vols (London: Macmillan and Co., 1889), vol. 7, pp. 255–312.

Yapp, M. E., 'British Perceptions of the Russian Threat to India', *Modern Asian Studies*, 21 (1987), 647–65.

Yapp, M. E., 'The Legend of the Great Games', in *2000 Lectures and Memoirs* (Oxford: British Academy, 2001), pp. 179–98.

Yarshater, Ehsan, 'The Development of Iranian Literatures', in Ehsan Yarshater (ed.), *Persian Literature* (New York: The Persian Heritage Foundation, 1988), pp. 3–41.

Yarshater, Ehsan, 'The Qajar Era in the Mirror of Time', *Iranian Studies*, 34 (2001), 187–94.

Yohannan, John D., *Persian Poetry in England and America: A Two Hundred Year History* (New York: Caravan, 1977).

Young, Robert J. C., *Colonial Desire: Hybridity in Theory, Culture and Race* (London: Routledge, 1995).

Zarrinkoob, A. H., 'Persian Sufism in Its Historical Perspective', *Iranian Studies*, 3 (1970), 139–220.

Zarrinkub, A., 'The Arab Conquest of Iran and its Aftermath', in R. N. Frye (ed.), *The Cambridge History of Iran*, 7 vols (Cambridge: Cambridge University Press, 1975), vol. 4, pp. 1–56.

Index

Note: 'n' indicates chapter notes.